The Hall of Mirrors

The Hall of Mirrors

Drafts & Fragments and the
End of Ezra Pound's *Cantos*

Peter Stoicheff

Ann Arbor

THE UNIVERSITY OF MICHIGAN PRESS

Copyright © by the University of Michigan 1995
All rights reserved
Published in the United States of America by
The University of Michigan Press
Manufactured in the United States of America
⊗ Printed on acid-free paper

1998   1997   1996   1995   4   3   2   1

*A CIP catalogue record for this book is available from
the British Library.*

Library of Congress Cataloging-in-Publication Data

Stoicheff, Peter, 1956–
    The hall of mirrors : Drafts & Fragments and the end of Ezra
Pound's Cantos / Peter Stoicheff.
        p.   cm. — (Editorial theory and literary criticism)
    Includes bibliographical references (p.   ) and index.
    ISBN 0-472-10526-4 (acid-free paper : hardcover)
    1. Pound, Ezra, 1885–1972. Drafts & fragments. 2. Pound, Ezra,
1885–1972. Cantos. I. Title. II. Series.
PS3531.082C2965   1995
811'.52—dc20   94-38210
                                                                    CIP

For Kathryn, Alix, and Christopher

Acknowledgments

Previously unpublished material by Ezra Pound copyright © 1994 by the Trustees of the Ezra Pound Literary Property Trust; used by permission of New Directions Publishing Corporation, agents. Grateful acknowledgment is given to New Directions Publishing Corporation for permission to quote from *The Cantos* (copyright © 1934, 1937, 1940, 1948, 1956, 1959, 1962, 1963, 1966 by Ezra Pound). Manuscripts, typescripts, and letters referred to, quoted, and excerpted in chapter 2 are published with the kind permission of the Donald Hall Collection, Special Collections, University of New Hampshire Library, copyright © 1994; Donald Hall, copyright © 1994; the Yale Collection of American Literature, Beinecke Rare Book and Manuscript Library, Yale University, copyright © 1994; James Laughlin, copyright © 1994.

The *Bloomsbury Review* reproduction in chapter 2 is copyright © 1986 by Owaissa Communications Company, Inc., and permission to include the reproduction is from them.

Portions of chapter 2 appear in different form in "The Interwoven Authority of a *Drafts & Fragments* Text," in Lawrence S. Rainey, ed., *A Poem Including History: The Cantos of Ezra Pound* (Ann Arbor: University of Michigan Press, forthcoming). Portions of the Afterword appeared in different form in "Poem's Poetics or Poet's Death: What Ends *The Cantos, Maximus,* and *Paterson?*" *Genre* 22, nos. 1–2 (spring 1989): 175–93, copyright © 1989, the University of Oklahoma.

Many people assisted and encouraged me in the writing of this book. In particular I would like to thank James Laughlin for his many years of patience and candor, his indispensible knowledge of Ezra Pound and modern literature, and his hospitality at Norfolk, Connecticut. Professor Ronald Bush served as guide and friend and helped immeasurably in correspondence and in working sessions at Caltech. Professors

George Bornstein, Ira Nadel, Eric Domville, Hugh Kenner, Jerome J. McGann, Carroll Terrell, Lawrence Rainey, and Richard Taylor assisted in various ways in the research, writing, and production. Tom Clark wrote a crucial letter years ago. Donald Hall hosted me at Eagle Pond Farm and wrote many letters of information and encouragement. Sheri Martinelli helped with "Canto 120." Ed Sanders shared some thoughts long ago in Toronto. Desmond O'Grady wrote many useful and entertaining letters. All gave time and information without which the book could not have been written. My special thanks go to Professors David and Ann Hiatt, and to longtime friend and mentor Professor Emeritus Douglas LePan. These people share responsibility for any value in this book, none for its weaknesses.

The help of Roland Goodbody in the Special Collections Department of the University of New Hampshire Library, Rick Hart of the Beinecke Rare Book and Manuscript Library at Yale, Cathy Henderson of the Harry Ransom Humanities Research Center at the University of Texas at Austin, and Jennie Rathbun of the Houghton Library at Harvard University was essential in preparing chapter 2.

This book could not have been completed without the generous assistance of President's Fund Grants from the University of Saskatchewan, and a Research Grant from the Social Sciences and Humanities Research Council of Canada.

Every effort has been made to trace the ownership of copyrighted material in this book and to obtain permission for its use.

Contents

Abbreviations   xi

Introduction: Pound Reads "Pound"   1

Chapter

1. "No Substitute for a Lifetime"   11

2. The Mirrored Reader: A Composition and Publication
   History of *Drafts & Fragments*   33

3. *The Cantos* Mirrored: The Self-Reflexive
   Canto CX   75

4. Reflecting on the Image: The Return to a
   Pre-*Cantos* Poetics   101

5. Choosing Blindness: Vorticism and the Narrative
   of Fascism   115

6. The Mirrored Self: The *Trachiniae* and a
   Lost Center   133

Afterword: "To 'See Again'"   153

Appendixes

Appendix 1. Magazine, Journal, and Volume
   Publications of *Drafts & Fragments* Cantos   171

Appendix 2. "From CXII" and Joseph Rock's *The
^2Muan-^1Bpo Ceremony or the Sacrifice to Heaven as
Practised by the Na-Khi*   175

Notes   179

Works Cited   203

Index   209

Abbreviations

Texts by Ezra Pound

ABC   *ABC of Reading.* London: Routledge and Sons, 1934. Reprint. New York: New Directions, 1960.

CA   Confucius's *Analects.* In *Confucius: The Unwobbling Pivot, The Great Digest, The Analects,* translation and commentary by Ezra Pound. New York: New Directions, 1969.

EPT   *Translations / Ezra Pound.* 2d edition, revised and enlarged. Edited by Hugh Kenner. New York: New Directions, 1963.

GB   *Gaudier-Brzeska: A Memoir.* London: John Lane. 1916. Reprint. New York: New Directions, 1970.

GK   *Guide to Kulchur.* London: Faber and Faber, 1938. Reprint. New York: New Directions, 1970.

J/M   *Jefferson and/or Mussolini: L'Idea Statale: Fascism as I Have Seen It.* London: Stanley Nott, 1935. Reprint. New York: Liveright, 1970.

LE   *Literary Essays of Ezra Pound.* Edited by T. S. Eliot. London: Faber and Faber, 1954. Reprint. New York: New Directions, 1968.

LEP   *The Letters of Ezra Pound, 1907–1941.* Edited by D. D. Paige. New York: Harcourt, Brace, 1950.

SR   *The Spirit of Romance.* London: J. M. Dent and Sons, 1910. Reprint. New York: New Directions, 1968.

WT   *Sophokles, Women of Trachis: A Version by Ezra Pound.* London: Neville Spearman, 1956. Reprint. New York: New Directions, 1957.

Other Texts

CWCMP   Ernest Fenollosa. *The Chinese Written Character as a Medium for Poetry.* Edited by Ezra Pound. San Francisco: City Lights Books, 1936. 9th printing, 1983.

SLW   *The Selected Letters of William Carlos Williams.* Edited by John C. Thirwall. New York: McDowell, Obolensky, 1957.

RP   "Ezra Pound: An Interview." In Donald Hall, *Remembering Poets: Reminiscences and Opinions.* New York: Harper and Row, 1978.

Manuscript Collections

EPAB   Ezra Pound Archive, the Beinecke Rare Book and Manuscript Library, Yale University, New Haven, Connecticut.

ULNH   Donald Hall Collection, Special Collections, University of New Hampshire Library, Durham, New Hampshire.

JLA   Personal Archive of James Laughlin, Norfolk, Connecticut.

When citing various cantos I have used the New Directions 1986 *Cantos* for reasons that are discussed in chapter 2. Cantos are cited by number and, when helpful, by page number, for example: LXXIV/436.

Introduction: Pound Reads "Pound"

A group of *Cantos* readers, nearing the end of their rich and daunting project, is in a state of some confusion. They each have the poem's third American collected edition, in printings ranging from the first in 1970 to the twelfth in 1991, and have proceeded through their texts at a similar rate. Nevertheless, one of the readers is inexplicably two cantos behind the others by the end of the fifth section, the *Pisan Cantos*. Later, beginning to discuss the poem they have finished, it becomes evident to them that one has read at least three cantos that another cannot remember—a Canto LXXII, a Canto LXXIII, and a poem titled "Fragments (1966)" dedicating *The Cantos* to Ezra Pound's companion Olga Rudge. Another reader recalls all three of those poems at the end of the text; another confidently remembers reading Cantos LXXII and LXXIII some days before (their celebratory fascism rendering them unforgettable) but in their numerically correct positions in the *Pisan Cantos* section, and encountering "Fragments (1966)" at the very end. Yet another reader is sure that a canto numbered CXX containing the memorable lines "Let the Gods forgive what I / have made / Let those I love try to forgive / what I have made" ended the poem, that there was no "Fragments (1966)," no Canto LXXII, no Canto LXXIII. One of them returns to his text and locates the lines of the "CXX" poem elsewhere, in a group of four fragments titled "Notes For CXVII et seq.," close to the end of *The Cantos*. But another whose text has a group under that title counts only three fragments in it, not four, and the lines of the "CXX" poem are not among them. In fact, there is no "CXX" in her text at all, and the other readers' relief that Pound at the end seems contrite and regretful (particularly given the fascist shrillness of LXXII and LXXIII, say a couple of readers to their uncomprehending companions) leaves her rather uncomfortable.

In an attempt to sort out these various problems, they arrange the printings of their edition chronologically, but the inclusions, exclusions, and repositionings refuse to settle into some comprehensible evolution. Canto CXX, in particular, poses thorny problems, since it is not included in the printings during Pound's lifetime but appears and then repositions itself rather awkwardly and inexplicably after his death in 1972. Nor do the Faber and Faber editions corroborate any one of the many *Drafts & Fragments* variations—its 1976 edition does not include the Canto CXX that New Directions, its source for the sheets no less, contained four years before.

They agree on one thing: asking that "the Gods forgive what I / have made" is a significant act, gathering as it does the religious and ethical resonances of error, sin, and their admission. In the case of Ezra Pound's *Cantos,* the site for many of this century's profound and identifying engagements between aesthetics, politics, the individual, culture, and history, the request has tremendous implications for interpretation. If it is included in the text, it might, as an example, permit one to soften a condemnation of the more unpleasant aspects of *The Cantos'* politics, and the anti-Semitism that accompanied them. It might also facilitate the separation between writer and text that generated much debate over the value of *The Cantos* since the Second World War. Or, if "what I made" refers both to his life and his text, it may just as easily fuse them as declare their difference.

What the readers do not know (though the confused state of their various texts hints at it) is that their options for interpretation are governed not only by the poem's semiotics but by its material production as well. Pound wrote the lines contained in "CXX," but it may be that he wrote them in a different order and scattered through a different poem, that he never recomposed them in their "CXX" variation and did not authorize their publication as a poem of that number to culminate *The Cantos.* The request for forgiveness therefore hovers over *The Cantos* as one of Pound's several explored, but not decisively chosen, possibilities for its termination. But critics, readers, and editors can remain uncomfortable with such momentous hesitation, particularly when the text that is denied resolution is the contentious and intricate *Cantos.* After all, the text must eventually achieve some canonical form, must it not?

It is perhaps best commemorative of the enterprise of writing *The Cantos* that its termination would frustrate, and continue to frustrate, such an assumption. The poem's exotic and unrehearsed negotiation between form and flux, interpretation and fact, narrative and lyric, reading and writing, language and what it signifies would find its ironic testament in a series of *Drafts & Fragments* texts, none of which stands as unequivocally "correct." Yet together, as a series of closural possibilities entertained by Pound, his readers, and his editors, and by extension fostered by the literary and political cultures that contained them, the various texts of *Drafts & Fragments* and the circumstances of their production tell us much about the poem they were to terminate.

In whatever form, or more accurately, across the accumulation of its many unresolved forms, *Drafts & Fragments* is the place where Pound attempts to create the paradise of natural and private harmony, and of limpid verse, that he had frequently predicted for the end of his long poem. To read the various portions of the volume where that paradisal vision fitfully and incompletely emerges is to encounter some of *The Cantos*', and Pound's, most powerful and luminous poetry. That vision, however, is only one dimension of the volume, compromised by many personal and poetic forces that seemed almost to conspire against its realization. The complex problem of defining and achieving a paradise, and the graphic absence of a satisfactory solution, pervade *Drafts & Fragments* as thoroughly as, or perhaps even more than, any mastery of the poem's expected paradisal close could. These final poems of *The Cantos* are dignified and deepened by Pound's expression in them of his distress over their partial failure, which he felt went beyond its boundaries of Cantos CX–CXVII to encompass much of the poem and its writer.

The full character of the *Drafts & Fragments* poems emerges, therefore, only when they are read within that context of the culminating volume in *The Cantos*. Pound's composition of them is inseparable from his sense of his long poem's imminent close and is shaped and troubled by that horizon. Too, as the last volume of *The Cantos*, sanctioned by the authority of that imposing text to which it now belongs, the volume is frequently regarded as Pound's intended close to the poem. Since the structure of *The Cantos* itself has been described so variously, it is not surprising that its final volume attracts a wide spectrum of responses. *Drafts & Fragments* has been interpreted as an indication of "Pound's refusal to provide a coherent ending," but also as the "open-ended and relaxed finale that [*The Cantos*] needs." It ends

Pound's long poem in "an appropriately indirect, but rather pathetic manner" offers another reader; yet another, though, senses among its "unforgettable words and images" a direct reference to Canto I, and hence a circular structure, in which the final fragments of "Notes For CXVII et seq." do not communicate pathos but a "hopeful warning to . . . fellow human beings."[1] Retroactively, through *Drafts & Fragments,* *The Cantos* has been read as incomplete, closed, failed, and successful, and its critical reception has tended to remain within this quadrangle of possibilities. Yet *Drafts & Fragments* generates not only readers' reassessments of *The Cantos* but contains Pound's own responses to it, periodically similar, but eventually operating outside the strict parameters of failure or success. The act of trying to write a paradise for his *Cantos* forced him to review the poem, and himself as well, and *Drafts & Fragments* thus becomes the fascinating site where Pound reads "Pound"—as he has been composed and refracted by *The Cantos*— where the poem becomes, in the language of CXIV, a "hall of mirrors." Its fragmentary form is but one of many indications that this personal and poetic reappraisal was extremely difficult for him. The composition and publication histories of the volume, in fact, suggest that it all but caused his abandonment of the poem during its writing.

In this study I have attempted to trace *Drafts & Fragments'* complex mixture of poetic and private exploration and reassessment. To do this I have avoided offering exhaustive interpretations of each canto and have chosen instead to trace the complicated dynamics of *The Cantos'* close from a specific and hardly conclusive set of perspectives, in the process examining the numerous passages in the volume relevant to that task. In chapter 1 I discuss Pound's evolving conception of paradise in his *Cantos,* of which *Drafts & Fragments* is to be the realization, but of which it is more truly the reconsideration. If the achievement of a paradisal close to the poem seldom exists untroubled by its own undoing, that tension is displayed in the composition and publication histories of these cantos, which offer the earliest indications of Pound's struggle and disenchantment with them, as I discuss in chapter 2. The process of composing *Drafts & Fragments* occasioned Pound's greatest awareness of *The Cantos'* infirmities and insecurities—entertaining the possibility of a paradise for his poem would illuminate and reflect the irresolvable conflicts that had remained latent in it for the 109 poems that precede its final volume. Their appearance troubles the waters of that paradise and in the process shifts Pound's relationship with the last poems during their composition, and afterward with *The Cantos* as a whole. As a result, their publication is less in accordance with his wish to see them in print than with peculiar circumstances outside the text that demanded their authorized appearance. Though the very inclusion of the *Drafts & Fragments* volume with *The Cantos* implies Pound's blessing of the close, the facts of its publication are that he did not actively pursue its appearance, and that its various forms mirror his readers' and editors' desires for the poem and its poet as much as they mirror Pound's. The case of the "Let the gods forgive what I / have made" lines, which have been editorially added, deleted, and then repositioned several times over the publishing history of the volume, represents one of a number of crucial inclusions and revisions that were not his. It illustrates how *Drafts & Fragments* has become, since its first appearance, a site where conflicting responses to his fascism, anti-Semitism, and other contentious issues of his inseparably public and poetic lives are interpreted and reconstructed. What we read as *Drafts & Fragments* is partly Pound's inconclusive text for the close of *The Cantos,* but the very fact of its incompletion has left it open to a subtle, equally endless refurbishing, creating an historically conditioned and evolving text of "Pound."

The measure of editorial and readerly control over these poems is partly a result of Pound's failing health during their publication, but it is also permitted by the ambivalence he felt toward the poems, itself a consequence of his intricate response to his life and *Cantos,* each approaching its close. To an extent the poem's uneasy termination is contoured by his declining health and effective exile from America between 1958 and 1968, the years of *Drafts & Fragments*' composition, editing, and publication, during which he frequently endured illness, fatigue, and despondency. His ability to participate actively in the volume's editing was severely diminished by these conditions at the time of its first authorized production and publication in 1968, and he died four years later in October 1972 without regaining the energy and health necessary to oversee such a demanding task. The final poems are as a result profoundly contoured by insights afforded the elderly, and by the imminence, the emerging threshold, of silence and death. But another of this study's implications is that the end of a modern long poem such as *The Cantos* is neither fully administered by the circumstances of its poet's life nor entirely contingent upon his death. These relationships probably occur as frequently as they do because a long poem does not begin until a poetics has been devised by its poet that is significant enough to be tested by its imposing stature. In most cases, this requires a mature vision; and, of course, the composition of the poem itself takes a long time. The assumption behind the view that the length of the poem coincides with the longevity of the poet, and that the poet's death marks its own, must be that the long poem is perpetually unfinished and that, had the poet persevered, the poem would have too. One critic, writing on *The Cantos'* termination, points out that since "Ezra Pound always was in *The Cantos*—indeed, his mind is the medium in which the poem operates—there is really no possible ending for the poem except death." (Another, speculating in a similar manner on the close of *Paterson,* wrote that Williams's "work will end only with his death; and the *Paterson* format, with its provision for letters, reminiscences, odds and ends, gives him a place for those things which interest him as he attempts to keep going").[2] The composition and publication histories of *Drafts & Fragments* (and, as I discuss in the Afterword, those of *Paterson* books 5 and 6, and *Maximus: Volume Three* as well) tell a different story. They urge us to recognize that Cantos CX–CXVII were not only the last group of poems Pound could muster the energy to write, but the last that his poem, his relationship with his poem, and his view of himself permitted to be written. This final act in the drama of *The Cantos* is not a tragic admission of defeat by death and time, but a somber and intricate contemplation of the lure of silence, of escape from the labyrinth of the poem to a reacquaintance with the self and with doubt, and to a new mode of perceiving the world unmediated by language.

One of the distinguishing characteristics of the *Drafts & Fragments* volume, even upon a cursory reading, is its frequent replacement of the paradise Pound seemed to desire for it with the poignant expressions of human frailty and incoherence that the last "complete" poem, CXVI, most famously contains:

> But the beauty is not the madness
> Tho' my errors and wrecks lie about me.
> And I am not a demigod,
> I cannot make it cohere.

The reasons for this, I think, are to be found in Pound's act of writing the poem's termination, which caused him to reflect upon his *Cantos,*

its partly distorted revelation of him, and the extent of its success or
failure in joining the aesthetic with the political. As I discuss in chapter
3, the volume's first canto introduces its many levels of equivocation;
Canto CX is powerfully self-reflexive, and it simultaneously contains
and redesigns *The Cantos'* various predictions of closure. Beyond CX
The Cantos' earlier nonclosural principles of imagism and vorticism
complicate any coherence that would close the poem, as I discuss in
chapter 4. It becomes evident that many nonclosural characteristics in
Drafts & Fragments have little to do with "unstable events" that the
poem relates,[3] for *The Cantos* has largely been "about," and written
in the language of, what Marjorie Perloff calls "the poetics of indeterminacy."[4] The nonclosural dynamic in *The Cantos* is its early vorticist
method, whose mandate is the continuation of pattern, whose model
is the semiotic principle in Fenollosa's *The Chinese Written Character
as a Medium for Poetry,* and whose elementary particle is the Poundian
image, which contains the nucleus of perpetual poetic motion. In chapter 5 I examine how these early principles eventually conflict with the
several teleological narratives gradually absorbed into the poem, which
envision a poetic close structured by what Robert Casillo in *The Genealogy of Demons* calls a "fascist myth of order."[5] By trying to satisfy
The Cantos' various narrative demands for closure Pound spurns its
early vorticist request for incompletion—a problem that cannot be resolved without an acknowledgment of its existence and then the relin-
quishing of the demands of one side or the other. In the midst of the
attempts by various readers and others connected with Pound at the
time to organize a close to the poem, his own expression of the problem
can be discerned, and his abandonment of *The Cantos'* political narratives and return to a prefascist stage of the poem detected, though not,
perhaps, with the assurance and volume that some would wish.

The Cantos had always relied on the mediation of its discourse, on
the masking of the poet by the personae of other texts; in *Drafts &
Fragments,* suddenly, the voice is that of Pound's encounter with the
self that the poem has so long concealed, and that now is almost
virtually unknowable, as I examine in chapter 6. If *The Cantos'* end is
orchestrated by its self-contesting dynamics, which culminate in
Pound's examination in *Drafts & Fragments* of himself and his poem,
this self-consciousness is one of the evocative dimensions of the *Drafts
& Fragments* volume, and possibly a reason why, along with the *Pisan
Cantos,* it is a most accessible and revealing section of the poem, read

with great empathy and emotion. In the *Pisan Cantos* the introspection concerns Pound's own situation, incarcerated in a cage, humbled by the magnitude of historical forces and by nature's inexorable patterns and beauties. The protean shapes of the final volume indicate how that introspection is complicated by a shifting appraisal of his political views and of his personal relationships, and of their effect on the poem itself, no longer suspended in a state of imminent harmony, and no longer an unquestioned medium for the poet's exclusive articulation of his "tribe." In *Drafts & Fragments* Pound believes he no longer occupies a central position as spokesman for anything but himself and sees his own reflection instead as scattered around the circumference of the political and cultural influence he sought since his early years in London. Such fragmentation and marginality, he eventually believed, came perilously close to defining his *Cantos* too, whose words were reduced to evidence of his "unsound mind" in 1946, and whose final plea to its readers not to be "destroyers" (CXVI) went unheard, for Pound, by the "600 more dead at Quemoy" ("Notes for CXI") and by the emergent political powers of the 1950s and 1960s in America, Europe, and the East.

Some of these characteristics of closure, or its absence, are peculiar to *The Cantos,* but the authorial self-examination, and the return to the poem's earliest poetics, are not entirely so. The backward glance in the case of *The Cantos* is a result of Pound's desire to return to a point in the poem and his career free of their particular overt, and covert, political and racist voices, but in other long poems of the twentieth century the pattern occurs as well, though for slightly different reasons. It suggests that the modern long poem is always a poem in conflict with itself, that the characteristic of length creates the limitless potential for the poem's successive stages to contest its earlier mandates. It is constantly imperiled by its own growth, and by the anxiety that no closure can satisfy all the requests of its perpetually burgeoning and protean self. *The Cantos* began partly in order to test the poetics of imagism and vorticism, to see if they had the stamina to travel the extended path of the long poem, and not just the local two-line space of "In a Station of the Metro." If Milton wrote a long *Paradise Lost* to justify the limitless ways of God, Pound (and other modern writers of the long poem, too) began his longest work to justify the poetics of his time in the enlarged field of action of the long poem. *Drafts & Fragments,* the furthest point in *The Cantos* from those original dynamics, is the clearest index of their stamina, and the site of greatest self-revelation in his "tale of the tribe." *The Cantos* becomes an ironic model for at least two long poems in this way—William Carlos Williams's *Paterson* and Charles Olson's *Maximus*. While *The Cantos* offers later poets such as these the assurance that the modern long poem can be written, it simultaneously embodies a code of self-termination that its progeny will struggle unsuccessfully to break. In the Afterword, I examine this structural legacy of *The Cantos* by looking at how *Paterson* and *Maximus* attempt to transcend that code and instead embody its characteristics of self-investigation, authorial self-revelation, and unstable termination.

It was to be an irony, not lost on Pound, that a poet who sought through *The Cantos* and his many other writings a measure of political and cultural authority, and embodied it for many, would find himself incapable of managing its close in a manner satisfactory to himself, and thus of controlling the poem that had seemed to acquiesce to his inviolable mastery for so long. A recognition of this irony, too, is involved in our response to *Drafts & Fragments,* a text that partly reveals a person behind the many masks and voices, behind the often frustrating didacticism and inflexible beliefs, whose poetic methodology has been admired, but whose ideologies have been questioned. In 1970 one biographer, Noel Stock, wrote that Pound will be remembered "because he was one of the few to whom is granted the gift of giving words to that which is beyond words," a gift that will supersede "the broadcasts and the manias, the economics and the sense of justice."[6] And in response to Pound's Bollingen award, Dwight Macdonald wrote in 1949 that the judges were finally able to separate "Mr. Pound the poet" from "Mr. Pound the fascist, Mr. Pound the anti-Semite, Mr. Pound the traitor, Mr. Pound the funny-money crank, and all the other Mr. Pounds whose existence has properly nothing to do with the question of whether Mr. Pound the poet had or had not written the best American poetry of 1948." In the *Drafts & Fragments* poems, composed between the two statements, Pound delivers a very different and less sympathetic judgment. He senses that neither those other Mr. Pounds, nor their broadcasts and manias, could be entirely ignored any longer, and that their acknowledgment late in life and poem would irrevocably complicate any possibility for a paradisal close. From this perspective the statement in CXVI that he "cannot make it cohere" is not so easily an admission of defeat or failure, but a recognition of how coherence

is ultimately foreign both to the poem and to the self. In *Drafts &
Fragments* he exchanges some illusions of the equation between authority and coherence for alternative perceptions—not unaccompanied by
defensiveness or confusion, however. Its poems tell us it is neither an
easy transaction nor one that is fully accomplished, but one that,
though perhaps originally unintended, just may permit a version of the
humanity *The Cantos* and its many different readers have sought.

Chapter 1

"No Substitute for a Lifetime"

—you
a poet (ridded) from Paradise?
—William Carlos Williams

By the summer of 1958, when Pound began to write the cantos that would become *Drafts & Fragments*, he had just left St. Elizabeths, and *Thrones de los Cantares XCVI–CIX* was virtually complete. At the time, he mentioned to Charlotte Kohler, the editor of the *Virginia Quarterly Review*, which had recently carried Canto XCIX, that his "characters . . . are somewhere in paradise."[1] And one and a half years later, while struggling to complete the poems, he told Donald Hall in an interview for *Paris Review* that he was composing the "Paradiso" for his *Cantos* (*RP*, 243). The statements seem rather puzzling. For one thing, *The Cantos* had already accumulated and expressed many dimensions of its paradise. A large number of texts had influenced its vision of paradise by the late 1950s, and Pound had given them various amounts of space in *The Cantos*. In Homer's *Odyssey* and Ovid's *Metamorphoses* he had seen mythological representations of the divine; the most recurrent in *The Cantos* is Aphrodite. St. Anselm's *Monologion*, Dante's *Divine Comedy*, and Grosseteste's *Hexameron* offered Neoplatonic visions of paradise. And texts by Confucius, Joseph Rock, John Adams, and Paul the Deacon generated *The Cantos'* images of an earthly paradise of custom, economic health, and society's harmony with nature. Numerous individuals from history inhabited this composite paradise; some were artists of various kinds (Mozart, the troubadour poets, the sculptor Gaudier-Brzeska), still others were politicians and statesmen (Malatesta, Mussolini, Thomas Jefferson). Its worldly sites were various: fourteenth-century Italy, eighteenth-century America, Tibet, ancient Egypt, thirteenth-century Provence.

Furthermore, many statements in *The Cantos* itself fractured any hope of a linear pattern of ascent such as the one that Pound mentions to Hall—Dante's in the *Divine Comedy*. Surely the poem's predictions that it weave "an endless sentence" in Canto VII, that it attempt to "Day by day make it new" in Canto LIII, that "there is no end to the journey" in Canto LXXVIII, suggest a poem not burdened by a teleology, paradisal or otherwise. In Canto XXV Pound winces at Titian's fate that he "be constrained to finish said canvas" and notes in Canto LXXIV that, for Allen Upward, to "end my song" meant suicide. And the statement "Nor began nor ends anything" permeates *Drafts & Fragments* itself, occupying its very center in CXIV. How curious, then, that Pound would speak not just of a paradise but, to Hall, of a Dantean "Paradiso," with all the systematic closure that might imply, while writing a late portion of the poem that frequently reveals his disapproval of enforced endings.

The statements of a polyphonic and complex poem such as *The Cantos,* however, cannot be represented quite so simply. For each of its testaments to open-endedness there is another to closure, and those of the latter kind begin to accumulate beyond the midpoint of the poem. Canto LXVII's "to determine form you must determine the end / (that is purpose)" is one, the definition of "end" as "purpose" here not entirely excluding the alternative meaning of "a close." Another is Canto LXXVI's "things have ends and beginnings," directly contradicted by the later meditation in CXIV, and yet another the hint of future revelation in the *Pisan Cantos*' refrain of the Homeric "with a name to come." And *The Cantos* incorporated several teleological narratives as well: the Confucian tao or way from ignorance to sensibility, the Social Credit realization of a debt-free society after the evils of usury, the journey from what one critic terms "the darkness of history to the light of the sun,"[2] the climb from Hades to the paradisal mountain of Taishan, the recreation of the Diocesian visionary city of Ecbatan through the ideals of fascism.

Pound acknowledges his poem's contradictory urges toward open-endedness and a paradisal close while caged at Pisa at the end of the Second World War, where his earlier skepticism of closure was no doubt tested by the immediacy of the very notion of paradise:

> I don't know how humanity stands it
> with a painted paradise at the end of it

without a painted paradise at the end of it

(LXXIV/436)

It is a contradiction provisionally resolved only two pages later (the intervening one, notably, connecting song's end with suicide). There, in a passage crucial to the vision of paradise, and of closure in *The Cantos,* he follows the example of the Chinese emperor Yaou mentioned later in the same canto, who "seized the extremities and the opposites / holding true course between them" (LXXIV/442):

Le Paradis n'est pas artificiel
    but spezzato apparently
it exists only in fragments unexpected excellent sausage,
        the smell of mint, for example

(LXXIV/438)

Contrary to Baudelaire's vision of it in *Les Paradis Artificiels,* it is of nature and not a contrivance. Like form itself in the poem, it could emerge from flux, recede back into it, then reappear unannounced. Though its potential exists permanently, it is realized only in fragments, and thus is not necessarily synonymous with closure: appropriate to a poem whose individual cantos equated completion with artifice and whose first, beginning "And then" and ending "So that:" already disputed a more traditional unity.

When Pound spoke in 1958 and 1960 of a paradise for his poem's last cantos, he did not mean that he hoped to close it with a secure and triumphant paradisal declaration, therefore, since that possibility is not commensurate with its earlier expressions of fragmentation. Yet, if we are to believe him, he did intend his late (and what would prove to be his last) cantos to display, or at least confirm, a paradise somehow. The cantos composed during the Pisan imprisonment, the St. Elizabeths hospitalization, and the *Drafts & Fragments* composition years of 1958 to 1960 are undeniably fascinated with paradise—while it is named five times in the first seventy-three cantos, it occurs twelve times in the forty-three cantos in and beyond the Pisan volume. In part, his comments, and the poetry of *Drafts & Fragments* itself, suggest that he intended there to strip away whatever obscured the various expressions of paradise *The Cantos* had already contained at different points in its evolution, and to isolate and reveal the core of the poem's vision. To this extent the writing of paradise involved Pound, as it does his readers, in reexamining his *Cantos,* to see what remained fundamental and constant in that vision, a process that also demanded his reassessment of it, frequently to be undertaken in *Drafts & Fragments* itself.

The most consistently influential intertext for *The Cantos'* evolving paradise is Dante's *Paradiso;* Pound's reference to it in the interview with Hall, and its permeation of *Drafts & Fragments,* suggest that even after writing most of the last poems Dante's text reverberated in Pound's imagination. Pound's reverence for the *Divine Comedy,* first articulated at length in 1910 in *The Spirit of Romance,* is sustained for the next fifty years, during which his *Cantos* would collect and reexpress its various meanings remarked upon in that early volume. The title of the 1959 volume *Thrones de los Cantares XCVI–CIX,* a direct reference to Dante's *Paradiso,* hints at how significant Dante's paradise was for Pound's conception of his own.[3] *The Spirit of Romance* devoted to Dante's poetry almost twice the space accorded any other subject, and the bulk of that to the *Divine Comedy,* which Pound called "the tremendous lyric of the subjective Dante." For the *Paradiso* Pound can barely find adequate descriptors. More than an exquisite arrangement of imagery, it was an almost magical grouping of sounds whose transcendent lyricism was fused with the visionary quality of the experience the poem recorded. That lyricism is inseparable from the original Italian and, as Pound argues in *The Spirit of Romance,* cannot be translated into another language without the sacrifice of poetic effect. This verbal dimension of paradise would be characterized by a direct and luminous perception that *The Cantos* manifests as insight and wisdom, a chthonic wisdom where word, world, and insight merge, where expression and subject and understanding are united. Pound had first considered this notion in *The Spirit of Romance* too, where, as Christine Froula writes, he recognized that "the 'paradise' of the Latin poets is not purely thematic but also stylistic."[4] To Pound, reading Dante required the development of a new linguistic sensibility, and a new ear for the melopoeia not encountered in any English verse. The first reference to the *Paradiso* in his poem is troubled by the question of whether he can fuse vision with the sound of words to recreate what is best in Dante's epic in his.

> The fire? always, and the vision always,
> Ear dull, perhaps, with the vision, flitting

And fading at will.

(V/17)

The passage seems uncannily to predict the "spezzato" aspect of the paradise his *Cantos* will later acknowledge; if so, it implies how closely aligned with thoughts of the *Divine Comedy* Pound's meditation upon paradise would always be.

Pound also saw a tremendous clarity of expression in the *Divine Comedy*, a lucidity that becomes intrinsic to the vision of paradise itself. Pound's imagism, which pushed for "hard light, clear edges," as he wrote to Amy Lowell in 1914 (*LEP*, 38), had revered this quality in language as well, and throughout *The Cantos* Pound celebrates texts that are composed out of it. The Ur-Cantos and Canto II are indebted to such a text, Browning's *Sordello*, which Pound exclaimed in 1934 held "a certain lucidity of sound that I think you will find with difficulty elsewhere in English, and you very well may have to retire as far as the Divina Commedia for continued narrative having such clarity of outline without clog and verbal impediment" (*ABC*, 191). That lucidity was also in Noh drama, which he wrote in that year was "too beautiful to be encumbered with notes and long explanation.... quite lucid"(*LEP*, 31), and whose disappearance in the later stages of *The Cantos* is notably reversed in *Drafts & Fragments*.

With the exception of Browning, who "had attained limpidity of narration and published Sordello at the age of 28" (*ABC*, 191), writers and literary epochs tended to achieve clarity, economy, and simplicity for their language only after a long apprenticeship. Hardy accomplished it in his later poetry ("Now there is a clarity.... the harvest of having written 20 novels first" [*LEP*, 294]), Villon at "the end of a whole body of knowledge, fine, subtle, that had run from Arnaut to Guido Cavalcanti" (*ABC*, 104), Dante in his *Paradiso*. One of the features of *Drafts & Fragments* is that it occupies this position, both in his career and his poem, where Pound would be concerned that preparation must give way to mastery, if it is ever going to. As early as this passage in Canto V we read of the self-doubt that later encloses *Drafts & Fragments'* mood, for here he worries that he is not equal to the task, that the development of such verbal precision is beyond his powers, and that his vision of paradise, unlike Dante's, will be "flitting and fading / At will." The Pisan volume gives the first indication that such a fusion of insight and language is truly imperiled in *The Cantos*, if not impossible, and that insight exists only beyond language, ineffable and silent: "Wisdom lies next thee, / simply, past metaphor." The volumes *Rock-Drill* and *Thrones* temporarily dispute that assertion, sounding the depth of language as an impenetrable barrier to understanding, but the silence mentioned by name and approached in tone in *Drafts & Fragments* will attest to its final and complex significance for Pound. To him, Dante's achievement in the *Paradiso* is the paradoxical and mysterious evocation of silence in language, the "mystic ecstasy" (*SR*, 141) that "may not be told in words" yet is enacted so superbly that it is "almost impossible to convey, except by longish quotations" (*SR*, 138). The mood of silence in *Drafts & Fragments,* which becomes Pound's own in the last decade of his life, seems in part to stem from his perceived inability to accomplish the same in his poem—the hush of a personal infirmity coupled with the inarticulate voice of poetic failure.

Another reason Pound retains his gesture toward a unified paradise for the end of his poem is that the glow of Dante's achievement surrounds him for at least the five decades after writing about it in *The Spirit of Romance,* and because the 109 cantos in between become a long initiation into writing to prepare him for this final task of emulating it. Not coincidentally, the line immediately before the opening of *Drafts & Fragments*—"You in the dinghy (piccioletta) astern there!" (CIX/774)—looks ahead to *The Cantos'* paradise by invoking the early stage of Dante's, where his readers are cautioned that he is about to move into spiritual territory uncharted before by poets, and into a region of his poem that only the most faithful and attentive might follow ("O voi che siete in piccioletta barca...": O ye who in a little bark, eager to listen, have followed behind my ship...turn back.... The waters I take were never sailed before" [2. 1–7]).[5] The early part of the *Paradiso,* looked to by Pound as his own approaches, also includes Dante's description of the poverty of language and memory to render and recall paradise fully ("e vidi cose che ridire...": "I saw things which he that descends from it has not the knowledge or the power to tell again; for our intellect, drawing near to its desire, sinks so deep that memory cannot follow it" ([1. 5–9]), a cautionary message that Pound will acknowledge in various ways in *Drafts & Fragments,* so frequently concerned with maintaining memory and shoring fragments of lucidity against the ruin of verbal misuse and imprecision.

Many passages in *The Cantos* itself, and elsewhere in Pound's writing as well, alert us to his consistent suspicion of "the Aquinas map" that Dante's poem so effortlessly traveled by, since its order of ascent followed a Christian system ("ecclesiastical lumber" he termed it in *The Spirit of Romance* [146]) with which *The Cantos* had no relationship.[6] Yet the curve from spiritual vacancy to divine fulfillment, from misdirected to directed will articulated in the *Divine Comedy* is drawn, if jaggedly, in *The Cantos* too. As Ronald Bush has shown, Pound "reinterpret[s] the religious, emotional, and psychological system that in Dante stands behind the drawing of the soul toward God"[7] and effectively replaces it with Allen Upward's concept of primitivism while composing the Ur-Cantos that anticipated his long poem. The apotheosis that Dante creates in his *Paradiso* as an identification of human with divine will becomes, by *The Pisan Cantos,* the resolution of individual and political will with the patterning of nature, Pound's "green world" so reverently described there. And later, in *Rock-Drill* and *Thrones,* "nature" would be internalized, so that paradise would be a harmony between the individual's disposition or inner nature, the nature of the green world, and economic and political nature, a hypostasis of sorts that is encouraged in *Rock-Drill* (and intermittently sustained in *Thrones*) with the quotation of an Egyptian monarch Khati that begins Canto XCIII: "'A man's paradise is his good nature.'"

Thus, for instance, Pound could write in 1944, in *An Introduction to the Economic Nature of the United States,* that his *Cantos* traced a Dantean path that "begins 'In the Dark Forest,' crosses the Purgatory of human error, and ends in the light." The statement refers not so much to any strictly Dantean substructure as to *The Cantos'* progress toward clarity and lucidity. And just before beginning to write CX, *Drafts & Fragments'* first poem, in the summer of 1958, he could tell Kohler that his characters had passed "through Hell and Purgatory and are somewhere in Paradise. When you paint on a big canvas... you have to start colors down here... but it all ties in." The second description suggests that Pound, looking back, regarded his poem as a kind of mystery cycle, which is how he described the *Divine Comedy* in *The Spirit of Romance,* as "a great mystery play, or better, a cycle of mystery plays" (*SR,* 154), possibly because each, like his *Cantos,* spanned an enormous history and equated natural with political and individual order.

This description also attests to the tenacity of certain metaphors of composition in Pound's imagination, for he had written thirty-seven years before to Felix Schelling, after the completion of the first eleven cantos, that they were a "preparation of the palette,"[8] an identification of *The Cantos* with painting that is crucial to an understanding of the dimensions of the paradisal gesture Pound wanted to make in *Drafts & Fragments*. The poem had gathered qualities of painting about it from its Ur-Cantos stage, and its very genesis was in many ways inseparable from Pound's interest in visual expression. Now in 1958, to equate paradise with color emphasized the optical brilliance of Dante's, the stunning illumination summoned in the *Paradiso* through Dante's invocation of Apollo, and by his early repetition in Canto 2 of "videre." *Drafts & Fragments* is more infused with light than any volume of *The Cantos*, a symbolic enactment of its own desired visionary qualities of understanding and insight. This tremendous luminosity, combined with the reverential quiet that extends from CX's opening line, creates poetry that frequently seems to meditate upon "the heart of light, the silence," Eliot's own homage to Dante. And when the paradisal vision is imperiled in *Drafts & Fragments*, it is by a darkness so pervasive and powerful that it too, like the silence, seems to predict Pound's own emotional state for much of the last decade of his life.

So when Pound was about to write the poems that would become *Drafts & Fragments*, which he hoped would merge paradise and coherence into closure, Dante's *Divine Comedy* had long since become a most significant structural source, an intertext for imagery, a model of melopoeia and of a supreme, lucid articulation of the divine: an initiatory text whose successful emulation by Pound in *The Cantos* would be a paradisal experience in itself. Writing a paradise for *The Cantos* involved acquiring and then sustaining the poetic ability to reenact its lucidity and melopoeia. Yet it also demanded gathering various other paradisal texts invoked in *The Cantos* into a coherent vision, to reveal how justice, divine will, and various dimensions of love—truths articulated in the *Paradiso*—were not simply transitory, the isolated expression of one text. They were shared by other texts and concepts Pound had worked with over the years, and were represented by everything from the "ABSOLUTE" in *Gaudier-Brzeska*, to the retention of substance within changing form in metamorphosis, to Frobenius's *paideuma* or "complex of the inrooted ideas of any period" (*GK*, 58) to the energy that creates the "rose in the steel dust" in Canto LXXIV.

Pound spent years in *The Cantos* accumulating these individual expressions of divine, natural, and human will. But within the poem they would remain merely as surface details if they were not eventually allowed to reveal a common energy. One can detect Pound's concern about this particular problem as *The Cantos* gains in length, and as it amasses more and more of these separate expressions. In 1927, at the beginning of a letter to his father in which he compares the structure of *The Cantos* to the "subject and response and counter subject in a fugue," he worries that the poem is "rather obscure, especially in fragments" (*LEP,* 210), and in 1936 he writes to Basil Bunting that the "poet's job is to *define* and yet again define till the detail of surface is in accord with the root of justice" (*LEP,* 277). When Hall interviewed him in 1960, Pound still felt that *The Cantos'* paradise depended upon his ability to "clarify obscurities" and to "make clearer definite ideas"—an act of what he terms coherence in *Drafts & Fragments,* which he finally represents there as the ability to discern "the gold thread in the pattern" in CXVI.

Although the presence of Dante's *Paradiso* is formidable throughout the cantos that Pound wrote between 1917 and the Second World War, it is not until *The Pisan Cantos* that he begins to reconstruct the Dantesque fusion of will, love, and natural, private, and civic order in the individual, and to begin the process of writing the paradise that has been predicted for so long in the poem. *Rock-Drill* and *Thrones* extend this beyond the *Pisan's* individual subject to encompass a political order whose exemplars are the Shang Dynasty, Justinian's Byzantium, Mussolini's Italy, and Napoleon's France, each represented by a host of sometimes obscure texts that can make it difficult for Pound's readers to follow him, as so many have lamented.[9] Yet Khati's "A man's paradise is his good nature" supplies a persistent refrain in those volumes, which frequently recalls Pound from the labyrinth of this political and economic intertextuality to the individual arcanum of *The Pisan Cantos.* And the volumes' obvious gesture of relating inner nature to political and economic nature, at times lapsing into obscurity and even insignificance, is often redeemed by the Confucian insights at the core of the attempt.

The simultaneity of individual and political order is the subject of the Confucian writings that Pound uses in *The Cantos* (Canto XIII's "If a man have not order within him / He can not spread order about him" is the first Confucian citation in the poem), and one of the reasons Confucius becomes, along with Dante, a most apparent and consistent intertextual source in the three volumes that precede *Drafts & Frag-*

ments. In Confucius's words in Canto XIII, Pound would later see a secular version of Dante's "directio voluntatis"—what Pound would translate as "direction of the will": "And if the reader will blow the fog off his brain and think," Pound wrote in *Jefferson and/or Mussolini* in 1933, "he will find this phrase brings us ultimately both to Confucius and to Dante" (15–16). The basis for Pound's interest in Confucius, introduced in Canto XIII, is amplified in Canto XLIX, whose vision is one of economic justice (represented by an absence of debt) emanating from the ruler's inner serenity and order. This "dimension of stillness" is not exclusively rendered in a social context, however, for the style of portions of the canto is reminiscent of Li Po's reverence for nature's serenity, and has at least two of Li Po's poems as intertexts.[10] But Pound's interest in Confucius at this point is more truly with his extension of personal order into political action, with the thought that a "good ruler keeps down taxes" (LIII/267). The China cantos seldom depart from this interpretation, and it is only in *Rock-Drill* that Pound begins to join Confucius with Dante, and to employ Confucius as a metaphysician as well as a social thinker. And it is in *Thrones* that he directly states what *The Cantos* has to that point already implied, that the two are not antithetical: "*meta ta physika* / meta, not so extraneous, possibly not so extraneous."

This is another reason for Confucius's presence in *The Cantos:* his emphasis on this "unwobbling pivot," the essence shared by man and nature that brings harmony to the world, the "one thing that flows through, holds together, germinates" as Pound would translate him in *The Analects* (CA, 263) in 1950. His concern for a harmony between the political and the poetic had emerged, as Tim Redman argues, during the years he wrote for A. R. Orage's *New Age* in London.[11] Confucius's tao, Frobenius's paideuma, and Dante's "directio voluntatis" were manifestations of this equation, primary to Pound's evolving view of *The Cantos* and of himself, for he increasingly shunned the Mauberley-like figure of the aesthete for that of the political reformer whose media were poetry and essays. Pound's embrace of Mussolini, an extension of his attraction to Confucius, occurred in part because it gave him "the illusion of effect,"[12] the sense of being a poet who is central and consequential in the world of politics and human affairs. A quotation from a letter by John Adams to Thomas Jefferson, "Litterae nihil sanantes" (literature curing nothing), appears in Canto XXXIII and then again in CXVI, effectively the boundaries before and after Pound's active involvement with fascism. The sense of being marginal to political power generates his attraction to it in the 1920s and 1930s; the quotation's repetition in *Drafts & Fragments* hints at his reassessment of the relationship between literature and political involvement that occurs in that volume and implies that the political is eclipsed by the poetic and private, in a dramatic return to the poetry of the earliest cantos, and to the poetry that predates even them.

By *Rock-Drill,* Pound equates Dante and Confucius rather firmly (he would more properly call it "hammering" to Hall) along these lines: "Justice, directio voluntatis, / or contemplatio as Richardus defined it in Benjamin Major" (LXXXVII/576) and fuses them with Richard St. Victor's words from the *Latin Patrology* ("Animus humanus amor non est": The human soul is not love, but love proceeds from it) and John Heydon's from *The Holy Guide:* " 'From the colour the nature / & by the nature the sign!' " (XC/605) in the great ode to love, perception, and justice that assists in focusing Pound's paradise, Canto XC. Here, through the influence of Confucius, Pound begins to orchestrate the two major dimensions of the paradise *The Cantos* has frequently contained but only intermittently connected—the spiritual paradise and its "forméd trace" in the social and political world, the *paradiso terrestre.* Much of the two volumes that precede *Drafts & Fragments* approaches this equation ponderously, encumbering it with textual examples of financial reform such as Alexander Del Mar's *History of Monetary Systems.* Yet the Dantean concept of paradisal divine justice that is measured by love merges, despite these intrusions, with its Confucian counterpart in the social order whose measures are sincerity and filiality. The family, particularly in Canto XCVI, the first canto of *Thrones,* and in the rest of that volume, becomes a central representation of this terrestrial order—"a filiality that binds things together" (XCVIII/686)—and evolves into *Throne's* emphasis on harmonizing family, commerce, love, and government into a paradise of simplicity and coherence that the poetry itself, ironically, often has to struggle to contain—

> To trace out and to bind together
> From sonship this goes to clan
> and to avoid litigations
> > out of the field, from the trees,
> Food is the root

> Feed the people
>
> (XCIX/695)

—a bond instructed by Confucius's *Four Books:*

> Kung said: are classic of heaven
> They bind thru the earth
> and flow
> With recurrence,
> action, humanitas, equity
>
> (XCIX/698)

This "binding" or, later, coherence, has many intertexts in *Thrones,* of which Confucius's *Sacred Edict* is the main, but not sole, example. Their accumulation prompts Pound to observe in Canto XCIX that *The Cantos* "is not a work of fiction / nor yet of one man," and that its paradise is a multitude of voices "with Chou rite at the root of it / The root is thru all of it" (708). It is a crucial recognition in the poem that its poet is a listener, reader, and gatherer of texts, capable neither of the single authorship of its utterances nor of supreme control over its form. Instead, there is "a must at the root of it / not one man's mere power" (XCIX/709), an informing intelligence that integrates Confucian filiality and Dantean *caritas* (XCIX/720) in the *paradiso terrestre* with the *Divine Comedy*'s attributes of harmony and lucidity in poetry:

> The father's word is compassion;
> The son's, filiality.
> The brother's word: mutuality;
> The younger's word: deference.
> Small birds sing in chorus,
> Harmony is in the proportion of branches
> as clarity (chao[1]).
> Compassion, tree's root and water-spring
>
> (XCIX/708)

In 1922, in his letter to Schelling, Pound had foreseen closing his poem by "100 or 120 cantos," and it is noteworthy that Canto XCIX, on the threshold of that achievement, stands out from much of *Thrones* because of its integrative character, as if it is drawing the poem to an end. Canto C, however, gives no indication that such a milestone has been achieved.[13] The absence of any gesture toward closure there in fact suggests that to distill the foundations of *The Cantos* was a task more imposing than Pound had originally hoped it would be, and that he required more time.

The canto's end,

> nous to ariston autou
> >   as light into water compenetrans
> that is pathema
> >   ouk aphistatai"
> >   thus Plotinus
> >   per plura diafana
> neither weighed out nor hindered;
> >   aloof.
> >   1 Jan '58
> >   (C/722)

is notable in this regard. The quotations from Plotinus ("nous ... ": the mind in itself most wonderful; "pathema ... ": affection is not separate from it) follow two from Cavalcanti and Villon concerning love. Together they swerve *Thrones* temporarily from its ideological didacticism toward a vision of Pound himself, divorced from his economic and political apparatus, private and introspective. The composition date included at the end of the canto acknowledges this return to the poem as an act of private record and briefly exposes as illusory any imminent coherence of the political, economic, cultural, and aesthetic that discards the personal. The earliest sign of *Drafts & Fragments'* composition appears in typescripts from the same time, and Canto C's close is one brief anticipation of *Drafts & Fragments'* insight that any such act of coherence that ignores Pound's own past and present life is artificial and unconvincing. James Wilhelm, writing of Confucius's influence on *Rock-Drill* and *Thrones,* points out that these volumes' emphasis on the extrapersonal is Pound's way of suggesting that "a social paradise is a necessary prelude to a lasting psychic one."[14] Yet if so, Pound is reversing the Confucian maxim that his poem has presumably already affirmed but deferred since Canto XIII, that social order cannot be achieved in the absence of inner order, an insight that *Drafts & Fragments* would once again offer, in dramatic contrast to the priority established in *Rock-Drill* and the early part of *Thrones.*

This gradual reversal in *Thrones* of the cultural over the personal is facilitated by many things, as we will see, but one of them is Pound's

encounter with texts describing a geography of silence and private contemplation, and which almost miraculously harmonize with aspects of
Dante and Confucius: Joseph Rock's 1947 *The Na-khi Tribe of Ancient
Tibet,* and 1948 *The ^{2}Muan-^{1}Bpo Ceremony or the Sacrifice to Heaven
as Practised by the Na-khi.* Pound first saw Rock's texts in 1955 while
writing *Thrones*[15] and was attracted to Rock's discovery of the contemporary Tibetan tribe, the Na-khi, that had apparently remained entirely
separate from outside influence for thousands of years. Their society,
retaining its original forms and structures, customs, mythology, and
language, becomes a symbol of an earthly paradise for Pound. At the
time that he discovered Rock's texts, Pound needed precisely the imagery that they offered, imagery of a natural landscape so in harmony
with individual will and political custom that it perfectly integrated
Dante, Confucius, and the historical expressions of political virtue that
Rock-Drill and *Thrones* otherwise contained somewhat uneasily. So
timely was Pound's discovery, in fact, that he could hardly restrain
himself from employing it, hence Canto XCVIII's cryptic and spon-
taneous reference to a Na-khi rite that celebrated nature's coherence
and spirit:

> Without ^{2}muan ^{1}bpo . . . but I anticipate.
> There is no substitute for a lifetime.

> (691)

But it was the outline of Rock's personal situation, so coincidental
to Pound's own when writing his paradise, that may also have attracted
him. Rock spent twelve years researching the Na-khi tribe, but all his
writings were destroyed during their shipment to the United States in
a submarine attack.[16] Rock would go on to salvage his work by returning to Tibet and rewriting his study, hoping (as he writes in the preface
written at the foot of Mount Kinabalu) "that Providence will grant me
enough time to [rewrite the new book on the tribe]." Pound saw in
Rock's situation a surprisingly appropriate analogy to his own. In the
Hall interview Pound mentioned that *The Cantos'* "writing is too obscure as it stands," and although he dismissed the possibility of "a
comprehensive revision," he obviously entertained one of "elaboration,
clarification." The sentiment is more a product of the years after Pisa
than before, and an important part of the self-reflexive aspect that we
will see operating in *Drafts & Fragments* particularly. His trial in

Washington, which redefined Pound for the American public and his readers, is crucial in this respect. Its "Pound" was not the writer of *The Cantos* but the author of the Rome Radio broadcasts; the poem, the international product of a lifetime's reading and interpreting, the field on which the modernization of Western poetry was being played, had been superseded by broadcasts heard by a handful of people.[17] It was an irony that, if unrecognized by Pound at the time, did not elude him when writing his poem's last volume. Much effort had been spent by his detractors combing the broadcasts for the indictable phrase, the revealing word. Yet, as for *The Cantos,* Pound later wonders in *Drafts & Fragments'* CXVI, "who will copy this palimpsest?" (797). The charge of treason was based on the contents of his broadcasts (which he believed reflected his desire to reform America, not to betray it),[18] yet his *Cantos,* when briefly invoked, was cited merely as the incidental trace of his mental incompetence. Fourteen years afterward he would lament in CXVI, with a pun on the verb, that "my errors and wrecks lie about me" (796). In a curious and temporarily invisible way, the fact of Pound on trial placed his poem on trial too, an interrogation that would recur years later in the very different court of the *Drafts & Fragments* poems.

Thus in Canto CX he would, echoing a line from *The Waste Land,* refer to *The Cantos* as "these fragments shored against ruin," as expressions retrieved from their own destruction at the hands of an uninterested audience, or a culture no longer retaining poetic expression at its center. We might sense here that for Pound the composition of *The Cantos* became an increasingly defiant protection of "the forméd trace" of culturally and politically significant utterance from distortion and abandonment, and that in Rock's difficult act of recovering his own text (and simultaneously the record of the Na-khi tribe) Pound saw a metaphor for his own act of rescuing and writing his poem in its later stages. And in Canto CX's allusion to Rock's ordeals, and in the translation of portions of his *The ^{2}Muan-^{1}Bpo Ceremony* that comprises most of "From CXII," we can sense an involvement with Rock that leaves the intertextual to consider the relationship between writer, text, and culture.

The combination of spontaneity and restraint in the Canto XCVIII reference to Rock, then, assumes a deeper meaning for Pound's conception of his poem's close. Although Rock's imagery is entirely appropriate to the terrestrial paradise that he hopes to describe, Pound also realizes that the relationship between the texts and their writers is even more significant for his purposes now. Yet "the palette" for that personal dimension of paradise is still not fully prepared; it cannot be approached, really, until *Thrones* has answered Pound's desire at the time to connect the political and economic strands of the terrestrial paradise that he is in the midst of writing, a feeling no doubt sustained by his politically charged situation at St. Elizabeths.

Pound's inclination during the years 1946 to 1958 was to search for, or reassert, the social model that would have interpreted him differently. The first St. Elizabeths canto begins with the ideogram for "sensibility," and invokes the virtuous government of the Shang dynasty.[19] A brief nod toward Galileo, a similarly misperceived figure, and then on to the Confucian ideogram *chih*[3], the firm moral center from which the actions of an individual, or a state, should spring:

LING[2]

Our dynasty came in because of a great sensibility.

All there by the time of I Yin

All roots by the time of I Yin.

Galileo index'd 1616,

Wellington's peace after Vaterloo

 chih[3]

(LXXXV/543)

In part, the passage describes the terrestrial paradise often expressed in *The Cantos,* defined by a society whose economic center was debt free, whose political energy was philosophically founded and humane, who recognized and recorded intellectual achievement, and whose design was peace, not destruction. Several printings of *The Cantos* that include *Drafts & Fragments* could be said to end that way with the last line of one of the "Notes for CXVII et seq." fragments: "To be men not destroyers." But an urgency to communicate this terrestrial paradise to the state that would imprison him runs throughout *Thrones,* as if his situation was the measure of its justice. Edward Coke, who initially appeared in Cantos LXII to LXVII as an interest of John Adams's, reappears insistently from Cantos XCVII to XCIX as a validation of Pound's belief in his own innocence of the treason charge. Coke's *Institutes of the Laws of England,* which argue for the supremacy of the Magna Carta and of the pragmatic common law over the prerogative of the king, eventually led to his imprisonment for treason under King James and then Charles I, a situation predicting Pound's own. *Rock-Drill* and *Thrones* seem permeated by this urgency for Pound to revalidate himself, to convince an audience, through the sheer weight of relentless historical lesson, of its poet's unjust treatment.

If *Thrones* seems difficult and obscure, particularly in its second half, the reason may be that Pound was writing almost mechanically now, insisting upon seeing his situation in political and economic terms when it had asked from the time of the Pisan volume to be treated in private and self-exploratory ones. There is a sense of obligation to the outer dimension of *The Cantos'* paradise in these poems (even in the departure of *Rock-Drill* and *Thrones* as a whole from the meditative disposition of the Pisan volume) and of his moving swiftly to complete it. Certainly the poems after Canto C shorten in length quite noticably, and their composition is much more hurried, their typescripts less emended, than was usual for Pound. All the while Rock's texts begin tentatively to sound in these poems, first in Canto XCIX,

> Let him analyze the trick programs
> and fake foundations
> The fu jen receives heaven, earth, middle
> and grows
>
> (712)

where the [2]Muan [1]bpo ceremony opposes artifice and reasserts a Confucian middle, and then (maybe not so coincidentally) in Canto CI, where their beautiful geography, emblematic of nature's intelligence (and reminiscent of the landscape at the end of Dante's *Purgatorio*),[20] is consistently used to resonate with some of Pound's favorites of the moment—Jules S. Simon, George Kennan, McNair Wilson, and others. Rock's description of the Na-khi landscape devoid of people ("Not a human soul dwells here") begins Canto CIV, too—"Na Khi talk made out of wind noise, / And North Khi, not to be heard amid sounds of the forest"—invoking a scene conducive to the private contemplation that Pound seems to be moving toward. But it is quickly eclipsed by Pound's obscure presentation of the (to him) unjustly executed Serb Draja Mikhailovitch:

> But when the young lout was selling the old lout
> the idea of betraying Mihailovitch
> The air of the room became heavy so that young S.
> Resigned from the F.O. and "went into the City"
>
> (738)

Ultimately, reference to Rock's fabulous discovered world remains sporadic and restrained until Pound purges the monetary and political from *The Cantos*' system.

Yet if *Thrones* deflects the personal that the Pisan poems had so exquisitely bestowed upon *The Cantos,* it simultaneously reintroduces the possibility for encountering that most formidable dimension of paradise through the Na-khi texts of Rock. Thus it anticipates the last stage of *The Cantos* that will turn once again to face a private and visionary paradise assessing and then transcending the political and economic. The intensity of the private voice in *Drafts & Fragments* is partly a response to its postponement after *The Pisan Cantos,* and it will be released in *Drafts & Fragments* with commensurate power. *Thrones* both defers and foresees the explosion of Rock's, Dante's and Confucius's influence (and then reassessment) at *The Cantos*' close, Pound's age and experience having accumulated to the point ("There is no substitute for a lifetime") where its expression can no longer be held in abeyance. Its lengthy deferral, though, will bring with it a different set of problems, for the "Pound" that is to be reencountered has been repeatedly traced over and remade through the history of writing *The Cantos,* and through the many personae that have been constructed by the conflicting political, personal, artistic, and economic demands of the accelerated years he lived in, effectively obscuring it from the Pound who writes *Drafts & Fragments.* The personal arcanum had been suspended, quite possibly, because any exploration of the self in the poem would be perplexing and irresolvable, troubling if not preventing both its paradise and its close.

There were the problems of poor health, political exile, and emotional suffering, too, which complicated any such exploration. Certainly Pound experienced powerfully depressive states after returning to Italy from the United States in the summer of 1958, which made composition of any kind arduous, and at times impossible. The condition may have been due to physical factors, combined, however, with the consequences of the very self-examination that old age and the writing of this portion of his *Cantos* involved, and with the many disorienting changes that characterized his life at this late stage.

Like Mauberley, Pound was out of key with his time when beginning to compose the last cantos, suddenly freed into a world that had gone on without him for the last fifteen years. After his release from St. Elizabeths he described himself as having "popped out of a booby hatch like a cork out of a champagne bottle. But I was not prepared for what I would find on the outside.... I came out like Rip Van Winkle, and it is hard to catch up from such a long sleep."[21] He returned to Italy from the United States to live in his daughter's Brun-.nenburg castle in the Tyrol, a location that was intended to provide him with time to work on the next stage of his poem, and to prepare *Thrones* for publication in the summer of 1959. A young admirer, Marcella Spann, joined him there, and they lived together with Pound's daughter Mary de Rachewiltz and his wife Dorothy. His longtime companion Olga Rudge was not far away, in Rapallo. Domestic strain was inevitable, and it forced him to leave Brunnenburg within a year, to take several trips with Spann and his wife, and finally to make a complete departure for Rome in the fall, where he lived by himself for several months.

Once the *Thrones* cantos were ready for publication in the fall of 1959, he became increasingly introspective, "oppressed always by some sense of not having done what he should with his life," as his wife put it.[22] By late 1959, in Rome: "I write but I never get to the end of the line";[23] and, in a letter to Archibald MacLeish, "I got to Rome after a year and collapsed, have been no use to myself."[24] In a January 1960 letter he wrote of getting "stupider and stupider," of not being able to compose poetry, but only of sorting and assembling some recent material comprised of "various drafts cut from the *Thrones*. Some may be worth saving."[25] He was able to write the emerging cantos infrequently, when he had the energy, but an "aphasic losing of the thread of memory"[26] constantly impeded him. As he told his New Directions publisher James Laughlin by 1960, "need twenty hours sleep a day to make one coherent sentence or approx."[27]

Pound's exhaustion and physical infirmities, experienced at precisely the time he began trying to work in earnest on the next volume of *The Cantos,* are a crucial factor in the apparently incomplete and provisional character of the eventual *Drafts & Fragments* volume. Yet its poems were composed twelve years before he died, twelve years during which, if compromised by ill health, he was nevertheless active in the literary field. He gave many public readings, traveled to the United States for an honorary degree and to London for the funeral of T. S. Eliot, and sustained his enormous correspondence. The silence on *The Cantos'* front is notable, therefore, because it cannot entirely be explained by these external impediments but involves in addition the complicated tensions that were disturbing *The Cantos'* paradise, and the "doubt" as Pound would later call it—a difficult reappraisal of his personal relationships in the present and the past—that came to characterize his old age.

It is one thing for Pound to imply in theory that *The Cantos'* paradise will bind together what had been constant in the poem's expression, and to combine with it this urge to return to the private and the personal. It is another to accomplish it in a long poem whose protean aspect seems certain to prevent distillation and consensus, in an environment fraught with irresolvable tensions that would expand beyond the domestic ultimately to encounter the origins of Pound's fascism and anti-Semitism and their expressions in his life and poem. A coherence of *The Cantos'* myriad statements and almost infinite texts and sources would not be a simple task; and to achieve it within a poetry that is suddenly both emotional and personal would seem an unattainable vision for a poet who has, with few exceptions, been hidden by the many intertexts and voices of *The Cantos.* Inevitably, one wonders how Pound could have misconstrued for himself the apparently irresolvable complexities of his own poem and have been blind to its accumulation of the very usurious excesses it had always abhorred in language and in culture. In hindsight, we might interpret his paradisal gesture not only as an attempt to gather and rearticulate *The Cantos'* many themes, then, but simultaneously to validate the poem itself through the coherence of closure, and thereby redeem it, and him. His confident forecast that the poem "all ties in" in the summer of 1958, not surprisingly, gives way to greater concern not long after that, when the composition of the final poems actually begins. He writes to Norman Holmes Pearson later that year, for instance, that he foresees a close not in the confident terms he speaks of to Kohler, but as more provisionally guided by his own shifting response to the poem: "Cantos won't be finished until my demise, shd always reserve possibility of death-bed swan."[28] His hope here is that the poem will continue as long as he does, no doubt generated at least in part by his own anxiety that he simply cannot fulfill the closural demands he has placed upon *The Cantos* in its later volumes—upon a poem that has anticipated paradise yet disputed closure, acknowledged the significance of endings yet constantly deferred them, asserted the reciprocity of cultural, political, economic, and personal order yet diverted self-examination. Guided by a desire for *The Cantos'* redemption, attracted to the expression of the individual arcanum, and entangled within the paradox of closure and open-endedness, the composition of the last poems begins.

Chapter 2

The Mirrored Reader: A Composition and Publication History of *Drafts & Fragments*

Knowing within myself the manner in which this Poem has been produced, it is not without a feeling of regret that I make it public. What manner I mean, will be quite clear to the reader, who must soon perceive . . . every error denoting a feverish attempt, rather than a deed accomplished.

—Keats, preface to *Endymion*

Neath this altar now Endymion lies

—Canto CX

These complications facing a paradisal close for *The Cantos* emerge in expressions of doubt and reassessment in the *Drafts & Fragments* poems, as I will discuss later, but they are also apparent in the volume's composition and publication histories. For Pound, writing an individual arcanum raised the specter of self-exploration, and of reinterpreting his political and racial views. As we will see, the volume's first poem, CX, becomes the tentative entry into that difficult ordeal. For many of Pound's readers, however, such an expression was an attractive possibility, for any remorse might dispel the shadow of his obsessions that threatened to obscure the poem's centrality and stature and would reinvigorate its New Critical readings. As a result, *Drafts & Fragments* becomes a critically constructed text pushed and pulled by various expectations for *The Cantos'* close, and by interpretations of Pound, that its writer either refused to or more possibly could not accommodate, given the problematics of closure he faced at this point in the poem's evolution.

Those expectations are visible in the history of the *Drafts & Fragments* texts, held in part by a readership hoping that *The Cantos* would achieve a particular coherence, and that Pound might offer an expression of remorse at its conclusion—activities that the composition history suggests he considered but that he did not fully carry out, either in intention or in text. Louis Montrose describes the New Historicist mandate in Renaissance studies as one of distinguishing between "the Renaissance text and our text of the Renaissance,"[1] and it is a crucial type of distinction to keep in mind when reading *Drafts & Fragments,* whose construction reaches far beyond the complex intentions of Pound to a circumference defined by his readers' expectation of coherence, and by their desire that an expression of personal remorse might extract the poem from its larger ethical controversy and return attention to the text itself. The publication history of *Drafts & Fragments* shows rather graphically, that is, a distinction between our text (and author) of *The Cantos,* and Pound's.

For a number of reasons, the *Drafts & Fragments* volume is the least authorially sanctioned of any in the poem, and as much the product of readers' and editors' wishes and necessary interventions as of Pound's. Its title, for instance, was not Pound's creation, the contents of its posthumous printings had not been entirely his choice, and its sequence, at least at two critical locations in those texts, had to be decided by others. More importantly, its appearance as the termination to *The Cantos* was occasioned neither by Pound's sense of the volume's completion nor even by his desire to print it as a record of *The Cantos'* evolving paradise beyond *Thrones.* Instead, its first authorized appearance as a volume in 1969 was generated by external circumstances—it was the necessary counterattack on a 1967 pirated edition of poems (crudely printed by a disdainful Fuck You Press) whose preemption of Pound's control over the pace and character of publication effectively prevents us from knowing whether he would otherwise have made his last cantos public as a volume, and in what specific form.

The full history of *Drafts & Fragments'* composition is an unwieldy knot, and untying it is no easy matter, largely because the poems did not develop discretely, or even sequentially. Passages from one, partially composed, would be moved to another; other passages would find no permanent place. Possibilities for a canto would be discarded and then resurrected or left undetermined while other cantos evolved.

Canto CX's opening lines were changed several times, its eventual contents an amalgamation of at least three differently numbered typescripts, and Canto CXV sustained at least two distinct versions well into the years of journal publication after 1962. Since Pound moved frequently from 1958 to 1960, when most of the composition took place, various people typed and retyped for him, their copies taking time to come back by mail. Meanwhile, significant changes would be made in the versions he retained, overtaking the copies that eventually returned.

Nevertheless, though its edges are sometimes blurred, an informative pattern to the composition process emerges. Pound had completed the fourteen cantos of *Thrones de los Cantares* by early 1958 and was already anticipating the stage of *The Cantos* that would follow. Its first trace appears even before the composition of Canto C in fact, in a St. Elizabeths typescript of late December 1957 titled "Canto 110 (or 111 or 112)" (fig. 1).[2] In it Pound transcribes portions of the 1662 Connecticut Charter (abbreviating the source as "Conn Ch" in the top right corner), which harmonizes in Canto XCIX with Coke's *Institutes* as the expression of correct government. The Connecticut Charter maintained the principles of its predecessor, the 1639 Fundamental Orders of Connecticut, which asserted the authority of the citizens of the region and the establishment of general assemblies presided over by an elected governor and magistrates whose power could, under circumstances of neglect or absence, be usurped by the people. Written shortly before Pound was identifying Canto C as a private record, though, its attraction for him was not only political. He briefly extended the ideals of self-government and liberty to marriage through the phrase "TO HAVE AND TO HOLD," introducing the issues of power and control into the domain of human relationships, for instance, issues that were to dominate parts of *Drafts & Fragments*' composition for the next four years. And its life as a physical document bore an uncanny resemblance to Rock's texts, surviving in dramatic fashion James II's attempts to annul it through Joseph Wadsworth's ploy of hiding it in the now-famous Charter Oak while the king's representative sought to return it to London. Wadsworth was one of Pound's maternal ancestors, and although the Connecticut Charter material eventually vanishes as the post-*Thrones* poems begin to take shape, the Wadsworth connection (obliquely introduced and then abandoned in Canto LXXIV) was extracted and retained.

```
CANTO 110 ( or 111  or 112 )

Chas , the 2nd   Gods Grace    '62
            1162 --  But Linnaeus  --
To whome theis  ... whereas .. Navigacons
Discoverers , of diverse
             Islands, Places , Plantacons
         ... & Commerce  increased
Obedias  Brewen..
               Mathew Camfeild
                     Body  Politique
                       and meere  mocon
Ordeyned
       Our heires and  Successors..
                    Woollcott  , Talcot  ..
                        perpetual  ..
                                 Common Seal
One Governor, one Deputy
                 and  12 Assistants
                      2nd. Thursday  May  & October
A general  meeting .. take their
                         Corporal Oathes
                             Ship, transport  and Carry
-- there    or on the Sea   goeing  thither

liberties &  immunities  appoint  judges  make Lawes
                                  Direccons
    not contrary to those of England
                          Fines, Mulcts, Imprisonment
                             under their Common Seale


may wynn   and invite
                published in writing
                      and under their  Common  Seale
against    vs, our  heires  and Successorw   ...
                to Assemle, Martiall , Array
                      ..Warlike posture  ..
detriment or annoyance  Law  martiall   in
                                such cases   onely
( & that they not take to piracy )
             ayders , Abettors
                    and not hinder  Fishinge  ..
                         as shall be necessary for Salting
                            by Norrowgancett
and on the South by the Sea
          Mynes, Mynerals Precious Stones  Quarries
                    TO HAVE AND TO HOLD
As of our Mannor East Greenwich   in Soccage ,
                         not in Capite
Onely the Fifth  parte  of all Oare    Gold and Silber
      our Selfe in Westminster
                      23  rd April

writt Privvy
              HOWARD
```

Fig. 1. "Canto 110 (or 111 or 112)." EPAB Box 71, Folder 2754.

The background to the personal, however indistinct, was there and was focused into the specific personal reference, the Connecticut assembly's recognition of his action—"20 shillings to Wadsworth"—in another draft, unnumbered, composed sometime after his arrival in Italy in July.[3] Headed "this part is for adults," it repeats the more familiar paradisal tropes of Dante and of Rock's Tibetan geography and contains a nonchalant rendering of Confucius, "the gent's job is to watch the language." But the gestures are interrupted, as Bush points out in a detailed account of *Drafts & Fragments'* composition, by a more somber mood, introduced through a Na-khi suicide ceremony, regarded now as an inevitable corrolary to the ^{2}Muan ^{1}bpo that Pound had "anticipated" earlier in *Thrones* as part of his paradise ("without ^{2}muan ^{1}bpo, no reality"):[4]

> Oaks on Mt Sumeru
> and with eyes of coral and turquoise ,
> can you see with such eyes on Mt Sumeru
> had Ash .   queen
> eyes of turquoise
> and will you walk with the oak's root
> yellow iris in that river bed

As a result of their assimilation by the Chinese, the Na-khi were forced to abandon their own marriage customs for the Confucian system of arranged marriages, and the suicide ceremony that Pound briefly quotes was carried out by young lovers prevented from marrying each other. The tension between marriage and true love in the Na-khi account doubtless held relevance for the difficult triangle of relationships emerging at the time involving Pound, Dorothy, and Marcella Spann—en route to the departure for Italy the three traveled together to Pennsylvania and New Jersey (their relationship apparently confusing some along the way) and shared a stateroom on the boat trip. And a description of "serenitas" in the typescript suffers a similar interruption, this time by a brief image of Pound's own more infernal emotions—"Ixion, the unstill wheel" (to reappear at the end of CXIII as "the mind as Ixion, unstill, ever turning")—dissolving the earlier connection between the Na-khi sexual tension and Pound's into a less-determinate world of personal pain.

In Italy that summer he continued to work with and reorganize the material contained in these typescripts, but as the year went on the domestic situation at his daughter and son-in-law's Brunnenburg castle deteriorated, the personal difficulties growing with the number of people sharing Pound's company and attention. Pound's attraction to the Na-khi suicide ceremony, his translations of Sophocles' *Elektra* and *Trachiniae* in 1949 and 1950 respectively, the powerful introspection of the emerging poetic sequence—all suggest that a tangle of possession, love, devotion, guilt, and jealousy upset the balance between Pound and his family, dominated Pound's psychological environment, and influenced his compositions at the time. In the midst of this, a short trip to Venice with Marcella Spann in the fall of 1958 spurred the exuberant opening to the eventual *Drafts & Fragments* CX.[5] Of the many versions of that number slowly to emerge, one began as an ode to love, blending its spiritual and physical forms through references to the Madonna in the Venetian Torcello cathedral and to Astarte, the Syrian Aphrodite,

> Thy quiet house at Torcello ,
> > Alma Astarte ,
> The crozier's curve runs in the wall ,[6]

Predicting the first forty lines of *Drafts & Fragments'* CX, the typescript culminated with the passage

> The purifications
> > are snow, rain , artemisia,
> > also dew, oak , and the juniper.

The influence of the somber and personalized lines from the earlier "this part is for adults" draft is detectable now ("Can you see with eyes of coral and turquoise / or walk with the oak's root?" [cf. CX/ 777]), darkening the opening meditation on love, newly fused with sections of Rock's [2]Muan [1]bpo ceremony (which would later become much of *Drafts & Fragments'* "From CXII"). The typescript then repeated some old refrains—the economic and artistic health of the Medici reign, of America during Adams's presidency, and of England's descent into debt-ridden weakness (the "staggering and disraellibitched empire")—lines that would disappear and resurface in different locations as a sequence of post-*Thrones* poems evolved and then be discarded altogether. Its penultimate page, to suffer the same fate, contained a passage reminiscent of the notebook entry "Canto 110 (or 111 or 112)," and its final page, containing the personalized Wadsworth reference again, outlined what would become the first half of *Drafts & Fragments*' "Notes for CXI," up to "Oct. 31st, Wien."

Trips through parts of Italy with Dorothy and Marcella Spann were intended to reacquaint Pound with the past, but they turned sour at times, intensifying the claustrophobia of the present and idealizing the earlier years of heady friendship and love. One of these trips, in January 1959, took in the Lake Garda region, which held the sites of Mussolini's Salò Republic, Catullus's birthplace at Sirmione, and the town of Brescia. It generated a typescript titled "CXI" that introduced a landscape mixed with moments of serenity, jealous tension, and a touch of sensuality, beginning with the lines

> And in thy mind beauty, O Artemis ,
> as of mountain lakes in the dawn ,
> Foam and silk are thy fingers ,
> Kuanon
> And the long suavity of her moving

and ending with

> the holiness of their courage forgotten,
> The Brescian lions effaced.
> hsin 新 to go forth by day[7]

Though it contained nothing of *Drafts & Fragments*' eventual namesake "Notes for CXI," in late 1959 and early 1960 these lines and the lengthy passage they surround would take the place of the Rock, Medici, and Connecticut Charter material deleted from the earlier Venetian CX typescript ("Thy quiet house at Torcello, / Alma Astarte," Folder 2756) to form the middle section of the eventual *Drafts & Fragments* CX, lines 41 to 85.

The dynamics of composition and revision that began with the "Canto 110 (or 111 or 112)" and "this part is for adults" texts and culminated in the early CX versions and the "CXI" typescript reveal the discrepancy between Pound's earlier vision of an economic and political paradise in *Rock-Drill* and *Thrones,* and its greatly reconstituted version in what would become *Drafts & Fragments.* Pound's eventual solution was to forfeit the dream of merging natural, political, and economic dimensions of a paradise for his *Cantos*, and instead to scatter their private and ritualistic tonalities (the Wadsworth residue from "Canto 110 [or 111 or 112]" and Rock's ²Muan ¹bpo ceremony from "this part is for adults") across an emerging, more introspective opening to a post-*Thrones* sequence.

By March 1959 Pound moved with Dorothy and Marcella Spann to Rapallo, where he had lived on and off from 1925 to his arrest in 1943, and until the following October maintained a frequently uneasy home there. The opening of the developing sequence continued to pose problems too, and CX and CXI would turn out to be the last poems to take shape in it. Meanwhile, several other cantos developed only slightly less arduously, and when in October 1959 Marcella Spann left (possibly at Dorothy's insistence), she took with her Pound's gift of a series that had been written by that point, containing a provisional CX, a "CXII" and "CXIII," and four poems numbered "114" to "117."⁸ She retyped the poems during the next several months, with the exception, it seems, of the CX, which Pound meanwhile altered extensively.⁹

The differences between this group and the eventual versions of *Drafts & Fragments* display the evolution of paradise and closure at this stage in Pound's poem. A four-page "CXII" contained most of the Rock ²Muan ¹bpo material from the early CX typescript that now comprises *Drafts & Fragments*' "From CXII," the suicide ceremony material that darkens *Drafts & Fragments*' Canto CX (extracted and expanded from its first appearance in "this part is for adults"), and a final two pages again from the early CX that repeated the attempt to resuscitate a political and economic dimension for the sequence.¹⁰ A six-page "CXIII" (fig. 2), composed in May 1959 according to the typescript's internal dating, contained the passages that now make up *Drafts & Fragments*' CXIII, and another that would eventually become the final fragment of "Notes for CXVII et seq." as well. It began with forty-seven lines that Pound would extract sometime during the first four months of 1960 and turn into the last movement in *Drafts & Fragments*' CX (from "hsin / that is, to go forth by day" to the end; ll. 84–131 [780–81]), leaning the volume again toward a deeper despair, and inaugurating much of the revisionist reading and self-reflexivity that underlies it. In those lines the mood of the canto descends from the "panache" and "gaiety" of its 1958 Venetian opening ("Thy quiet house at Torcello, / Alma Astarte"; this section is ll. 1–40 in CX)

CXIII

hsin 新

hsin 新

                                   that is
                             to go forth by day

That love be the cause of hate
                   something is twisted
Awoi   5 Feb.

bare trees walk on the sky line, but that one valley reach
                                 the four seas.
mountain sunset inverted

La Tour, San Carlo gone
          and Dieudonne,
                 Voisin

Byzance a Tomb, an end. Galla's rest, and thy quiet house in Torcello.

"What! What!" says the auzel here.
"Tullup" said that bird in Virginia,
               their meaning?

Wars are the desctruction of restaurants.

               Quos ego Persephonae
                not with jet planes

The holiness of their courage forgotten
            and the Brescian lions effaced

Until the mind jumps without building
and there is no chih   止 chih

           and no root

Bunting & Upward neglected;
          all the resisters blacked out

From Time's wreckage shored,
             these fragments shored
             against our ruin

and the   旦 sun
             new with the day

Mr. Rock still hopes to climb at Mount Kimbalu

his fragments sunk (20 years)

13,455 ft. facing Joselton, Borneo,

Falling spiders and scorpions!
           Give light against falling poison!

a wind of darkness hurls against forest

Fig. 2. First collection "CXIII." Reorganization of passage sequence into *Drafts & Fragments* CXIII, and eventual dispersal of remaining passages into *Drafts & Fragments* CX and "Notes for CXVII et seq." fragment #4. Crossed out lines do not appear in *Drafts & Fragments*. EPAB Box 71, Folder 2752.

                         the candle flickers;
                                        is faint
lux enim -
          versus this tempest.

The marble form in the pine wood.

                         The shrine seen and not seen

From the roots of sequoias

                    pray   pray

                    There is power

Awoi or Komachi
                    The oval moon

Then a partridge shaped cloud over dust storm.

The hells move in cycle.

                    No man can see his own end.

CXIII
11.37-95 .The Gods have not returned. "They have never left us."
(end quote)
                    They have not returned.

Cloud's processional and the air moves with their living.

Pride, jealousy and possessiveness

                    3 pains of hell
& a clear wind over garofani

                    over Porto Fino   3 lights in triangulation

          Or apples of Hesperides fall in their lap
                    from phantom trees

The old countess remembered (say 1928)
                              that ball in St. Petersburg
and as to how Stef got out of Poland ...
          Sir Ian told 'em help
                         wd/ come via the sea
(the black one, the black sea)
                         Pétain warned 'em

And the road over apple-boughs
                    mostly grass covered
          and the olives to windward
                         Kalenda Maja!
Li Sao, Li Sao, for sorrow
          but there is something intelligent in the cherry-stone

     Canals, bridges, and house walls
                         orange in sunlight
but to hitch sensibility to vitality

                              that is the question, my Marlow,
grass versus granite

                    for the little light and more harmony
Oh God of all men, none excluded

& howls for Schwundgeld in the Convention
                              (our constitutional
                              17..whichwhat
Nothing new but their ignorance
                              ever-perennial

Parsely used in the sacrifice
                    and(calling Paul Peters)

                    12% does not mean one, oh, four. 104%
                                             ~~recd.~~
                                             ~~March~~
                    ~~(stamp in ms.)~~   1959

~~"Oh well, we'll fight anyhow"~~
                         ~~sd Patocki~~

~~Gawd hellup yu if yu trust (them damn limeys)~~

                    ~~by the black sea"~~
                         ~~Ian Hamilton.~~

          ~~(vide Beck, "Last Report")~~

~~That was tuned (was it tuned?) to some british print shop.~~

~~Vide Mr. D. Kaye out of Perrault.~~

Error of chaos. Justification is from kindness of heart
                    and from her hands floweth mercy.

As for who demand belief rather than justice.

And the host of Egypt. The pyramid builders,
                    waiting there to be born.

No more the pseudo gothic sprawled house
                    out over the bridge there.
                                   (Washington Bridge, N.Y.C.)
                    but everything boxed
                    for economy,

That the body is inside the soul.
                    The lifting and folding brightness
                    the darkness shattered,
                         the fragment.

CXIII
11.96–end (146)

That Yeats noted the symbol over (Paris)
                              that portico

And the bull by the force that is in him.
                    Not lord of it--
                              mastered--

And to know interest from usura

Sac. Cairoli - prezzo giusto
                    In this sphere is Justizia.

In mountain air the grass frozen emerald
                    and with the mind set on that light
                              saffron, emerald
                                        seeping.

"but that kind of ignorance" sd the old priest to
              Yeats in a r/y train, "is spreading every day
from the schools to say nothing of several other varieties."

Article X for example - put over, and 100 years to get back to
              the awareness of _____
                              what's his name in that convention.

And in thy mind, beauty,
                    O Artemis.

As to sin, they invented it - eh?
                    to implement domination.
eh? largely.

              There remains grumpiness.
       malvagità

Sea, over roofs, but still the sea and the headland.

And in every woman, somewhere in the snarl is a tenderness,
                    A blue light under stars.

The ruined orchards, trees rotting. Empty frames at Limone
       and for a little magnanimity somewhere.

And to know the share from the charge
                    (scola altrui)

God's eye art 'ou, do not surrender perception.

And in thy mind beauty O Artemis:
                    Daphne afoot in vain speed.
When the Syrian onyx is broken
       Out of dark thou, Father Helios, leadest,
but the mind as Ixion, unstill, ever turning.

Thru the 12 houses of heaven seeing the just and the unjust,
        tasting the sweet and the sorry.

Pater Helios - turning.

"Mortal praise as no sound in her ears"
                            (Fortuna's)

And who no longer made gods out of beauty

                            this is a dying.

Yet to walk with Mozart, Agassiz, and Linnaeus.
        *
        Here take thy mind's space.

And to this garden, Marcella, ever seeking by petal, by leaf-vein
        out of dark, and toward twilight.‡

And over Li Chiang, the snow range is turquoise.

Rock's world that he saved us for memory

        a thin trace in high air.

And with them Paré (Ambroise) and the "men against death."

Tweddell, Donnelly--
        Old Pumpelly crossed Gobi.

"No horse, no dog, and no goat."

        "I'd eat his liver, told that son of____
and now bi god I have done it."
                    17 Maggio
                    why not spirits

But for the sun and serenitas
                    (19th May '59)
H.D. once said "serenitas"
                    (At this et cetera)
            at Dieudonne's
                    in pre-history.

No dog, no horse, and no goat.

The long flank, the firm breast
                and to know beauty and death and despair.

To think that what has been shall be.

                Flowing -- ever unstill.

* *Drafts & Fragments* includes: "'neath overhanging air under sun-beat"
‡ *Drafts & Fragments* changes "twilight" to "half-light"

La Faillite de François Bernouard or a field of larks at Allegre.

"Notes for
CXVII et seq."
fourth fragment

                "es laissa cazer"
     so high toward the sun and then falling.

              "de joi sas alas

    to set here the roads of France.

Two mice and a moth my guides

   To have heard the farfalla gasping
            as toward a bridge over worlds. (lepidoptera)
   That the kings meet in their island
            where no food is after flight from the pole.
   Milk weed the sustinence
            as to enter arcanum.

To be men not destroyers.

through the lines of jealousy and sensuality taken from the earlier "CXI" ("And in thy mind beauty, O Artemis" to "to go forth by day"; ll. 41–84 [778–80]) to a personal and far more somber expression of self-doubt, fear, and remorse. The sequence of passages in this first collection "CXIII" would also be reordered, moving its fifth page to the beginning to open the poem with the lines "Thru the 12 houses of heaven / seeing the just and the unjust, / tasting the sweet and the sorry," (cf. CXIII/786), in the process invoking "The Seafarer" as part of *Drafts & Fragments*' dramatic engagement with Pound's pre-*Cantos* verse. And "114" merged the themes of jealousy and possessiveness that began to appear in the early "CXI" with self-examination ("Yet these had thrones. / and in my mind were still, uncontending—") and personal reminiscence ("William murmuring: Sligo in heaven, when the mist came, / To Tigullio. / And that the truth is in kindness") to comprise a poem very similar to *Drafts & Fragments*' CXIV.

It is the "115" of this first collection, though, that most clearly displays the tensions between Pound's original paradisal vision for the sequence and the somewhat darker tones of *Drafts & Fragments* itself (fig. 3). This long early version, composed in July 1959,[11] contained passages that would in the months and years to come disperse into three cantos or canto fragments: "From CXV" and "Notes for CXVII et seq," first fragment and third fragment (the latter is CXX in New Directions printings prior to 1981). The first collection's "115" becomes, in this sense, a crucial vortex for the volume, into which the hope of inscribing a paradise rushed and from which a residue of three troubled and personal canto fragments emerged, products of Pound's difficult reworking of this dimension of his poem. In the portion that would later be recast into *Drafts & Fragments*' "From CXV," Wyndham Lewis was presented here as an example of the "courage" to resist the apparent decline of European energy and awareness ("Su! coraggio. / do not accept it"). Set beside this were Pound's own expression of remorse ("I have tried to write Paradise— / let the Gods forgive what I have made. / Let those I love try to forgive what I have made") and spells of personal serenity ("for the blue flash and the moments, / benedetta Marcella"). The canto terminated with a glance toward Pound's recent domestic problems ("When one's friends hate each other / how can there be peace in the world? / peccavi"), tinged with remorse over troublesome friendships of the deeper past ("Their asperities diverted me in my green time. / Their envies"). In essence, it uneasily

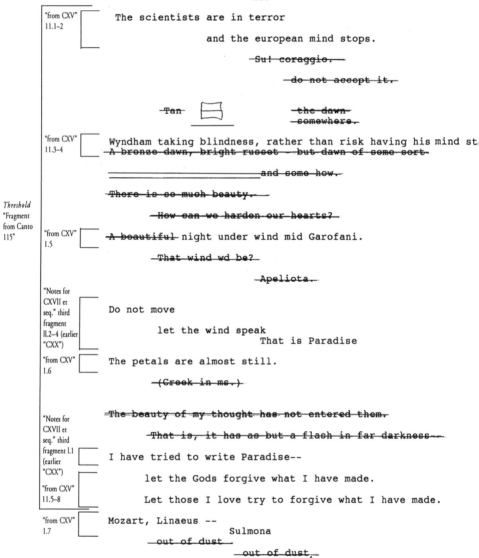

The scientists are in terror

and the european mind stops.

~~Su! coraggio.~~

~~do not accept it.~~

~~Tan~~ ☐ ~~the dawn~~
~~somewhere.~~

"from CXV" ll.3–4

Wyndham taking blindness, rather than risk having his mind st
~~A bronze dawn, bright russet - but dawn of some sort~~

~~and some how.~~

~~There is so much beauty.~~

~~How can we harden our hearts?~~

"from CXV" l.5

~~A beautiful~~ night under wind mid Garofani.

~~That wind wd be?~~

~~Apeliota.~~

"Notes for CXVII et seq." third fragment ll.2–4 (earlier "CXX")

Do not move

let the wind speak
That is Paradise

"from CXV" l.6

The petals are almost still.

~~(Greek in ms.)~~

"Notes for CXVII et seq." third fragment l.1 (earlier "CXX")

~~The beauty of my thought has not entered them.~~

~~That is, it has as but a flash in far darkness--~~

I have tried to write Paradise--

let the Gods forgive what I have made.

"from CXV" ll.5–8

Let those I love try to forgive what I have made.

"from CXV" l.7

Mozart, Linaeus --
Sulmona
~~out of dust~~
~~out of dust,~~

Threshold "Fragment from Canto 115"

Fig. 3. First collection "115." Eventual dispersal of passages into *Threshold* "Fragment from Canto 115," *Drafts & Fragments* "From CXV," *Drafts & Fragments* "Notes for CXVII et seq.," fragments 1, 2, and 3 ("Canto 120" in *Anonym Quarterly* and "CXX" in New Directions 1972, 1973, and 1975 printings). Crossed-out lines do not appear in *Drafts & Fragments*. EPAB Box 71, Folder 2767.

~~The gold thread in dark pattern at Torcello~~
~~The wall still stands.~~
~~There is a path by a field almost empty~~
~~Ub.   '43~~
"God damn it,
~~it is your future utility~~
~~I am thinking of."~~

~~'45:~~
~~"fa un affare,"~~
~~he said, "chi muore oggi."~~
~~Since when has been action.~~
~~Poiche' 'l superb' Ilion~~
~~and Europe crashed without Maud's assistance~~
~~(ref. Yeats on burning)~~
~~and to get this into simple language,~~
~~and not transmit private discouragements.~~

~~The gt inscription: @ Behistien~~

~~"They LIED."~~
~~which the arcivescovo thinks, as Ari. sd. about something~~
~~or other (monopoly,~~
~~Thales)~~
~~common practice.~~

"Notes for CXVII et seq." second fragment l.1

m'amour
        ~~ma vie~~

m'amour
        ~~ma vi'~~

"Notes for CXVII et seq." first fragment

for the blue flash and the moments,

        benedetta Marcella,

the young for the old
                That is tragedy.

And for one beautiful day there was peace.

        Brancusi's bird
                in the hollow of pine trunks

or when the snow was like sea foam,
                Twilit sky leaded with elm boughs,
under the Rupe Tarpeia,
                weep out your jealousies

To make a church

                or an altar to Zagreus.

Son of Semele   (greek)

~~Two chicks~~ without jealousy,
                        like the double arch of a window

or some great collonade.

~~Great trees over an avenue~~

"from
CXV"
ll.8-10
When one's friends hate each other
                    how can there be peace in the world?

~~peccavi.~~
            Their asperities diverted me in my green time.
~~Their envies.~~
                ~~Their paradise?~~
                                ~~their best~~
~~for an instant.~~

~~? to all men for an instant ?~~

                            ~~Beati!~~

~~the sky leaded with elm boughs,~~

                ~~above the vision~~

                            ~~the heart~~

~~"the flowers of the apricot blow from the East~~
                                    ~~to the West~~
~~I have tried to keep them from falling."~~

"from
CXV"
ll.11-14
A blown husk that is finished
                        but the light sings eternal
a pale flare over marshes
                where the salt hay whispers to tide's change.

placed heroic courage, located in past figures, against a sense of personal weakness in the present, all the while searching vainly and somewhat remorsefully for reconciliation within a joyless day-to-day existence ("There is so much beauty. / How can we harden our hearts? / ... And for one beautiful day there was peace.")

Canto "116" of this collection was perhaps the closest of its companions to a final *Drafts & Fragments* form. One difference was of voice, in an isolated yet key point in the poem where Pound lamented that coherence seems unattainable: "Tho my errors and wrecks lie about me. / And I am not a demigod, / The damn stuff won't cohere / If love be not in the house / there is nothing." The frustration there over intractable "stuff" that resists coherence would be softened in a later version of 1960, where "damn" is abandoned in favor of the more chastened and less adversarial "I cannot make it cohere." And the substance of the passage would be altered too, from a sense that something ("stuff") obstinately thwarts coherence to a very different admission that it is Pound himself who "cannot make it cohere." The final version, that is, recognizes a personal involvement in the resistance of Pound's *Cantos,* and life, to coherence and significance. This admission, in fact, was contained in the mostly deleted "117,"[12] where Pound saw himself as "outliv[ing] one's intelligence / with the young waiting a systhesis [*sic*]," little more than "a pitiless stone— / stone making art work / and destroying affections."[13] A dearth of kindness does more than injure those closest to him there—it extends to undermine the validity of all he has worked on, and to make *The Cantos* (for that seems to be the allusion) appear forced into a semblance of success (through the pun on "making art work") by an unfeeling creator, a far cry from the supposed Odysseus-Pound who listened sympathetically to Elpenor in Canto I and humbly sought the counsel of Tiresias there.

At the age of seventy-two Pound had moved from Washington to Brunnenburg, and within a year from there to Rapallo. By the fall of 1959, after Marcella Spann's departure, he was back in Brunnenburg, depressed and troubled. By the beginning of 1960 he had left his family temporarily and moved to Rome by himself. Donald Hall, poetry editor for *Paris Review,* contacted him there about doing an interview for the magazine's Writers at Work series; Hall and George Plimpton (*Paris Review*'s editor) proposed that Pound be paid for the interview (breaking with precedent in this matter) if they carried some of his unpublished work (*RP*, 126–27). A reluctant Pound agreed to meet Hall in January of the new year, admitting that "there are fragments of new Cantos. but ... whether fit to release???" (*RP*, 128)[14] and offering instead some old letters written to Basil Bunting, and some recent lines not included in *Thrones* (left over from a volume called *Versi Prosaici* published the previous summer).[15] Also contained in the list were some recent translations of Horatian odes that synchronize with the attention to age, reputation, and poetic skill in his first collection, including 1.31 ("Grant me now, Latoe / Full wit in my cleanly age, / Nor lyre lack me, to tune the page") and 3.30 ("This monument will outlast metal and I made it / More durable than the king's seat, higher than pyramids. / ... / Bits of me, many bits, will dodge all funeral, / O Libitina-Persephone and, after that, / Sprout new praise").[16] The interview seems to have renewed Pound's confidence in continuing with *The Cantos,* for Hall's response to the fragments of post-*Thrones* poems that Pound showed him was generous and encouraging at a time when, as Pound put it to Hall, he was emotionally "in fragments." (Indeed, Hall had to work very hard to reassemble Pound's answers over the two-day interview into some kind of coherence, predicting the kind of refashioning that would take place in later interviews, and in the various *Drafts & Fragments* texts themselves.) The extra *Versi Prosaici* material had just been printed, however (though Pound had apparently forgotten about any such arrangements until reminded of them in March),[17] and, coupled with Hall's strong approval of the paradisal elements in the new canto sequence Pound showed to him, it seemed to Pound the only material available for *Paris Review* to carry. Judging from a 24 March letter to Hall, Pound hoped to comply with *Paris Review*'s conditions in other ways and to avoid publishing parts of his newly emerging *Cantos* sequence:

> Further mess. ... "Listen" has printed "Versi Prosaici." I don't know where or when they got text. I hv. proby/ lost the U.S. copyright anyhow. ugh gawd hellup all pore sailors Have you struck any other snags. ... wd the attempts to translate Horace fill the bill. (ULNH)

And just after, another letter: "am struggling with problem of what can do instead. Hurled toward a date line and all other materials are @ Brun. save one copy 110–117 fragments that I am struggling with" (ULNH). That copy was the sequence he had sent with Marcella Spann (including its provisional CX), and in a very short time Pound substantially reworked parts of it to send to Hall for the *Paris Review* project. Pound offered the cantos reluctantly though, only after the *Versi Prosaici* material was unusable, and after the Horace translations were offered and (presumably) quietly rejected by Hall. While Pound's swift reworking of the early collection was stimulated by his own vision for *The Cantos'* next stage, it was generated in equal measure by the external circumstances of collecting as quickly as possible, in the absence of anything else, some new poetry for *Paris Review*.

Pound sent Hall two separately edited and reworked groups of cantos, developed from the early collection, for his possible use in *Paris Review*—one (which I call DH1) in early April, the second (DH2) in May.[18] He also wanted Hall to act as a kind of secretary, retyping the poems into cleaner copies that Pound could then emend. As Hall wrote to Laughlin in 1982, when recalling the situation: "I was (gladly, gladly) being his secretary for a brief time there."[19] In addition to revealing Pound's fluctuating and conflicting responses to writing a close for *The Cantos*, the two groups display how significant a reader's role could be in the composition and final form of such a sequence, for Hall's preference for the personal and paradisal dimensions of the early collection, so evident in the description of his response to them in *Remembering Poets*, encouraged Pound's tentatively paradisal vision for the poems.

By this point Pound had absorbed into CX the passages from its earlier Venetian "Thy quiet house at Torcello, / Alma Astarte" version, from the "CXI" typescript, and from the early collection "CXIII," resulting in the sequence of lines in *Drafts & Fragments'* Canto CX. Of the various, less drastic changes that CX underwent during this process, those involving the first two lines provide a glimpse into the complex introduction of the private and meditative voice that had already begun to pattern Cantos CXIII through "116" in the first collection.[20] The opening lines "Thy quiet house at Torcello, / Alma Astarte," of the Venetian typescript were refashioned by the time of the DH2 group to replace "Astarte" with "Patrona" (protectress or, more fittingly given Pound's new liberty, patroness of a freedman), and sometime later the specific location "at Torcello," and "Alma Patrona" (the freedom, perhaps, no longer so easily appropriate), were both deleted.[21] The result— "Thy quiet house / The crozier's curve runs in the wall"—is that "Thy" is invested with tremendous interpretive weight, leaving aside the Madonna/Aphrodite union to include now whoever Pound believes holds for him the prospect of domestic security and peace. More significantly, it can also refer directly to Pound, as if he is speaking to himself here, thus permanently installing the hushed and introspective voice that will thread through the volume, and further displacing the political and economic paradise that a post-*Thrones* volume was to express.

Pound evidently struggled with "115" again too, for the DH1 "115" retained only a portion of the first collection version, the lines from "Ub. '43" to "like the double arch of a window / or some great collonade."[22] Significantly, the passage did not include what Hall liked best, the "I have tried to write Paradise" lines that Pound would remain unsure of essentially for the remainder of *Drafts & Fragments'* history, and that later would become a hotly debated inclusion. The editing procedure of "115" into the truncated version sent to Hall recalls the contraction of what became "In a Station of the Metro" from thirty lines to two. Although some lines that Hall did not receive would later find their way into *Drafts & Fragments'* "From CXV" and "Notes for CXVII et seq.," many were deleted entirely. A definition of a semantic paradise—"and to get this into simple language"—was taken out, possibly because it spoke too directly of his creative frustration to be included in a paradise. Also among the eventual suppressions is part of the Confucian passage from XIII/60:

> And Kung said, "Without character you will
>   be unable to play on that instrument
> Or to execute the music fit for the Odes.
> The blossoms of the apricot
>   blow from the east to the west,
> And I have tried to keep them from falling."

This passage recalls its earlier context, which employs Confucius as the model for the connection of language and action, and its deletion now implies that the Confucian vision that was to bind a paradise together has lost its appropriateness for Pound. And the extraction of the lines "out of dust— / out of dust" recognizes his poem's apparent failure to inscribe Canto XC's Dantean vision of spiritual love as well:

> out of Erebus, the deep-lying
>   from the wind under the earth,

                              m'elevasti
        from the dulled air and the dust,
                                    m'elevasti

                                                        (606)

These differences between the long "115" of the early collection and the short DH1 version reflect Pound's difficulty in arbitrating between the various forms his paradise might take—from the relieved gesture of personal remorse and the serenity of the Na-khi landscape to the more anxious expressions of unresolved self-confrontation. Evidently, Pound was not yet ready to go to his readers either with easy self-remorse or with an unequivocal paradise. The next version of "115," however, contained in the DH2 group, would use many of its passages, differently contextualized, to offer an alternative to these possibilities.

The first collection "116" was included, with its alterations in the crucial "I cannot make it cohere" passage. But "117" was omitted entirely, even though it culminated with the same self-disparagement already registered in its predecessor. Pound may have sensed that the tone in "117" was harsher, more relentless, and extended too far what "116" already articulated. "116"'s last lines—"A little light like a rush light / to lead back splendour"—implied a brighter successor and also had the weight of an approaching close. To include a "117" in its present form would be to admit that private demons could thwart *The Cantos* at its termination. Furthermore, "117" was personal in a very restricted way—it commented on Pound's effect on others, on their sacrifices to his life of "making art work," and was not encountering the larger question of the political and racial aspects of his life.[23]

Apparently Hall assumed that the DH1 group represented Pound's final vision for a sequence to follow *Thrones*, because his request for further typescripts from Pound was stimulated by a concern over the precision of his typing-copying, and did not anticipate significant conceptual changes. As he wrote to Pound in May of that year, "If you will correct and assemble a final mss. and return it to me, I'll copy it again (or amend the copy I keep, rather) and return to you your annotated copy—so that you'll have one."[24] The DH2 group, though, turned out to be quite different. It contained a sequence of numbered pages that included mostly completed poems from CX to "116"; the exception was "115," which was not included in the numbered sequence, but appended to it, almost as a defiant afterthought.[25] Compressed and utterly reconceived, it is with only small differences identical to *Drafts & Fragments'* "From CXV." In it Pound has moved beyond recalling Wyndham Lewis rather nostalgically as one of the "resisters" in the early collection's "115" to perceiving him as representative of a point in his own life when resistance also meant being "diverted from my green time," a most crucial moment in the volume where Pound examines his fascism and anti-Semitism, as I will discuss in chapter 5. Just as significant is the conflation of the "blown husk" passage with the personal "my green time" through the deletion of the intervening lines, allowing the "blown husk" now to refer both to Pound himself and to his *Cantos*. In essence, in the new "115" wistful memory is exchanged for clearer self-examination, and the flirtation with self-pity yields to the humbler vision of an eternal process that encompasses him and his poem: "A blown husk that is finished / but the light sings eternal."[26]

This second canto group sent to Hall in April 1960 is the final collection of post-*Thrones* cantos that Pound compiled. The publication history of these cantos between 1962 and 1966 suggests that Pound remained uncertain of the final form several of them were to assume. Even his desire to have them appear in print is disputable. Hall had sent James Laughlin, Pound's New Directions publisher, a copy of the DH2 typescript in June 1960, and Laughlin wrote to Pound, upon receiving it:

> Let me say that there is some really marvellous stuff in this new material. Absolutely beautiful. I've asked Hall to let me know as soon as possible exactly what portions "Paris Review" plans to use, and then perhaps you will instruct me about placing the new Cantos in various magazines here.[27]

Receiving no answer, he queried Pound again in August of that year. Pound eventually dictated the various selections, but their placement was neither his choice nor, apparently, his interest. His selections often included more than one version of the same canto, indicating that even between 1962 and 1966, the years of magazine and journal publication, he was still undecided as to the final form of much of what would become *Drafts & Fragments'* content. In particular Cantos "113," "115," and "116" saw several different versions, and portions of versions, submitted by him. A "Fragment from Canto 115" published in the Belfast journal *Threshold* in 1962 (fig. 4) resurrects crucial lines

FRAGMENT FROM CANTO 115

```
The scientists are in terror
          and the european mind stops.
          Su ! coraggio
                         do not accept it.


Tan   |‾‾|
      |__|



                         the dawn
                         somewhere.
Wyndham taking blindness, rather than risk having his mind stop.
A bronze dawn, bright russet - but dawn of some sort
                         and some how.

There is so much beauty.
               How can we harden our hearts ?
A beautiful night under wind mid garofani.
          That wind wd be ?
                         Apeliota.

Do not move
          Let the wind speak
                         That is paradise
The petals are almost still.
                    Απηλιώτης

The beauty of thought has not entered them
          That is, it has as but a flash in far darkness-
I have tried to write Paradise-
          let the Gods forgive what I have made.
          Let those I love try to forgive what I have made.
```

Fig. 4. "Fragment from Canto 115." *Threshold* 17 ([spring?], 1962): 20, from 1959 first collection version of "115." Lines 16–18, 23, 24–25, rearranged, become the *Anonym Quarterly* "Canto 120" and "CXX" in the New Directions 1972, 1973, and 1975 printings.

from the early collection version, for instance, that contain the "Let the Gods forgive what I have made" passage, as if Pound is still attracted to an expression of personal remorse but is unsure of what its provenance should be. (See appendix 1 for a full description of the *Threshold* publication history.) In the same year, *Paris Review* carried "From Canto 115," the poem appended to DH2 that is essentially *Drafts & Fragments*' "From CXV." It is not surprising, then, that when Laughlin suggested the idea of a post-*Thrones* volume including this material to Pound in 1965, his response was merely conciliatory: "I will try to look into the question of draft of cantos. I haven't much here. Please let me have a list of what has been printed where, as far as you can."[28] The difficulties posed by writing a paradise and responding to its alterations, coupled with frail health, generated Pound's almost virtual abandonment of the *Drafts & Fragments* poems at this provisional point in their evolution.

During the process of typing clean copies of these two collections that he received from Pound in the spring of 1960, Hall made two carbons of each page. Shortly thereafter, Hall lent a student (Tom Clark, who was writing an honors thesis on *The Cantos*' structure) his own copy of the DH2 group (from a CX to "116," not including the appended "115"), which were then retyped by a friend of Clark's, and a carbon made, which remained in Clark's possession. From 1963 to 1967 Clark lived in England, studying Pound's poetry at Cambridge. He returned to the United States in 1967 and while in New York City

> bumped into Ed Sanders while walking down St. Marks Place, between 2nd and 3rd Aves. . . . Sanders said, as I recall, "Got any manuscripts we can instantly freak into print?" It was a fairly casual question. Sanders was a zealous and aggressive underground publisher; I was poetry editor of the "Paris Review," and as such, usually had various manuscripts in hand.[29]

The copied version of the second set of Hall typescripts was retyped on Gestetner paper and mimeographed on a machine in Sanders's apartment on Avenue A, the "secret location in the lower east side" of the edition's cover (fig. 5), to produce three hundred copies by the Fuck You Press. Sanders, a student of classical languages, added the Greek

CANTOS 110-116

Ezra Pound

printed & published
by the FUCK YOU/ press
at a secret location
in the lower east side
New York City
USA
1967
cover by Joe Brainard

The FUCK YOU/ press

peace peace

in the name of
GASH COW

Fig. 5. Title page to *Cantos 110–116*. New York: Fuck You Press, 1967.

words in longhand, as well as those Chinese ideograms that he could decipher and reproduce. The complete process of publication took only a few days: most of the copies were sold ("at a high price" recalls Laughlin) to the Phoenix Bookshop in New York, while the rest were shared by Sanders and Clark and distributed to friends. Hence the resulting edition, *Cantos 110–116,* is an edited copy of a copy of DH2. Accidental changes do exist between the DH2 text and the pirated volume, but, except for a couple of visual misreadings in its Canto CX, no substantive errors were introduced into the edition.[30]

Laughlin first saw it a short time after its release in the fall of that year and immediately asked Sanders to the Russian Tea Room, where he treated his guest to a piece of his mind and some lunch. Laughlin reasoned that the pirated edition demanded a quick rebuttal from New Directions "to get some copyright protection." He wrote to Pound about the Sanders edition and requested that Pound arrange what he would like to see in the volume. As he told an interested party in September 1968:

> One reason for putting this New Directions *Drafts & Fragments* out fast, is to try to stop some more piracies of the Ed Sanders kind, his disgusting mimeographed version which he had made up from typescripts which he must have gotten from one of the poets to whom Ezra had sent them.... Pound's lawyers have gotten after Sanders, and he says he won't do it again, but with an anarchist like that you never know. It was on the basis of this piracy that I was able to persuade Ezra to do some work in putting these Drafts & Fragments into shape and let us bring them out now.[31]

A few months earlier Laughlin described Pound's situation, and the likely outcome of the pressure he exerted on Pound to fashion the material for publication:

> I now hear from him in Venice that the work is proceeding, though it is slow, because his eyes are in bad shape. It sounds as though what we will get will be about 20 to 30 pages of the portions of Cantos 110 to 117 which he has completed. So I think we will have to have some title such as "Draft of Cantos 110 to 117." There is precedent for this title as the first 30, when they were first done here, were titled "A Draft of Thirty Cantos."[32]

Shortly thereafter, Laughlin would revise this provisional title to its present one (probably because he received the unprecedented incomplete versions of three cantos—CXI, CXII, and CXV—that were not "in shape" in the usual sense). During the spring and summer of 1968 Laughlin was in contact with Pound concerning the proofreading of the typescripts Pound had mailed him and offered suggestions for changes. Pound's replies were often no longer than one or two words, implying not only ill health and poor vision, but a weariness with the whole procedure.[33]

In preparing the material for Laughlin, Pound seems to have worked from the second set of typescripts he received from Hall in 1960; he probably emended in his own hand, according to his daughter, and had Olga Rudge type the edited copy. Pound's major decisions here, though, were the choice of the DH2 appended "115," and two of the three fragments that would become the New Directions 1968 "Notes for CXVII et seq.," extracted from the first collection's "115." The second fragment, part of which was initially contained in that poem, was written out in longhand by Pound in 1959. It contained a final passage ("That the light / stand & / grow solid"—that Pound apparently chose not to include in published form, preventing the poem from moving beyond the personal tone that already suffuses it (fig. 6). What is now the fourth fragment in New Directions printings after 1979 (the third in their previous versions) is from the first collection's "113." It appeared in *Sumac* in the winter of 1969 under Laughlin's heading "Notes for a Later Canto."[34] There is no clear evidence that Pound chose the heading "Notes for CXVII et seq." for the 1968 edition, and indeed if he had Laughlin would presumably have used it in the *Sumac* printing. In the proofs, signed in Venice by Pound on 23 August 1968, these fragments are not given a number; they are included under the heading "Fragments of CANTOS" and are preceded under that heading by what are now the two "Addendum for C" fragments. The title "Fragments of CANTOS" does not imply, as "Notes for CXVII et seq." does, that Pound necessarily envisioned *The Cantos* extending past the final line of CXVI ("To be men not destroyers") in 1968. Instead, it directs the volume's title toward the provisional character of a nevertheless finite number of cantos, and not toward the possibility of *The Cantos*' continuation into new territory. Pound may have dictated the specific title ("Notes for CXVII et seq.") for these fragments later; the Latin, Laughlin speculates, suggests Pound's

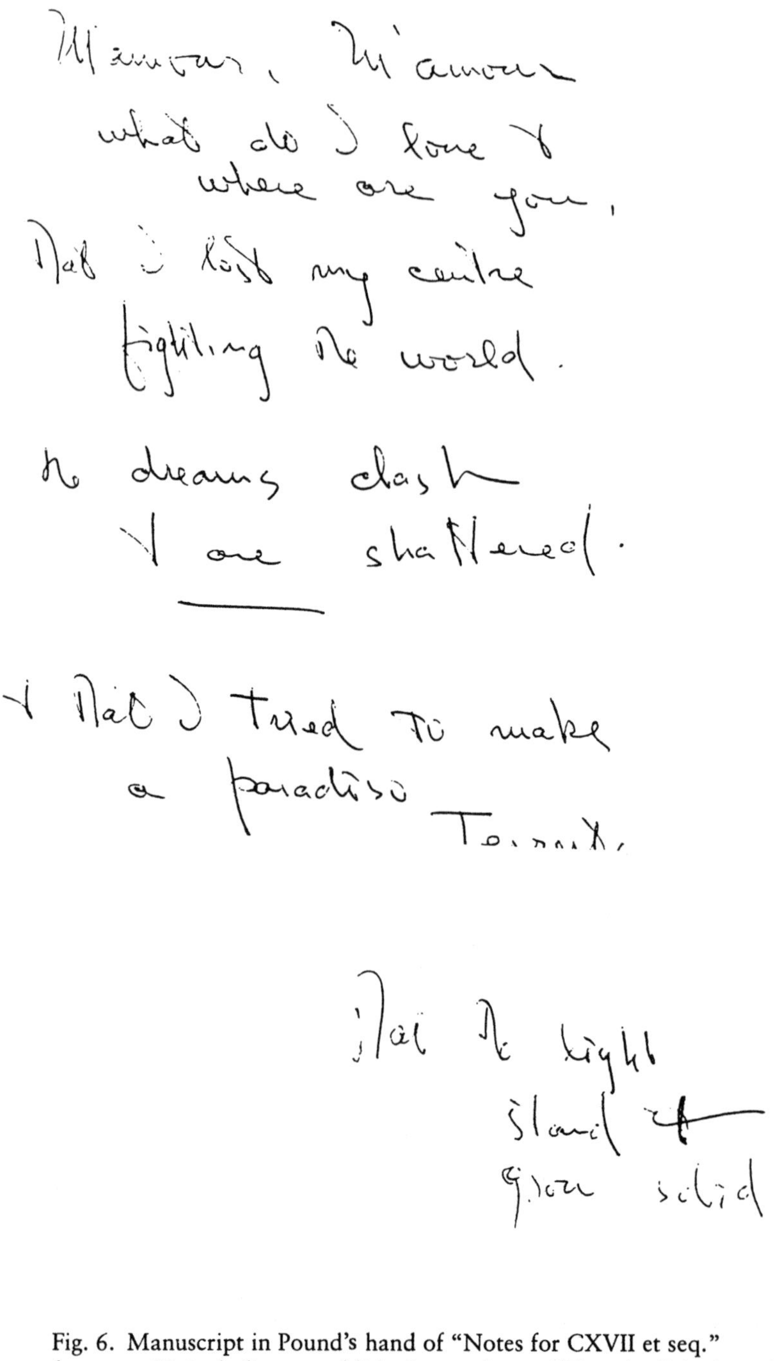

M'amour, M'amour
what do I love &
    where are you,
That I lost my centre
    fighting the world.

The dreams clash
    & are shattered.

———————

& That I tried To make
    a paradiso
        Terrestre,

That the light
    stand &
    grow solid

Fig. 6. Manuscript in Pound's hand of "Notes for CXVII et seq." fragment #2, including unpublished second page "That the light / stand & / grow solid." 1959. EPAB Box 71, Folder 2775.

authorship. However Eva Hesse, to whom Laughlin turned for editorial advice on *Drafts & Fragments,* wrote Laughlin that she was "most suspicious" about the heading:

> Did Ezra really think that one up? . . . [It] implies that he proposes to go on beyond 116, which I am sure was really intended to be THE END. This gives critics an opportunity to claim that he's now stuck and can't finish the job. . . . [It] helps to sustain Olga's myth that he's still "working on the Cantos," but it places the whole status of the Cantos in serious jeopardy, don't you think?[35]

Hesse's response astutely foresaw how editorial decisions concerning *Drafts & Fragments'* content had the potential (fulfilled later, as we will see in a moment) to affect readings not only of the isolated volume, but of the entire *Cantos.* In its conviction that Canto "116" was to be "THE END," though, the response also reflected the readerly usurpation of such crucial decisions.[36] In this case there were no consequences, but in the later case of the ephemeral "CXX," whose mere existence as a published text may be the result of readers' intervention, the effects are still being felt.

A similar editorial problem faced Laughlin concerning "Addendum for C," the two fragments that Pound included ("as an afterthought" grumbled Laughlin to his confused printer)[37] in the 1968 typescripts under the title "From Canto C." The first originally appeared in *Vice Versa* in 1941 with the title "Canto proceeding (circa 72)," the second in a letter of 12 March 1941 to Pound's friend Katue Kitasono, headed "Lines to go into Canto 72 or somewhere." The problem Laughlin faced was dizzying: to integrate into a 1968 volume two 1941 fragments originally intended for the territory around Canto LXXII (a poem that had not been printed with *The Cantos* by 1968) but now given the number C by their author for a volume beginning with Canto CX. Laughlin first wrote Pound asking, somewhat incredulously, "Am I right that you now want it [the first fragment] to be hitched evnetually [sic] onto, or into, # 100?" and suggested to Pound that it be "put at the end of the book, with the [CXVII] fragments. Would that be OK?" Pound's response was an ambiguous "yes," which left Laughlin with the problem of whether it was to the first or second of his questions and, if to the second, precisely where at "the end of the book" the fragment should go.[38] The next day, Laughlin wrote his printer to say that he hoped "we can persuade [Pound] just to have it at the back, among the fragments, with some indication that it eventually belongs with Canto 100, so that we won't foul up our title [*Drafts & Fragments of Cantos CX–CXVII*]."³⁹ Two months later, Laughlin wrote to Douglas Paige, the editor of *The Selected Letters of Ezra Pound,* which first published the 1941 letter to Kitasono, for permission to use the fragment from it. There he claimed that Pound "doesn't seem yet to have decided which Canto they [the lines] are finally to reside in, but just wants them put at the end of this collection."⁴⁰ Thus, in the absence of much authorial guidance, Laughlin had to place them himself between CXVI and the CXVII fragments. In making the decision, Laughlin may have reasoned that all fragments appearing after CXVI should assume an historical order, and thus the 1941 fragments should lead.

By the time Laughlin saw the Sanders piracy and started the process of creating *Drafts & Fragments,* New Directions' forthcoming 1970 *Cantos I–CIX* was still two years away, and publication of a separate volume seemed more likely to "get the special attention . . . to head off piracy." This decision resulted in the first authorized text (printed in 1968, distributed in 1969), and a limited edition of 310 copies hand printed by the Stone Wall Press in Iowa City under the direction of Kim Merker (of which 100 were for Faber and Faber in London, 200 for New Directions, and 10 for the Stone Wall Press). Laughlin anticipated receiving one hundred dollars per copy for the Stone Wall edition and declined to advertise it, rightly assuming that it would "sell itself by word of mouth."

One of the more interesting questions concerning the authorship of the end of *The Cantos* involves the appearance of "CXX" in the 1972 New Directions volume (the "third printing" of the 1970 first American collected edition) and its subsequent four printings, its omission from Faber's 1976 edition (and reinsertion in 1981), and its recent role as the penultimate fragment in "Notes for CXVII et seq." in New Directions printings eight (1981) through twelve (1991). These eight lines, it turns out, followed a curious route in their journey from the first collection "115" forward into "CXX" in the 1972 New Directions *Cantos,* and then backward into the "Notes for CXVII et seq." fragments in 1981. Laughlin may have included the "CXX" lines for copyright protection, because they were printed in 1969 without Pound's name in a journal called *The Anonym Quarterly,* out of the State University of New York at Buffalo, under the title "Canto 120." The lines were excerpted, by someone using the pseudonym "The Fox," from the 1962 *Threshold* fragment of the 1959 first collection version of "115" (which Pound had omitted from the two 1960 groups sent to Hall). The *Anonym* poem is in many respects that phantom reader's composition, for it extracts lines 16–18, 23, and 24–25 from the *Threshold* "Fragment from Canto 115" and reassembles them into a different order (23, 16–18, 24–25; see appendix 1). The title "CXX" seems to consider the three "117" fragments to be sequential separate cantos, producing numbers "117," "118," and "119" (one type of misreading that the specific numbering of those fragments permits). The recomposer was also likely aware, as Pound's early biographer Charles Norman was (and he might have been the source), that Pound had written in 1959 of how he still "hoped to make it to 120," maintaining his prediction to Schelling over thirty years before.[41] The act of placing them in that terminal position reflects a particular reading of *The Cantos* that insists on an organic unity to the poem (so definitively as actually to rearrange lines from a differently numbered, and apparently abandoned, canto). Equally important is that it sympathetically privileges a narrative of Pound's ideological self-awareness and remorse and demands the cathartic close that will exonerate the poem and its poet. The author of the canto may be Pound; at the moment we cannot tell. If it is, he invested a great deal of energy in covering his tracks: energy matched only by those who want to uncover them. Furthermore, the difference between authoring the lines and authorizing their publication is enormous, and Pound, it seems, simply did not do the latter.[42]

A case of such posthumous resurrection of authorship occurred in 1986, when the Denver *Bloomsbury Review* carried an article by Scott Edwin Ewing that argues that "allowing considerations other than artistic to influence our thinking about Pound's *oeuvre* is a temptation to be resisted."[43] It notes his occasional "desire to be fair" to Jews, invokes his friendships with individual Jews, and quotes Katherine Anne Porter's 1950 statement in the *New York Times* that his "so-called anti-Semitism was . . . only equalled by his anti-Christianism," in an attempt to neutralize Pound's racism and prevent it from "inter-fer[ing] with the appreciation his *oeuvre* deserves." Significantly, the article is illustrated with a reproduction of a manuscript, titled "Canto 120" at the bottom, and signed there by Pound (fig. 7). The reproduction gives no indication, however, that the signature, while Pound's, is a photocopy from the seventh leaf of Gianfranco Ivancich's *Ezra Pound in Italy: From the Pisan Cantos*.[44] It is added to the reproduction to give authority to a manuscript that in reality lacks it, for the manuscript is a visual copy, written longhand by the art director of the review in 1986 to illustrate the article. Its emulation of Pound's handwriting, and its inclusion of his photocopied signature, erroneously confirm for the hopeful that Pound indeed authored the poem. It is no coincidence that "Canto 120," asking forgiveness for "what I made," [*sic*], would be chosen to illustrate an article containing such a thesis, and though the act of copying may have been innocent enough, it clarifies how crucial it is to substantiate the authority behind this particular poem before invoking it as proof of Pound's remorse at the end of his life.

Thus the canto's line sequence, and number, may or may not be Pound's. The latter possibility seems more likely, for otherwise his decision not to submit the poem to Laughlin in 1968, or anytime in the next four years, while supposedly publishing it anonymously at Buffalo, remains inexplicable. Too, under whose authority was it reintroduced in 1981 within the CXVII fragments?[45] If the lines are not Pound's, we then must notice how large the discrepancy between an author's and his readers' desires can be, and how powerfully a reader's interpretation of the poem (and of its apparent relationship to its poet) can alter the text. If they are Pound's lines, his refusal to put them in *The Cantos* or, considering their pseudonymous publication in *The Anonym Quarterly,* to have them attributed to him, must be recognized when encountering their ostensibly sanctioned inclusion (and culminating position) in the 1972 New Directions *Cantos,* and their later seemingly authoritative appearance in the "Notes for CXVII et seq." fragments.[46]

Laughlin, whose motives have always been exemplary, may have had copyright as his foremost reason for including the poem in the 1972 text, but a lingering desire to see it there may have deflected him from pursuing less aesthetically invasive methods of obtaining it. There are other ways of getting copyright, and in this case one might have been to publish the poem in some less crucial context than the end of *The Cantos;* Laughlin published it in *The New York Times* as part of Pound's obituary, in fact.[47] No copyright is recorded in the Library of Congress for "Canto 120" in 1969, when the poem appeared in *The Anonym Quarterly,* or for 1972, when it appeared in *The New York Times*.[48] The 1972 *Cantos* inclusion of "CXX" may have been an

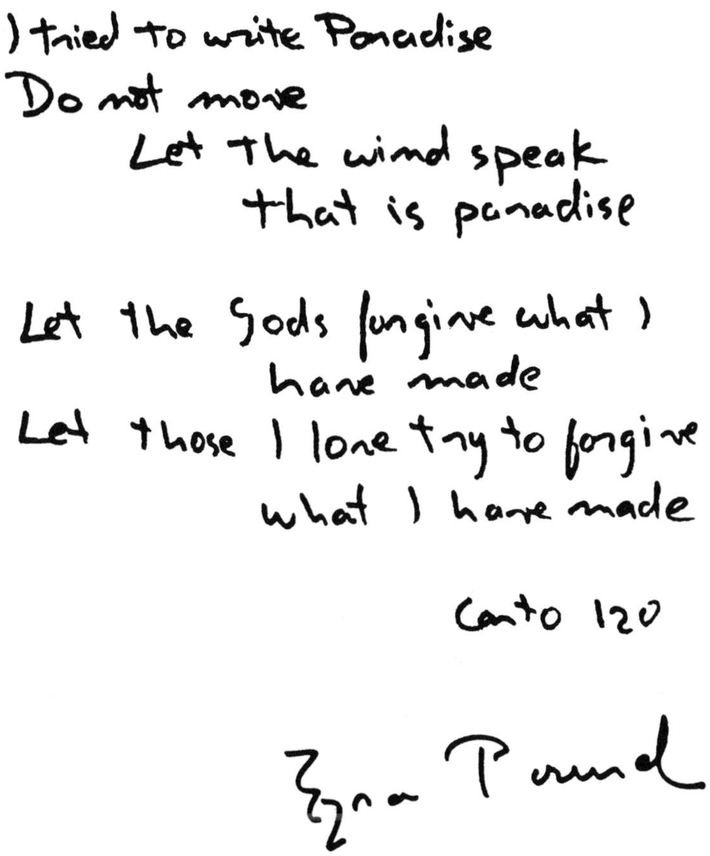

I tried to write Paradise

Do not move

Let the wind speak

that is paradise

Let the Gods forgive what I

have made

Let those I love try to forgive

what I have made

Canto 120

Ezra Pound

Fig. 7. Illustration for *Bloomsbury Review* 6, no. 4 (March 1986): 23. Artist's longhand "Canto 120" with attached signature of Ezra Pound from Gianfranco Ivancich, ed., *Ezra Pound in Italy: From the Pisan Cantos* (New York: Rizzoli), xiii.

effort to redress that legality, making the text even more the subject of external, not aesthetic, circumstances.

Pound showed Laughlin what the "ultimate" canto was to be in 1966, the poem (terminating the 1987 Faber and post-1979 New Directions texts) dedicating *The Cantos* to Olga Rudge:

> That her acts
>   Olga's acts
>   of beauty
>   be remembered.
>
> Her name was Courage
>   & is written Olga
>
> These lines are for the
>   ultimate CANTO
>
> whatever I may write
>   in the interim.
>
> [24 August 1966]

It offers another clue to any interpretation of *The Cantos'* teleology: since Pound never sent it to Laughlin for inclusion in *Drafts & Fragments,* we are left to assume that even by 1968, when submitting the material and signing the proofs, he believed in the possibility of extending his long poem to a later conclusion in which the Olga Rudge canto would figure as the close, or at least as part of it.

It is difficult, and perhaps inappropriate, to speculate on the fate of these last poems had this piracy on the high seas of *Cantos* texts not occurred. At one extreme are the possibilities that Cantos CX–CXVII would never have been included in the complete *Cantos* text, or that eventually they would have been included posthumously (taken from their magazine forms, which were often very different from their present ones) offered and read with the tentativeness such a gesture requests. At another extreme is the improbable vision of a text Pound arranged, named, worded, and sanctioned at greater leisure than the sudden response to the piracy, and to illness, required: a text, that is, devised and published entirely in accordance with Pound's wishes. It is improbable because during the late 1960s that serendipitous combination of vigor, health, and time was not his. It is improbable for another, and equally significant reason, too, which is related to Pound's reassessment of *The Cantos* during the composition of the *Drafts & Fragments* poems, as I will discuss in the following chapters.

Hence we have been given, over the last twenty-two years, at least six different versions of a volume titled *Drafts & Fragments*.[49] Each incorporates varying editorial decisions concerning sequence and content. Each responds in its own way to what its editor(s) hoped Pound intended, or to what they thought *The Cantos* requested in the absence of its author's full editorial participation: some including a Canto "CXX" and some not, one (the pirated version) including two versions of a Canto CXV and excluding the "Notes for CXVII et seq." fragments, one rearranging the fragments in a sequence different from the others, placing the troublesome foster child "CXX" among the CXVII family, putting the suppressed Cantos LXXII and LXXIII next, and then ending with the poem to Olga Rudge. The New Directions edition of 1989 maintains the changes of its immediate predecessor but restores the displaced Cantos LXXII and LXXIII to their numerically proper sites in the poem. (This latest restoration is problematic, and indicative of just how delicately any editorial decisions about a sequentially ordered and historically composed text such as *The Cantos* must be made and implemented. Though the cantos' numbers invite the restoration, to grant that request retroactively drapes the illusion of calm over what was an extremely disrupted moment in the text's composition, in effect erasing its history.) The five versions of a *Drafts & Fragments* text merely represent the number of editions and printings that actually contain different poems and sequences. That number does not include, for instance, the 1975 Faber *Cantos,* which refused entry to "CXX." Although it is identical to the New Directions 1970 edition (with the exception of small differences in particular spellings), it is so as a result of deliberate policy, not external circumstance, and thus the two texts exist in extremely divergent "bibliographical environments" of which the reader may be entirely unaware.[50] And the number scarcely begins to reflect the several, though less spectacular, differences in precise wording and spelling. If these were included, the number would be far higher.[51] Nor does it include the very different versions of individual cantos published in magazines and journals in the six years preceding its volume publication.

Since four of the six different volume versions (the exceptions are the pirated edition and the New Directions 1968/9 edition) have been part of a complete *Cantos* text over which readers may have believed Pound had exerted full editorial control, the assumed history of their predecessors has somewhat falsely sanctioned *Drafts & Fragments* for the reader. Although Pound maintained an evasive policy about his involvement in *The Cantos'* editing (writing in 1938 that he did "not care a hoot how much I am *edited*. I am not touchy about the elimination of a phrase" [Pound's emphasis]), the ironic fact is that *The Cantos* and its terminal *Drafts & Fragments* have frequently been read until recently with an unconscious belief, or at least conditioned hope, in the "monolithic authority" behind the text that simply is not present.[52] Ultimately *Drafts & Fragments* reveals, perhaps most clearly of all *The Cantos'* volumes, a textual instability that may be characteristic of each of them; its production underlines how *The Cantos* was never innocently subordinate to the dictates of its poet, but a product of the combined and interpretive "readings" of its readers and editors as well. In the case of *Drafts & Fragments,* readers and editors have resuscitated a volume whose maker may otherwise have let it collapse before it achieved the satisfaction of intact sequential numbering, a 120th canto, or the courtesy of closure.[53]

Thus the volume's contents and interpretation necessarily involve and implicate the long poem to which it is appended and help situate *The Cantos* in a judgmental debate over the nature of its achievement. It is partly for these reasons that it has been made to bear the weight of such editorial resurrection and reconstruction. A reading based upon the 1972 New Directions *Cantos* that includes "CXX" will differ from one based on the New Directions 1970 edition and the 1976 Faber edition, which do not. A reading based on New Directions' texts after 1979, and Faber's 1987 printing, will generate a third set of interpretive possibilities, for their camouflage of the "CXX" lines as the third "Notes for CXVII et seq." fragment is presumably to release the last line of the fourth fragment—"To be men not destroyers"—into the poem's final numbered position. The reading that believes the itinerant "CXX" to be the end will sympathetically regard "the last words of the entire epic [as] a gentle, almost muted prayer for forgiveness. . . . a startling ending."[54] A consequence of placing "Notes for CXVII et seq." at the end is the response, mentioned earlier, that sees *Drafts & Fragments* lending *The Cantos* "the open-ended and relaxed finale it needs," and that regards it as, somewhat mystically, "look[ing] beyond the poem" (just as Hesse had predicted it would). Yet, if we are to believe his statement concerning the Olga Rudge poem, Pound did not intend the "Notes for CXVII et seq." fragments to end *The Cantos* either (which unintentionally validates the claim that they "look beyond the poem," since they were not to close it). A third possibility, which, as we have seen, is not ignored by readers, is that CXVI (whose final lines are "A little light, like a rushlight / to lead back to splendour") ends *The Cantos*. This reading desires a conciliatory ending, in which the last lines ("Pound's final statement") longingly recall an earlier Pound, and possibly an earlier prefascist part of *The Cantos* too, for "splendour" refers not only to a crucial line about coherence in Pound's translation *Women of Trachis,* as we will see in chapter 6, but also to Hermes of Canto XVII ("Splendour, as the splendour of Hermes"). Confusing the issue still further is the fact that it also recalls the previously suppressed Canto LXXII, in which the self-sacrifice of a fascist girl is described by the term "splendour" as well. None of these responses is wrong, for there is nostalgia in CXVI, and remorse in "CXX." The point is that if these and future responses are to be valid, they must be made in accordance with a sufficient understanding of the historical dynamics and interwoven authority—Pound's, his editors', his readers', and even that of *The Cantos'* poetics—that has generated a text capable of so many definitive but divergent assumptions concerning its very provisional contents and significance. Otherwise, any *Cantos* text that includes the *Drafts & Fragments* volume will continue implicitly to sanction not only its version of the poem's ending, but consequently its reading of the whole poem, and obscure the fact of what turns out to be Pound's unresolved and uneasy response to it.

"CXX" was introduced into editions of *The Cantos* because the indeterminacy of its close permitted the substitution of various interpretations of "Pound," none of which he wanted to corroborate, for reasons that go to the very heart of his perception of his *Cantos* and himself at this late point in their composition. In the absence of such confirmation, Pound unwittingly releases his poem to a readership that is not without its own assumptions of what Pound and *The Cantos* are. The fragmentation of the final volume is not, therefore, merely an indication of how the practical sphere of publication and editing of cantos written after *Thrones de los Cantares* escaped his control. Considering that his health declined after the publication of *Thrones,* that his personal life and repeated geographical dislocations increasingly became an impediment to the laborious care such control demands, and that he was not always a vigilant self-editor, it seemed neither unusual nor unexpected for that to happen. Instead, though, Pound's problems with the option of a paradisal close he entertained for the poem as late as 1959 seem to have inaugurated his reconsideration of *The Cantos* and of the person it interpellated and, very possibly, as a response to that failure to "make it cohere," generated his silence.

The publishing history of *Drafts & Fragments* is certainly tangled, but it may do even more than hold a mirror to various interpretive desires for it and the larger context of *The Cantos*. In the wake of its unceremonious textual journey we may also recognize the current of Pound's own disenchantment with the poem, stimulated by the difficulty in untangling its various options for a close. His loss of control over these late cantos is not simply due to an inability to handle the practicalities of publication, therefore: the resistance he encountered in trying to write what could be the paradise to his long poem forced him to recognize that somewhere its own dynamics had eluded his control. Frequently, *Drafts & Fragments* ruminates upon how his vision of consolidating *The Cantos'* project to write paradise is compromised, making it the self-absorbed palinode to *The Cantos* that we now read more by accident than by Pound's design.

Keeping in mind that the impetus for the volume's publication did not come from Pound, then, we might explore options additional to the extenuating circumstances of old age and depression for the hyperfragmentary form of *Drafts & Fragments* and entertain the notion that he had some other reasons of a poetic, personal, and ideological nature for not publishing its lines in volume form until his hand was forced. In a sense, the *Drafts & Fragments* poems present an extreme version of the situation Bush uncovers in *The Pisan Cantos,* where the poems are "set in motion under the auspices of one set of poetic values"[55] and then significantly changed during their revisions as circumstances and personal attitudes intervene. If Pound had provisionally hoped for a close to his *Cantos* that would consolidate the paradise he had tried to write into it almost from the beginning, from the summer of 1958 through to at least May of 1960 he had begun to reconsider the foundations of that paradise, thus imperiling the termination the poem earlier seemed to request. The "spasm of defensiveness" that Bush sees finally shaping *The Pisan Cantos* is replaced in *Drafts & Fragments* by a deep reflectiveness that, while occasionally serene, is more often profoundly discomforting for its writer.

"It makes a great difference," Jerome McGann argues, "if, for example, an author writes but does not print a poem; it also makes a difference whether such a poem is circulated by the author or not, just as it makes a very great difference indeed when (or if) such a poem is printed, and where, and by whom."[56] These differences, so great in the history of *Drafts & Fragments'* text production, alert us to Pound's anxiety with closing *The Cantos,* and to his eventual disenchantment with at least some dimensions of the poem. The troubled composition of the last poems, and Pound's withdrawal from the usual process of their publication, illustrate both their new and difficult status for him, and his acknowledgment that *The Cantos'* structural finality is now inevitably to be placed "beyond the poem's horizon."[57] They also illustrate for us that any textual finality is CXIII's "hall of mirrors," a mirage more reflective of our "dream of the whole poem" (as Williams would write in book 4 of *Paterson*) than of *The Cantos* itself. In this manner, *Drafts & Fragments* becomes a vivid display of the historical dimension of text production and its consequences for interpretation. It is also the site where Pound acknowledges, contrary to the desires of some of his readers, that his poem, in keeping with its mandate to include history, must not avoid its own reconsideration and reinterpretation, processes undertaken in the *Drafts & Fragments* poems that pose difficult questions about the identity of *The Cantos* and of its poet. The publication history suggests, crucially, that Pound may never have felt comfortable with the intentions of closure that a published last volume for *The Cantos* might imply. The poems of *Drafts & Fragments* cannot, therefore, be read outside the context of their textual production, a history that is intrinsic to the volume's gestures of incompletion and self-interrogation (including the multiple identities, poetic and personal, which "self-" fitfully merges here). No matter how successfully any edition of *Drafts & Fragments* delineates the composite authorities that fashioned the poems, it can never communicate through the text itself how its mere existence is so historically determined by the occurrence of the pirated edition—a situation that removes the *Drafts & Fragments* cantos from the company of at least 107 of their forerunners, whose inclusion (though not necessarily textual precision) in *The Cantos,* however complex and multiply authored their texts, is at least fully generated by their writer.

Chapter 3

The Cantos Mirrored:
The Self-Reflexive Canto CX

> But how is it
> That this lives in thy mind? What seest thou else
> In the dark backward and abysm of time?
> —Shakespeare, *The Tempest*

Drafts & Fragments is a group of poems in which Pound responds in conflicting and unresolvable ways to his *Cantos,* generating the volume's repeated editing and reshaping after his death. The responses arise for Pound from composing what would likely be an end for his *Cantos,* which led him to a difficult reinterpretation of the poetic and political ideologies at its core and to withdraw gradually, through the writing, from some of its more strident and inflexible foundations. Though his declaration that his poem was "a botch"[1] can be interpreted as becoming modesty, it is safe to say that Pound wasn't known for that particular characteristic, and it is more likely that he did in fact develop insights after his release from St. Elizabeths that challenged many of the assumptions to which he had so vehemently clung before. Among the volume's composite authorities and historical circumstances, which have encouraged some of its closural possibilities, one can glimpse its new concerns of confronting the self, redefining a paradise, and of reevaluating *The Cantos'* poetics, fascism, and anti-Semitism, concerns that make it a reconsideration of, not a resolution to, *The Cantos.* The process begins tentatively in CX and culminates in "From CXV," CXVI, and the "Notes for CXVII et seq." fragments, the four points in the volume I turn to intensively here and in the following chapters, along with portions of the intervening cantos crucial to this larger debate.

75

In its original forms, *Drafts & Fragments'* opening image of the "quiet house at Torcello" represents the paradise Pound initially hoped to achieve in the volume, and which he would exchange in the final stages of its revision for a more complex version. The later deletion of "at Torcello / Alma Patrona" is one example of how the writing of the volume generated his reconsideration of the apparently secure paradise he spoke of to Hall and Kohler, for the earlier reference depicted a simpler paradise presided over by an archetypal redemptive and virginal goddess, to be replaced by a more complicated vision of the female, and sexuality, in CX and some of the subsequent cantos. The late alteration also shows Pound's embrace of the private and the personal initiating the confidential voice finally to be the territory of the volume, which *Rock-Drill* and *Thrones* had not fully encountered, since in the words' absence the significance of "Thy" expands to include Pound, as if he is his own listener now.[2] Evocative of "Alma Sol Veneziae" in his first volume, *A Lume Spento,* where he thanks the Venetian sun for "strength for the journey" ("Thou that through all my veins / Hast bid the life-blood run, / Thou that has called my soul / From out the far crevices"), *Drafts & Fragments* begins by summoning the same spirit of that city which had affirmed his artistic impulse some fifty years before, to give him "strength" for what is to be his final poetic voyage. As well as to Pound himself, therefore, "Thy" refers to Venice, where he launched his poetic career, and originates the powerfully reminiscential contour of the *Drafts & Fragments* poems.

The original image of the Torcello cathedral foresaw a location for *The Cantos'* paradise of insight, intelligence, and verbal limpidity, a sanctuary of harmonious resolution to the poem that *Drafts & Fragments* was to realize, but that remained elusive during its composition. Begun in the seventh century and continued under the Lombards in the ninth, Torcello cathedral was an example of architecture uncompromised by what were for Pound the excesses of design ruining the grace of later churches such as St. Peter's, which closes Canto CIX, and an analogy for his own realization of clear design and form—the "greater limpidity" he mentions to Hall—in *The Cantos'* last stage. Its interior—with an altar of white marble, a sarcophagus containing the bones of Heliodorus (the "Pater Helios" of CXIII), a mosaic of the bishop at the moment of death, his crozier slipping from his right hand, and of the Madonna, whose blue robe is decorated with a gold border, surrounded by vaults around which runs a golden interlace pattern—still

provides a consistent imagery for *Drafts & Fragments,* though less as
an affirmation of this earlier paradise than a reference to it as one of
many conflicting possibilities.

The "quiet house" that remains as the residue of CX's beginning is
an oasis between the self's concealment through most of its earlier seven
volumes and the cantos of *Drafts & Fragments* that reverse it. It is an
early indication that the process of writing *Drafts & Fragments* caused
a reevaluation of *The Cantos'* enactment of divine truths and developed
a humility that Pound briefly reveals as recently as Canto CVI ("Artemis out of Leto / Under wildwood / Help me to neede"). If the volume
records Pound's effort to reclaim a vision of paradise, the vision starts
here in this brief but auspicious moment at its beginning, a lingering
image not of poetic sound, but more paradoxically of an encompassing
silence within which the poet will dwell.

As CX progresses beyond this reworked beginning, it contains a
fusion of art and nature that will be both sustained and questioned
throughout the volume. Here it is the curling mosaic pattern reflected
in the waves of the surrounding lagoon:

> The crozier's curve runs in the wall,
> The harl, feather-white, as a dolphin on sea-brink
> I am all for Verkehr without tyranny
>   —wake exultant
>   in caracole
> Hast'ou seen boat's wake on sea wall,
>   how crests it?
> What panache?
>   paw-flap, wave-tap,
>   that is gaiety,
> Toba Sojo,
>   toward limpidity,
>   that is exultance,
>   here the crest runs on wall

                                                            (777)

The "crozier's curve" is the dying bishop's staff beginning to fall from
his hand within the golden interlace pattern of the mosaic at Torcello
(and would Pound not see himself here within the mosaic of *The Cantos,* modern poetry's aging ecclesiast beginning to fail?).[3] Its energy of
fluctuating curves is amplified in the following lines, where the feather-
white harl, the traditional pennant on the bishop's crozier, is placed

beside the dolphin on the brink of a wave, transforming the artistic energy of the interlace mosaic into the living energy of the dolphin cutting through the waves. An imaginary cross-section of the resulting image creates an interlace pattern itself, as if, through this liturgical and self-reflective figure, art and nature merge. It is a hopeful gesture, perpetuated by "Hast'ou seen," recalling an earlier *Cantos* passage of paradisal vision, from Jonson's *A Celebration of Charis: In Ten Lyric Pieces:*

> Hast'ou seen the rose in the steel dust
> (or swansdown ever?)
> so light is the urging, so ordered the dark petals of iron
> we who have passed over Lethe.
>
> (LXXIV/449)

In CX Pound reminds himself of the exhilaration in pattern, and the Jonsonian phrasing returns him to his first use of it in Pisa. Here the humility that the Pisan experience begins is recalled and strengthened, reversing the earlier *Cantos* by exchanging the descent into hell that formerly acted (since the *Nekuia* beginning in Canto I) as the entrance to paradisal vision and knowledge for that vision itself. And in the Latin root of "panache" is "penna," feather, and finally pen, and (along with Pound's gently humorous aside to himself as lover, duellist, and poet Cyrano de Bergerac) a recognition of the poet's utterance as the perpetuator of harmonies and patterns of recurrence.[4] Ideally, that utterance will not be the product of Pound's "tyranny" or mastery, endangering the tone of reconciliation and harmony only just beginning, but a paradisal agreement between his desire and the poem's capacity to inscribe it.

The harmonic patterns that are to characterize the clear and limpid paradise Pound hopes to attain in *Drafts & Fragments* reappear elsewhere in CX, to be contrasted later by his perception of *The Cantos* as "a tangle of works unfinished" in CXVI. The waves near the canto's opening merge with others, these drawn by Toba Sojo in his *Choju Giga* or *Scroll of Animals,* a twelfth-century children's book of animal drawings, which portray animals in a pool of water, deflecting ripples off the bank in a wavy pattern.[5] Their "exultance" combines with the wave pattern to recall the quiet house, itself surrounded by a "wake exultant," and he imagines himself presently beside its seawall, on which "the crest runs." The lines are reminiscent of a passage in Ur-Canto I that considered the genesis of the long poem in the context of Catullus's limpidity, of CX's Lake Garda location, of gaiety, of waves, of wakes, and of "home":

> As well begin here. Began our Catullus:
> "Home to sweet rest, and to the waves' deep laughter,"
> The laugh they wake amid the border rushes.

The Cantos will contain, from that inception, various allusions to the point of rest that it seeks—a constellation of poetry, delight, and nature—though, as he did in Canto LXXVIII ("You also have I carried to nowhere / to an ill house and there is / no end to the journey" [477]) Pound will at times doubt his ability to locate it. The image of the quiet house, then, also has significance within *The Cantos'* search for verbal limpidity and clarity that began in its embryonic stage, and that characterize the paradisal resolution Pound desires for his poem.

Toba Sojo's art leads "toward limpidity" because it recreates the "exultance" of the animals in simple signifiers, *Drafts & Fragments'* term for the "exuberance" that Pound attributed to nature in *Guide to Kulchur,* along with "delicacy" and "splendour" (*GK,* 282), other ingredients of the paradise *Drafts & Fragments* will recall in CXIV and CXVI respectively. Toba Sojo's drawings, in their simplicity, are a transparent sign that Pound has always hoped his *Cantos* would achieve too, escaping what he saw as metaphoric borrowing and confusion for accurate and direct portrayal. In CXVI a similar testament to the elementary and unadorned: "Disney against the metaphysicals" (796).[6] Twenty-five years before, in the *ABC of Reading,* Pound had articulated the need for poetry to emulate the "simplicity of statement" in prose, to produce

> an equal limpidity in poetry, where the perfectly simple verbal order is CHARGED with a much higher potential.... If you are trying to show what a man feels you can only do it by clarity. (*ABC,* 191)

Pound terms Stendhal's recognition of this "the great turning" in prose; its fusion of simplicity and clarity is part of Pound's desired paradisal limpidity in *Drafts & Fragments,* achieved by the trinity of "Mozart,

Agassiz and Linnaeus" in CXIII. That limpidity, so often manifested in *The Cantos* as wave patterns, is a reflection of the mind's abilities:

> Coke: the clearest mind ever in England
> vitex, white eglantine
> as tenthril thru grill-work
> wave pattern at Excideuil
>
> (CVII/758)

In CX the fusion of the wave image with limpidity (note Coke's absence now too) amplifies the symbol at the center of the waves, the quiet house. With "here the crest runs on the wall" he is adjacent to it, and to the last stage of *The Cantos,* whose paradise, like Dante's, is to be characterized by limpidity and clarity. After many typescripts, and the more than seven hundred pages of *Cantos* poetry since Pound began his quest in Canto I,[7] these opening lines of harmony and limpidity combine to build *The Cantos'* for its poet. Beyond in the volume, their pattern is disturbed by the many latent conflicts the poem has suppressed, which the pressure of a close and Pound's course of reassessment will reveal. But the pattern reappears periodically, placed in relief, like a gold thread in the mosaic of the volume, by the interference that surrounds and perpetuates it, recalling earlier poetry that connects gold patterning and utterance: the 1908 "Na Audiart," where he sets his words of desire in rose and gold, "The Tomb at Akr Caar," where four years later he has "read out the gold upon the wall," and again near the end of the CXVI: "But to affirm the gold thread in the pattern / (Torcello)."

The multiple significance of the German "Verkehr"—traffic, communication, and sexual intercourse—that Pound hopes in CX's beginning will be unaccompanied by tyranny can be traced throughout the volume. If read as sexual intercourse it introduces *Drafts & Fragments'* condemnation of the sexual repression that Pound feels is intrinsic to marriage.[8] Passages in CXIII: "Pride, jealousy and possessiveness / 3 pains of hell" and "sin, they invented it—eh? / to implement domination" are his response to this sense of tyrannical "Verkehr." In CXIV he refers to

> These simple men who have fought against jealousy,
> as the man from Oneida.
> Ownership! Ownership!

The "man from Oneida" is John Humphrey Noyse, who founded the Oneida colony in New York and began its system of polygamous "Complex Marriage," an early attempt to liberate sexual relations from social repression, no doubt recalled here in the context of Pound's situation after leaving St. Elizabeths and returning to Italy. Ruminating on this sexual tension, Pound frequently invokes the female form, as in CXIII:

> The long flank, and the firm breast
> and to know beauty and death and despair
> and to think that what has been shall be
> flowing, ever unstill

The beginning of the passage is reminiscent of Canto XX/90:

> And the light falls, *remir,*
> from her breast to thighs.

whose source (by way of the word "remir") is Arnaut Daniel's "Doutz brais e critz" (a poem, incidentally, in which the "auzel" of CX/780 is also mentioned):

> *Uns rics convens don tan gran joi atendi,*
> *Quel seu bel cors baisau rizen descobra*
> *E quel remir contra lum de la lampa.*
> Yes, that she kiss me in the half-light, leaning
> To me, and laugh and strip and stand forth in lustre
> Where lamp-light with light limb but half engages.

CXIII's "flowing, ever unstill" emerges from Pound's 1910 translation of Cavalcanti's "Donna mi priegha" (*EPT,* 175). There, two types of love are described: the "first perfection of love" is

> in a place always without pain
> because it is not an effect of physical quality
> it shines upon itself, a permanent effect

The "second perfection of love," in which desire passes "from potentiality to the actuality of sensual appetite ... when an appropriate object is presented to it," originates

From form seen . . . that, understood,
Taketh in latent intellect—
As in a subject ready—
                    place and abode,
Yet in that place it ever is *unstill*
                          (*EPT*, 135; Emphasis added)

Drafts & Fragments' "quiet house," originally divine in the presence of its goddess figures ("Alma Astarte" and "Patrona"), finally defers to this abode of the "second perfection of love," which is physical and sensual. As Pound goes on to write at the end of CXIII, its inevitable tensions ("Pride, jealousy, and possessiveness / 3 pains of hell") also resist the simpler paradise of resolution, for within it his mind too is "unstill, ever turning." The eventual paradise of *Drafts & Fragments* embraces such contradiction rather than obstinately denying it, discarding the "thrones / [that] in my mind were still, uncontending" for a vision of life and poem as "flowing, ever unstill" (CXIII/787), Pound's evolving sense of the impossibly reductive nature of a closural enterprise.

The contemplation of the sensual as a dimension of paradise returns Pound to Dante, but not to the *Paradiso*. The CX/777 quotation from Dante is a fragment of a conversation between Dante and Virgil in *Inferno* 5.73–75 in which Dante desires to speak with the two lovers of the Malatesta, Paolo and Francesca ("I'comincia 'Poeta, voluntieri / Parleriei a quie due che 'nsieme vanno, / e *paion si al vento* esser leggieri': "I began: 'Poet, I would fain speak with these two that go together and seem so light upon the wind'"). It applies both to the preceding image of the "crest run[ning] on wall," which, too, seems "so light upon the wind" and, in Dante, to the transitory nature of sexual desire and the tragedy of those who abandon themselves to it. The wind that is still for a little in Canto VIII/32 and the wind upon which Paolo and Francesca "seem so light" is the wind of the Second Circle of Hell, but it merges in CX with the Na-khi phrase "²Har-²la-¹llu ³ko" in the following line, taken from Rock's translation of the Na-khi *Romance,* which contains the suicide rite carried out by boys "with the girls whom they really loved and with whom they had carried on sexual intercourse,"[9] first appearing in the "this part is for adults" typescript of 1958. Rock interprets the rite as the result of the sudden growth of sexual repression in the Na-khi tribe since they were forced to assume

Chinese family customs informed by the Confucian system of arranged marriages. In CX, references to specific passages of the rite are placed beside the plight of Paolo and Francesca in *Inferno 5*, who suffer social rejection in the face of their enduring love:

> che paion' si al vent'
> ^{2}Hăr-^{2}la-^{1}llü ^{3}k'ö
> of the wind sway,
> The nine fates and the seven,
>   and the black tree was born dumb,
> The water is blue and not turquoise
> When the stag drinks at the salt spring
>   and sheep come down with the gentian sprout,
> can you see with eyes of coral or turquoise
>   or walk with the oak's root?
>
> (777)

Each of the phrases is taken, with some minor alterations, from the "^{2}Hăr-^{2}lla-^{1}llü ^{3}k'ö," the song the Na-khi lovers sing to each other in the ceremony, which propitiates the spirits of the wind who will otherwise torment the lovers eternally, as the wind in the Second Circle of hell torments Paolo and Francesca. The suffering the lovers endure from society's intolerance of their "Verkehr" is counteracted by the delight their love will yield them, for the lovers die believing "that they will live for ever young, in perfect happiness roaming with the wind and clouds, in the perpetual embrace of love, never to be reborn, never to be sent to an infernal region, but to live in a state of eternal youth."[10] If in Dante's cosmos sexual passion leads to hell, in Rock's description of the Na-khi system it leads through social banishment to paradise: a more appealing alternative, needless to say, both for Pound's personal situation and for this late stage of his poem, but also an indication that *Drafts & Fragments* confronts rather than reduces contradictory visions.

In the *Romance* the young female lover ^{2}K'a-^{2}ma hesitates to perform the ritualistic hanging that the ceremony demands, at once attracted to it and terrified by it. The *Romance* tells the story of ^{2}K'a-^{2}ma eventually killing herself after questioning why her lover has not yet carried out the ritual himself. If he had felt strongly enough about it, he would have been like the stag unable to lose the taste of the salt spring, or the lamb the taste of the gentian sprout. Upon finding her body, the male lover weeps, asking, if he gave "turquoise and coral eyes, will you be able to see? If I attach the roots of the pine and the oak, will you again be able to walk?"

Pound offers the girl's hesitation and eventual suicide, as well as the boy's failure to complete the ritual entry into paradise, as a measure of his own conflicting responses in the canto that is intended to begin the same ascent. Pound repeats the question later, but with the Jonsonian phrasing of the canto's beginning and of Canto LXXIV, extracting it from its Na-khi context and situating it more personally:

> can'st 'ou see with the eyes of turquoise?
>   heaven   earth
>   in the center
>   is
>   juniper
> The purifications
>   are snow, rain, artemisia,
>   also dew, oak and the juniper
>
> (778)

As in CX's revised opening line, Pound is speaking confidentially here, possibly asking himself ("can'st 'ou") if suicide is something he wants to consider at this point in his life. "Do I have the courage shown by the Na-khi girl," one might paraphrase this passage, "of placing my convictions in love before my life?" (Or, if "can'st 'ou" is interpreted as a question to the reader, does anyone?) But more in keeping with the tension between the visionary and the mortal that *Drafts & Fragments* sustains, Pound is considering the extent to which he can conceive of death's threshold itself ("Can I see from the perspective of one who is about to die?"), beyond which the world will remain in his absence and "what has been shall be" (CXIII), for though he is "A blown husk that is finished / . . . the light sings eternal" ("From CXV").

The turn from Dante to the Na-khi enlarges *Drafts & Fragments'* meditation upon the sensual—in both its luxurious and its painful figurations—that marks the revisionary nature of the volume, since *The Cantos* had formerly approved of the female only in the virginal state and condemned her otherwise as formless, threatening, castrating, usurious. These two aspects of the female represented a binary that *The Cantos* seemed incapable of resolving unless it sanctioned one, the virginal, and did violence to the other, an impossible solution that the poem chooses until Canto XCVIII, where "Leucothea gave her veil to Odysseus," and again with the reconsidered opening to CX. The problem is inherent in *The Cantos* really from its beginning, in contradiction to his earlier poetry, where he expresses his attraction to the troubadour tradition, which fuses sexual desire with the ideal of spiritual perfection and beauty. In *The Cantos* that hypostasis gradually erodes, and Cunizza, Helen, Circe, and the various female mortals and demigoddesses are condemned as chaotic disruptions undoing an otherwise male order of accomplishment and coherence. These male characteristics are precisely the ones he envisions for his poem as well (even through *Thrones,* which repeatedly portrays paradise in terms of the Confucian "filiality that binds things together") until *Drafts & Fragments,* when they are disturbed by *The Cantos'* earlier female tropes of disorder, irresolution, and silence.

Dante and Na-khi myth operate as initial meditations upon the sensual in *Drafts & Fragments,* introducing the volume's more humane, less pejoratively archetypal, rendering of woman. In CXIII, Marcella Spann is associated with the characteristics, formerly reserved for Pound's many masculine heroes, of discernment, curiosity, vision, indefatigable energy, the ascent from darkness to light: "Here take thy mind's space / And to this garden, Marcella, ever seeking by petal, by leaf-vein / out of dark, and toward half-light." "Thy" supplements its earlier first-line appearance in CX with the sensual context of Pound's relationship with Spann in the late 1950s, and "garden" is both, in private terms, the grounds of St. Elizabeths and of Brunnenburg. But it is also a figure for *The Cantos'* newly indeterminate ("half-light") paradise to which she leads (inhabited two lines earlier by Mozart, Agassiz, and Linnaeus); and *The Cantos'* solar symbol of masculine order must now share that redemptive potential with her—"Out of dark, thou, Father Helios, leadest"—at the end of CXIII.[11]

This integration of the sensual female as a crucial characteristic of paradise is followed by other similar accommodations in *Drafts & Fragments.* The gesture is not complete, as CXIII's "in every woman, somewhere in the snarl is a tenderness" makes clear, combining as it does (through "snarl") an image of cruelty with the more familiar *Cantos* presentation of the chaotic and ensnaring female. And Pound's CXVI interpretation of his poem as "cuniculi" (the reference is to Venetian canals, but it is also a conflation of the fatal labyrinth with female sexuality) at the very least calls this new version of woman into question. In this light, Pound's question in CXVII, to which we will return later in various other contexts—"M'amour, m'amour / what do I love and / where are you?"—becomes crucial, for in it is his awareness of the confusion that supplants *The Cantos'* simpler alternative paradise of transcendent females, excluded sensuality, male will, and order. Thus he writes in this CXVII fragment as if he were groping, suddenly blind, Canto V's vision having faded, an ironic incarnation of the Homer whose blindness was an avenue to deeper melopoeic vision in Cantos II and VII ("and / poor old Homer blind, / blind as a bat, / Ear, ear for the sea-surge; / rattle of old men's voices" [VII/24]) and whose epics originally provided a model for *The Cantos.*

Although it would overstate the case to say that *Drafts & Fragments* reveals Pound's new contrition, it is true that in the volume he no longer evades some of the sexual complexities that *The Cantos* had previously avoided. If, in fact, the specter of a secure paradise for *The Cantos'* termination was beginning to slip away, it was being replaced by a redemptive response to the poem itself "flowing, ever unstill," its previously scorned, but now reconsidered, female opposition to masculine accomplishment and form. Such revaluation is frequent in *Drafts & Fragments,* marked by the several reversals in CX ("under blue paler than heaven," "Here are earth's breasts mirroured," "'Neath this altar now Endymion lies," "bare trees walk on the sky-line," "mountain sunset inverted"), in CXIII ("blue light under stars" and "Sea, over roofs"), in CXIV ("sea, blue under cliffs"), and in "From CXV" ("Night under wind mid garofani"). The sense is of a world that was previously in Pound's "mind . . . uncontending" now being overturned, initially generating the "tempest" near the end of CX but finally an embrace of instability and uncertainty. Yet "tempest" here is multivalent, invoking not only Pound's emotional and possibly mental chaos, but also Shakespeare's equally final text, which, as *Drafts & Fragments* will, offers "a renewed and ennobled vision of nature"[12] and regards a predictable paradise, in Miranda's words, more "like a dream than an assurance" (1.1.45).

As in other ritualistic entries into paradise, *Drafts & Fragments* employs sacrifice in various forms, eventually offering up several of *The Cantos'* earlier convictions to a different vision of reality. Of the many references in the volume, those to sacrificial ceremonies are among the most numerous. Rock's *Romance* invoked early in CX introduces this, fused later in the same canto with the ²Muan ¹bpo sacrifice to heaven that Canto XCVIII had earlier, but incompletely, predicted ("Without ²muan ¹bpo ... but I anticipate") as necessary for "reality." The ²Muan ¹bpo ceremony that follows in CX, using the elemental remedies of snow, juniper, and oak, is designed to expel "unknown demons" and "evil impurities" from the community, which Pound maintains in Canto XCVIII cannot be done before "a lifetime" is completed. The ²Muan ¹bpo ceremony is intended more importantly to exorcise guilt and closes with the rather curious confession that "wrong we did not, but perhaps we did wrong.... Faults we have not committed, but perhaps we have committed faults." The contradictory language of the ritual is there because the faults and wrongs have been committed unintentionally in the course of human activity and introduces, however quietly at this point in the volume, Pound's emerging judgment of himself and the "faults" he begins to dwell on at this point in his life. The impurities that Pound transfers from the Na-khi to his poem here are thus in some sense personal ones, part of the self-revaluation that makes his a "mind as Ixion, unstill, ever turning" (CXIII), and that prompts him to consider that truth is not only divine but human as well, embodied "in kindness" (CXIV).

One of the influences on Pound's self-revaluation, and on this gesture toward "kindness" so prominent in the volume, is *The Analects*—the last of Confucius's *Four Books* to be translated by Pound at St. Elizabeths in 1950—in which Confucius speaks of the need for an individual to "see his errors and then go into his own mind and demand justice on them in precise, just, discriminating words." Pound would also find there a hymn of sorts to benevolence and generosity, articulated in terms predicting *Drafts & Fragments'* frequent move from the transcendent to the human: "Dwelling on high without magnanimity, performing rites without reverence, coming to funerals without regrets; why should I bother about 'em?" The Confucius of *The Analects* is in one scholar's words "not exalted as in later legend.... He has doubts and weaknesses as well as convictions and strengths,"[13] and Pound's attraction to the volume may have involved the recognition of just such a discrepancy between the legendary and the actual in his own life, and also of *Drafts & Fragments'* similarity with *The Analects'* more fragmented, less totalizing aspect than the previous Confucian texts he had translated. He called the volume itself "oddments" in his introduction to it. Beginning with CX's quiet house, whose referent is the Torcello cathedral above whose altar the dying bishop is depicted, and continuing through the Na-khi texts of Joseph Rock, purification and sacrifice are thus associated in *Drafts & Fragments* with personal revaluation and life's impending close. Whereas the impurities for which *The Cantos* previously sought remedies were frequently associated with Jews and women, here they are located within Pound himself (CXVI: "Charity I have had sometimes, / I cannot make it flow thru") and within his poem's own distortions and misperceptions: "to affirm the gold thread in the pattern."

To "affirm the gold thread in the pattern" is in one sense to have the poem corroborate the various dimensions of the paradise that Pound has envisioned for it, by *Drafts & Fragments* a difficult enterprise. The pattern referred to may be that of *The Cantos,* as if it is a mosaic or tapestry, in keeping with the analogy of painting that Pound uses for the poem from the beginning of its composition. In terms of *The Cantos,* "the pattern" is also nature itself, whose order is temporarily apparent, but mystical because inexplicable. If so, the gold thread is another metaphor for that principle of order, similar to "the something intelligent in the cherry-stone" in CXIII,[14] or the light that "sings eternal" in "From CXV," and to write paradise is to affirm its existence.

But of all *The Cantos'* volumes, *Drafts & Fragments* is the one where that optimism is also most directly questioned. A quotation from Camoens's *Os Luciadas* ("A sad case and worthy of memory") culminates a self-reflexive passage on art, and by extension Pound's, in CX:

> willow and olive reflected,
> Brook-water idles,
>   topaz against pallor of under-leaf
> The lake waves Canaletto'd
>   under blue paler than heaven,
> the rock layers arc'd as with a compass,
>   this rock is magnesia,
> Cozzaglio, Dino Martinazzi made the road here (Gardesana)
> Savoia, Novara at Veneto
> Solari was in that—
> Un caso triste e denho di memoria
>
> (778–79)

Pound had devoted a chapter of *The Spirit of Romance* to the sixteenth-century Portuguese poet and had included an extended treatment of the incident referred to here in Ur-Canto II. The line comments on the fate of Ignez de Castro, killed before her husband Pedro became king of Portugal: in *Os Luciadas* King Pedro seats the dead queen on the throne beside him at the succession ceremony. In the "Camoens" chapter in *The Spirit of Romance* Pound argues that the incident was already poetic, "written in deeds by King Pedro," and that a textual reconstruction can at best only duplicate it. Hence the scene in the poem may be "beautiful and full of music" but it does not rank as art:

> The tale of Ignez will perhaps never be written greatly, for art becomes necessary only when life is inarticulate and when art is not an expression, but a mirroring of life, it is necessary only when life is apparently without design; that is, when the conclusion or results of given causes are so far removed or so hidden, that art alone can show their relation.

The "Brook-water" recalls "Yeux Glaques" of *Mauberley,* Pound's indictment of poetry's weakness in the age of Gladstone and Ruskin, which softened artistic vision, that of the subject ("The Burne-Jones cartons / Have preserved her eyes / ... Thin like brook-water"), and imperiled a long poem like *The Rubaiyat* ("still-born / In those days"). "Topaz" recalls Mauberley's lifeless "Medallion" ("Beneath half-watt rays, / The eyes turn topaz") and the lament on partial vision in the Ur-Cantos and Canto V ("topaz I manage, and three sorts of blue"). Together they reassemble the poet-aesthete Pound was leaving behind in 1919 for the more politically engaged poet that he would soon become, as if Mauberley nostalgically represents a type of poetic identity that Pound now sees as one of several possible versions of selfhood. The references also introduce *Drafts & Fragments'* meditation on how art is made redundant by nature, which has "Canaletto'd" its own waters, and designed its own rock formations "as with a compass." Its rock along Lake Garda ("the road here (Gardesana)") is in fact "magnesia," magnetic, and holds within itself the power to produce what *The Cantos* has already privileged as supremely beautiful, the composition of iron filings into the rose in the steel dust. These scattered associations, in the company of the "pallor of under-leaf"—a reference to such a natural phenomenon, but also to the tenuity of the poetic page itself and the dearth of significance beneath it—combine in this passage to suggest the possible redundancy of Pound's art, now receding in insignificance as nature's designs become increasingly apparent, and as his death approaches. If CXIV's "Some hall of mirrors" invokes *The Cantos'* relentless intertextuality that in *Drafts & Fragments* is partly replaced by more personal references, the poem may be merely an example of what, in his Camoens discussion in *The Spirit of Romance,* Pound had called "art that mirrors art."

The first line of the quoted passage, "willow and olive reflected," recalls Pound's use of Upward's *Divine Mystery* in Ur-Canto I. There, describing Sirmio, Catullus's home, Pound writes,

> And all agleam with colors—no, not agleam,
> But colored like the lake and like the olive leaves,
> Glaukopos, clothed like the poppies, wearing golden greaves,
> Light on the air
> Are they Etruscan gods?
> The air is solid sunlight, *apricus.*

As Bush points out, in this early *Cantos* stage Pound is employing Upward's main theme in *The Divine Mystery,* "modern man's blindness to the spirits of nature."[15] The persistent return to the Ur-Cantos is difficult to ignore in CX and suggests that the revaluative process involved in the composition of the last cantos takes Pound back to the earliest stages of the poem's beginning. If the mandate at that time was eventually to render paradise in a poem long enough to permit such an achievement, by the end the attempt becomes secondary to the personal vision itself, questioned in CX ("Can'st 'ou see") but gradually affirmed as *Drafts & Fragments* progresses, in CXIII's "God's eye art'ou, do not surrender perception," and the volume's final ode to light and perception, CXVI. If *The Cantos* does not necessarily recreate beauty in itself, its poet has nevertheless borne witness to its existence, not only by "seeing the just and the unjust" like the Pater Helios who opens CXIII but also, in the line that follows, by "tasting the sweet and the sorry" like Pound's beleaguered Seafarer whose "age fares against him" and who "knows gone companions" (l. 95). Pound conflates the two now not just because the Seafarer is reminiscent of himself, isolated, old, voyaging, remembering, but because in the individual is the godly ability to perceive beyond the terrestrial to a paradisal world of coherence and significance. The potential is lost when "our heart grows quiet...when we forget that we are pilgrims,"[16] as Charles Singleton puts it in a discussion of the *Divine Comedy,* the very pilgrimage of

CX's opening image, with a seafaring boat approaching the quiet house, a house that, through Apuleius's "Cupid and Psyche," "is its own daylight, having no need of the sun." Perception must always be active, and one component of the "many errors" that will burden Pound in CXVI is passivity—invoking Canto LXXXI's "Here error is all in the not done"—that comfortably accepts the "still, uncontending" truths *Drafts & Fragments* is now placing under review.

The struggle to write paradise, imperiled by Pound's emerging revaluation of himself and his poem, is further troubled by "the view that Europe and civilization is going to Hell" (*RP*, 242), making it more appropriate to write an "apocalypse" (241) than a paradise. Certainly *Drafts & Fragments* reviews the past nostalgically, recalling many who were important to Pound and to his sense of cultural community in his lifetime, and acknowledging that his earlier plea to "black out the eroders...venerate honest men" in Canto XCIX/697 has gone unheard, and by now has been reversed: "Bunting and Upward neglected, / all the resisters blacked out."[17] "Uncle G.," Henry Cabot Lodge, Philander Chase Knox, are the others in CX; H.D., Yeats, Homer Pound, and Wyndham Lewis in later cantos.[18] The many inversions in the volume indicate this larger, and for Pound almost inexplicable, cultural amnesia that has hidden the past from the present. "The holiness of their courage forgotten" Pound says of them all, and of the many cultural mementos such as the sculpted lions of Brescia effaced by Second World War air bombings—a pattern that seems unlikely to stop, given incidents like the bombing of Quemoy ("Notes for CXI": "And 600 more dead at Quemoy— / they call it political") in the fall of 1958 while Pound is writing.[19] If *Drafts & Fragments* occasionally disputes Pound's later somewhat jaundiced view of his poem in CXVI, it is at this early point in the volume where the poem's record of an otherwise obliterated past (and of the friendship it witnessed, in restaurants like La Tour and Dieudonné) puts it in the company of the books given to Persephone in Propertius's *Elegies* ("sat mea sit magno, si tres pompa libelli, / quos ego Persephone maxima dona feram": "my not unworthy gift to Persephone," as Pound translates it in his "Homage"):

Quos ego Persephonae

chih[3]

                    not with jet planes,
The holiness of their courage forgotten
            and the Brescian lions effaced,
Until the mind jumps without building

止 chih³

and there is no *chih* and no root.
Bunting and Upward neglected,
        all the resisters blacked out,
From time's wreckage shored,
            these fragments shored against ruin

(CX/780–81)

The "chih³" encountered in *The Analects* Pound considers the most significant term in Confucius's vocabulary. While its meaning is "stop," it is used by Confucius there to mean having an ideological position and holding to it, suggesting that in CX, at least, Pound is still prepared to interpret his poem as an expression of tenacious commitment.

Yet the revaluative tendency that will overtake the volume later on is not entirely absent here either. Originally, the gold thread winding through the mosaic within the quiet house of the madonna at Torcello, and the "boat's wake on sea-wall" at the beginning of CX, were intended to continue the passage that ends Canto CIX:

San Domenico, Santa Sabina,
                    Sta Maria Trastevere
                            in Cosmedin
        Le chapeau melon de St Pierre
        You in the dinghy (piccioletta) astern there!

The final line, as we have seen, recalls Dante's *Paradiso* 2.1, in which the reader who has not meditated upon the more profound truths of life is admonished to revisit the shores of his mortal world, and not follow Dante to paradise. The shores to be revisited are now Pound's past, and his poem:

        From time's wreckage shored,
            these fragments shored against ruin[20]

Their confluence occurs in CX through the mediation of T. S. Eliot's *Waste Land*. Pound began Canto VIII with the line "These fragments you have shelved (shored)" (28), a reference to line 430 of Eliot's poem

("These fragments I have shored against my ruins"). In CX Pound has removed that earlier "shelved" and replaced it with the shore that the poem is to have reached at this point, as if he is trying to discern, 102 cantos later, whether *The Cantos* has in fact resisted its own ruin. We might also glimpse here Pound's reference to the poems of *Drafts & Fragments* just beginning, and thus to the fragments that are shoring up the larger trembling edifice of *The Cantos* itself. The insistence on the possibility of renewal, with the sun ideogram ("jih$^{4.5}$") and the reference to Rock's rewriting of his own ruined text ("Mr Rock still hopes to climb at Mount Kinabalu / his fragments sunk [20 years]" [781]) suggests as much. Pound then asks for "light" to be given "against falling poison," the impurity he has already located both within himself and his poem, a composite reference to Theophile Gautier's *The Comedy of Death,* whose personal relevance for Pound is apparent ("The hideous cuttle-fish and the monstrous polyp their tentacles all out-stretched . . . but to the surface I came again, for my breath failed me. A heavy mantle for aged shoulders is the mantle of the seas") and, if one critic is correct in her conjecture, to the Tao Dragon Boat Festival and tao's poisons of "spider, scorpion, lizard, snake and toad," undoing CX's opening image of a boat adjacent to paradise.[21] The reference may also involve the passage in "Notes for CXI" that reworks Dante's *Inferno* 17.19 and then incorporates much from that canto:

> And the sand grey against undertow
>   as Geryon—lured there—but in splendour,
>   Veritas, by anthesis,[22] from the sea depth
>   *come burchiello in su la riva*
>
> (783)

Geryon has a poisonous tail tipped with a scorpion's stinger, and a body more fantastically embroidered than the weavings of Arachne, who in mythology is changed by Minerva into a spider. Pound, predicting the passage in "Notes for CXI," may now see himself here as Dante, temporarily falling through hell on Geryon's back, surrounded as Dante is (and Paolo and Francesca, for that matter) by wind and darkness.

The significance of this passage of descent is not only in the many references that help to explain it, however, but in the momentous reversal of *The Cantos'* seascapes, where the surface of the water is life-giving, the submarine world terrifying and inconceivable. Wendy Flory argues that Pound's fear of moving beneath the surface in *The Cantos* is a fear of his own unconscious, which holds the guilt of anti-Semitism and fascism he more willfully ignores in previous volumes.[23] The paradisal CX opening, with the boat on the water, not surprisingly continues this imagery of denial, but this passage near the end of the canto introduces the volume's subsequent exploration of that deep and painful domain of private confrontation, CXIV's "genealogy of demons." In fact, *Drafts & Fragments* will arguably become the site of the most sustained attempt to do this, in the wake of *The Cantos'* persistent deflection of the self in every volume except perhaps *The Pisan Cantos,* turning the visionary descent into hell begun in Canto I away from the Homeric to the private.

This happens again closer to the canto's end, where "the marble form in the pine wood" is reminiscent of Canto XVII/79—"And the white forest of marble, bent bough over bough"—part of that otherwise paradisal canto's descent into hell, inaugurated by Hermes, who in "splendour" bears the golden bough in Canto I. The marble form is also Brancusi's sculpture, reappearing in "Notes for CXVII et seq." as "Brancusi's bird / in the hollow of pine trunks." Significantly, Pound in 1934 compares a speech by Mussolini to Brancusi's sculpture—"The more one examines the Milan Speech the more one is reminded of Brancusi, the stone blocks from which no error emerges, from whatever angle one look at them" (*J/M,* ix). The connection suggests that the "splendour" Pound refers to here is involved with an early stage of fascism that predates its more violent form, the form that compromises his reputation through his association with it during the Rome Radio broadcasts of the early 1940s. As we will see in chapter 5, it is partly this early and euphoric period of fascism, which for Pound was a political analogy to vorticist order, to which he seeks a "return" in CXVI, and it is also his involvement with the later menacing fascism that he now believes was a diversion of his truer political and poetic intentions. Through this detour, *Drafts & Fragments* again revives the entry into hell at the beginning of *The Cantos,* bending it now into a private context that will later encompass CXVI's otherwise elliptical reference: "A little light, like a rushlight / to lead back to splendour."

The enlightenment and vision that are invoked through the Nekuian descent in Canto I are reduced to a brief glimpse of light—"Lux enim"—by this point in *The Cantos*. The words are Grosseteste's, first translated by Pound in his essay on Cavalcanti (*LE*, 161) and repeated in Canto LV/298—"Lux enim per se omnem in partem" (For light of its very nature diffuses itself)—and in more fragmented form in Canto LXXXIII/528, where Pound also declares that "Le Paradis n'est pas artificiel." CX recalls its original paradisal image, the house that is its own daylight, through the mediation of the Grosseteste passage on light's self-reflexive nature. By this point so near the close of the canto, the self-generating light of paradise is threatened by darkness, Rock's climb by the loss of his work, Pound's Confucian calm by the tempest of his evolving self-recognition. Counteracting them is the canto's final passage:

> The shrine seen and not seen
> From the roots of sequoias
>
> pray 敬 ching[4] pray
>
> There is power
> Awoi or Komachi,
> the oval moon.

The shrine is possibly that of the Torcello cathedral, but more likely a reminder of the various rituals of purification that have begun to direct *Drafts & Fragments* in CX. The unstable sighting of the shrine recalls once again the distance between Dante's vision of paradise and Pound's that is "flitting and fading at will." The sequoias invoke Canto LXXXVII—"pine seed splitting cliff's edge. / Only sequoias are slow enough" (572)—the pine seed, in its haste, destroying the ground that gives it foundation, the sequoia more slowly realizing nature's inexorable processes, strength, self-renewal and (like the oak and cherry stone) intelligence. The forty-five year process of writing *The Cantos* may be as much a referent as is anything else here and stands as a reminder of the patience and time required to achieve insight, purgation ("there is no substitute for a lifetime"), and a vision of beauty (for "slowness is beauty," as Pound quotes Laurence Binyon in LXXXVII/572). There is an undercurrent of such measured and patient process throughout *Drafts & Fragments*, Pound's closing respect for nature's accomplishment of form and beauty through a time scale entirely separate from man's—"Time, space, neither life nor death is the answer" ("From

CXV")—starting with the descent to the underworld in Canto I, and closing in *Drafts & Fragments* with the "ching^4" ideogram. Although Pound translates it here as "pray," its proper meaning is "respect" (used earlier, in Canto LXXXVIII); in Confucian terms, such respect supplies the power to understand tao or "the Way" to peace within oneself, and thus again to the quiet house of the canto's opening.

Writing *The Cantos* had been a process of trying ("the vision, flitting / and fading at will") to inscribe the order perceived in nature, and of observing how nature expresses it in the form of beauty, such as Canto LXXIV's rose in the iron filings so famously represents. One of *Drafts & Fragments'* earliest versions of this is the "yellow iris in that river bed" in CX, a reference to Motokyo's Noh drama *Kakitsubata,* which Pound had included in the 1916 *"Noh" or Accomplishment,* whose theme he had interpreted as being that "beauty is the road to salvation," and whose central character, symbolized by the iris, changes into a "light that does not lead on to darkness." Narihira had been exiled from court long before, and written acrostics of regret to his lover Kakitsubata, whose symbol is the iris (and CX's obscure "yüeh$^{4.5}$ / ming^2 / mo$^{4.5}$ / hsien^1 / p'eng^2" might be read as Pound's acrostic to her.[24] One of Narihira's poems declares that "My body / Is not my body, / But only a body grown old" (*EPT,* 339), and Kakitsubata refers to her own apparition on earth as merely "the cracked husk of the locust" (340), generating both Canto VII's image of the soulless and insubstantial, the "Thin husks I had known as men, / Dry casques of departed locusts" (26), and "From CXV"'s more private description of a "blown husk that is finished." Her spirit reappears by the sea to a *waki* or priest, and it laments that she will probably never be reunited with Narihira. Her story of love, she tells the *waki,* "has no beginning and no end" (336), and thus she will wait eternally for the resolution she desires but cannot achieve, and her flowers will "flare and flaunt in their marsh / By the many-bridged cobweb of waters" (338). The yellow iris in CX introduces her to the volume, and through her the specter of love's and poem's irresolution. "From CXV" in particular will invoke the play again with reference to the light that "sings eternal / a pale flare over marshes."

The Noh cycle had large consequences for the beginning of *The Cantos,* for it demonstrated, as Bush points out, "how incidents could be given a sequence derived from a primary value structure and yet not

be locked into a Dantesque linear progression."[25] It is perhaps appropriate near the end of the canto that begins the abandonment, once and
for all, of a Dantean paradisal close and admits the impediments to it
of a personal and poetic nature that Pound now returns to the Noh as
a source of imagery and tone, for the "Awoi" and "Komachi" of the
penultimate line invoke Noh drama as well. In his 1916 version of
Fenollosa's Noh translations, Pound wrote that if the plays seem

> to "go off into nothing" at the end, the reader must remember "that
> the vagueness or paleness of words is made good by the emotion of
> the final dance," for the Noh has its unity in emotion. It has also
> what we may call Unity of Image.... the better plays are all built
> into the intensification of a single image: the red maple leaves and
> the snow flurry in Nishikigi, the pines in Takasago, the blue grey
> waves and wave pattern in Suma Genji. (*EPT*, 237)

Pound footnoted the phrase "Unity of Image" with the question he
poses slightly differently in *Gaudier-Brzeska:* "These plays are also an
answer to a question that has several times been put to me: 'Could one
do a long Imagiste poem, or even a long poem in vers libre?'" Pound's
original interest in the plays involved their unity of emotion embodied
in the image, evolving into an imagist poetics that would generate *The
Cantos.*

But it is partly their handling of closure, or more properly its absence, that returns Pound to the plays now. According to him in 1916,
any illusion that they fail to resolve themselves at the end is erased
once the reader understands the closing dance that unifies the plays'
emotion. This is their most important dimension for him at the time,
and he goes on to write in his introduction to *Shojo* that the Noh is
primarily a dance. Pound also included in his versions of the plays
Fenollosa's essay on the Noh, which argued that in its original form it
fused the Shinto god dance, the warrior court dance, and the Buddhist
pantomime into a drama of pure action and few words, on the threshold, like *Drafts & Fragments* again, of silence (*EPT*, 274). In CX the
dancelike celebration of movement and delight ("paw-flap, wave-tap,
/ that is gaiety") appears early, coupled with the wave patterns so reminiscent of many Noh plays, such as *Suma Genji,* whose title character
sings on the "sea-marge" and dances "Sei-kai-ha, the blue dance of the
sea waves" where "moving in clouds and in rain, / The dream overlaps

with the real" (235). "The Japanese people," Fenollosa writes, "have loved nature so passionately that they have interwoven her life and their own into one continuous drama of the art of pure living" (268), predicting not only the harmony of pattern that Pound temporarily achieves near CX's beginning, but also the metaphor of *The Cantos* as a tapestry or mosaic that occasions the image of Torcello and CXVI's "gold thread in the pattern." There is a powerful reminiscence in the Noh plays that Fenollosa translated, a desire to rectify the past that separated lovers from each other, as in *Nishikigi*, a past that contained "beauty lost in years," as Pound describes the play *Suma Genji*. Those in the present, conscious of the past but incapable of uniting with it except through divine intervention, have much in their hearts but "in our bodies nothing" (*Nishikigi: EPT*, 287). In another, *Kagekiyo*, an old man "blind...without his staff" (reverberating in this way with the bishop in Torcello's mosaic) who is "hated by people in power" (though we are not told why) has been separated from his daughter for a long time and does not want to be recognized by her. "I thought this would put dishonour upon you, and therefore I let you pass. Do not hold it against me" (320), he asks of her, and he begs that she ignore his suffering and "pray for me when I am gone from the world, for I shall then count upon you as we count on a lamp in the darkness...we who are blind" (321–22). The lines predict the muted presence of light in *Drafts & Fragments'* psychic cosmos of darkness, not only near the end of CX but particularly in CXVI's "A little light, / like a rushlight," and no doubt spoke newly to Pound of his relationship with his own daughter (already invoked through the Persephone reference in CX), with whom he is reunited while writing the volume, after the six months at Pisa and thirteen years in St. Elizabeths. Meanwhile, the chorus comments on Kagekiyo's heroic deeds in the past, and on how difficult it is for him to recount them now: "but oh!, to tell them! to be telling them over now in his wretched condition. His life in the world is weary, he is near the end of his course."

This is to suggest the general attraction of the Noh for Pound at this point in *The Cantos* and in his life—and he had reread the Fenollosa Noh translations for a new edition in 1954—but there were other more specific reasons why he turned to it again now.[26] Komachi, who appears in two plays, is a dramatic image of old age. "How sad a ruin is this: / Komachi was in her day a bright flower. / White of winter is over her head, / Over the husk of her shoulders," comment the two *waki* who encounter her. (If it seems extreme to connect a female character with Pound's own self-perception in 1958, it is worth noting his comment in 1916 that it is "quite usual for an old actor, wearing a mask, to take the part of a young woman" [225]). In *Kayoi Komachi* she is separated from her lover because he would not accept Buddhism, but they are reconciled and "both their sins vanish" (231), as Pound writes in his introduction to the play, which he labels an eclogue that is "very incomplete." Awoi is a character in *Awoi No Uye*, a "dramatization, or externalization, of [her] jealousy" (325) in which Pound sees affinities with Ibsen's sense that existence is a "contest with the phantoms of the mind" (324) that *Drafts & Fragments* is now beginning to identify as guilt and, in his domestic situation, jealousy.

As in the Na-khi ceremonies recorded in CX, an exorcism occurs in *Awoi No Uye* under the moon, at which the apparition of Awoi gazes "in sorrow." Her most potent statement in the play, accepting the irrevocable patterns of fate, is that "man's life is a wheel on the axle, there is no turn whereby to escape" (326), a concept filtered through the Na-khi ^{2}Muan ^{1}bpo ceremony at the end of "From CXII"—"Winnowed in fate's tray / neath / luna"—and then again through the myth of Ixion in hell at the end of CXIII—"but the mind as Ixion, unstill, ever turning"—against the volume's tentative statements of individuality and freedom. Through Noh drama the last four lines of CX return with the belief that respect and ritualistic prayer can transcend the pains of darkness, jealousy, self-recrimination, sin, and old age, as in their Noh counterparts, not beneath the poem's foreseen paradisal culmination in the eternal light of the sun, but beneath the Noh moon that is its symbolic reversal, as *Drafts & Fragments* is *The Cantos*'.

Chapter 4

Reflecting on the Image: The Return to a Pre-*Cantos* Poetics

> There would still remain the never-resting mind,
> So that one would want to escape, come back
> To what had been so long composed.
> —Wallace Stevens, "The Poems of Our Climate"

In CX Pound surrounds Dante's paradisal light in darkness and his silence in despair, reverses his ascent to descent, and troubles his love with insecurity. He reemploys the Noh, but with a sense of its new appropriateness to his personal situation at the time. He sustains *The Cantos'* search for purification but changes its previous sufferer, culture, to himself. He occasionally refashions the female as human, not impossibly transcendent, and through this accommodation explores the nonclosural alternative to masterful resolution. He embraces complexity, initially with the confidence of recasting it into harmony, but eventually with the understanding that it will prevent poetic resolution. With each of these reinterpretations, the shape of *The Cantos'* paradise is modified, making *Drafts & Fragments'* poems less its accomplishment than its interrogation, even its palinode.

The model that Dante's *Paradiso* consistently provides is again crucial in understanding the extent of these various reversals. The limpidity and clarity of expression that Pound discovered there before writing *The Spirit of Romance* are symbolized by the light that infuses Dante's poem, beginning with its invocation to Apollo and the description of God as one who "moves all things . . . and shines in one part more and in another less," a light that allows Dante a new understanding that surpasses the capacity of language to relate. "I saw things which he

101

that descends from it has not the knowledge or the power to tell again," Dante marvels near the beginning of the *Paradiso,* and the understanding he gains there, potentially obscured by the failure of memory that "cannot follow" the intellect, is in terms of light, variously a trope for knowledge, beauty, clarity, limpidity, simplicity, and God, within whom they all inhere. When Dante loses the power of sight in canto 25 of the *Paradiso,* he is counseled to "make up for it with speech" (26.6), and *The Divine Comedy* that results culminates with his understanding that what he tells of is a *semplice lume,* a simple light (33.90) that the intellect cannot adequately represent except through speech, itself "scant . . . and feeble" (33.121–22). The symbol for this divine simplicity throughout the *Paradiso* is the circle, visually pure and eternal, whose area is incapable of translation to another form, and Dante as poet compares himself at the end of his poem to a "geometer who sets all his mind to the squaring of the circle and for all his thinking does not discover the principle he needs" (33.133–35) when in the presence of the *vista nova,* the strange vision of light. The vision is possible for Dante because his mind is "smitten by a flash wherein came its wish" (33.141), and so he achieves God, Beatrice, and his poem.

The tangle of unfinished works that Pound regards *The Cantos* as in CXVI is one of his admissions that he has exchanged Dante's simplicity for an obscuring complexity (which he had noted, much more offhandedly, in the 1927 letter to his father) and not received Dante's "flash" of insight that transcends time and space. If genius is the capacity to see ten things when the ordinary person sees only one, as Pound rephrases Confucius in *Jefferson and/or Mussolini* (CA, 210; J/M, 88), and in "Notes for CXI" ("I, one thing, as relation to one thing; / Hui sees relation to ten"), the greater poet merges the ten back into one to make them inhere in each other, the way an apparently simple circle silently coheres a multitude of numbers and equations that represent it. Pound had been attracted to analytical mathematics as a site of simplicity and intuition at least since his discussion in chapter 9 of *Gaudier-Brzeska,* where he stated that it escapes mere description for "the universal, existing in perfection, in freedom from space and time" (GB, 91). This mathematical achievement is one that Pound hopes *The Cantos* will share as well, eventually to escape "the barb of time" for an intuitive poetic expression that sees "where the line had to go" (91), to "cause form to come into being" (92). And it was there, at the end of that chapter in *Gaudier-Brzeska,* that Pound repeated the question he asked in his Noh discussion of "whether there can be a long imagiste or vorticist poem" (94).

Now, at the end of his *Cantos,* he regards it almost as an expanding equation that, like Camoens's poem, is "like talk about art...a criticism of the form" (*GB,* 91), whose complexity cannot be reduced to a simple intuitive vision at its own close; though nature's "rock-layers [are] arc'd as with a compass" in CX, his poem has abandoned simplicity for complexity, CXVI's "tangle." By enlarging "his empire" of *The Cantos,* as he says analogously of Napoleon in "Notes for CXI," he has "diminished his forces" and now hopes to evade the "twisty thoughts" of CX (from *The Shih Ching,* and repeated in ideograms in "Notes for CXI") through images of simplicity and vision, to "see again" where the line, the gold thread in an otherwise complex pattern, must go, in poems where the word is eventually canceled in favor of nature's unmediated speech—the clear discourse of the "Jade stream" in "From CXII," the whisper of the salt hay to tide's change in "From CXV," the speaking wind in the first collection's 115 lines that temporarily become the itinerant "CXX."

Drafts & Fragments as a result is perhaps more fraught with a semiotic anxiety than any other portion of *The Cantos,* and recalls earlier, simpler pre-*Cantos* texts by Pound more insistently than any other volume does. CX's "That love be the cause of hate, / something is twisted" recalls Pound's translation of Li Po's "Poem at the Bridge at Ten-Shin," where an old man remembers jealousy as "the cause of hate!" The "auzel" eight lines later first appeared keeping the company of lovers with its song in Pound's 1920 translation of Arnaut's "XII." Added to this are the references to Pound's "Homage to Sextus Propertius" (whose intimation of death is also recalled, at the end of CXIII: "When the Syrian onyx is broken"), Noh drama, Western myth again, the Ur-Cantos and, in the CXVII fragments, Bernart's Provençal poetry ("'es laissa cader' / so high toward the sun and then falling, / 'de joi sas alas'"), rapidly turning *Drafts & Fragments* into a reencounter with the poetic simplicity that has otherwise eluded the complex poem he is trying to close. Pound's curious inclusion of "Addendum for C" may find one of its motives in this context of verbal simplicity to which he hopes to return his *Cantos:* its "'A pity that poets have used symbol and metaphor / and no man learned anything from them'" suggests his antipathy to figural excess, and his location of it now in *The Cantos.*

This complexity is partly a result of distance, of separation from the object of perception, and the geometer struggling in the *Paradiso* to "square the circle" sees its area as it were from the outside, extracts that area by translating it into mathematical terms, and then fails to reapply it to another geometric shape. Somewhat the same holds true for our understanding of history—in retrospect a pattern emerges that we try to account for, to extract some quantity from, and ultimately the assessment distorts. So Pound in "Notes for CXI" offers Mme. de Rémusat's eyewitness accounts of Napoleon in her *Memoirs* as correctives against the geometry of heroism that has been drawn around him and points out that his rule was for the first "ten years a blessing," the last "five a nuisance." Talleyrand, Napoleon's minister of external relations, notably fought against the verbal misuse that can obscure history's patterns or fabricate them where none were, at the Congress of Vienna in 1814, as Pound mentions in "Notes for CXI" as well, followed by a recent example of misleading terminology in the description of the six hundred Quemoy deaths as "political." The examples are circles of analogy (borrowed, in the case of Rémusat, from *Thrones*) drawing inward to Pound's truer subject in *Drafts & Fragments*, the verbal obscurity and complexity of *The Cantos*, eventually confronted when CXVI's gold thread in the pattern accumulates its various associations, including that of the medieval Torcello mosaic, an image of verbal precision and clarity that he attempts to locate in his poem. As he wrote to W. H. D. Rouse in 1934, a contemporary "decadence of thought . . . [is] due to lack of observation of words. . . . It may be an illusion that the Middle Ages tried to define their terminology. Certainly the last half century did not" (*LEP*, 262). Our interpretation of the past has simultaneously distorted and complicated it, made potential heroes like "Notes for CXI"'s "Roche-Guyon stoned to death at Gisors" into villains, and vice versa. There is a measure of self-defense here in Pound's inclusion of La Rochefoucauld d'Enville (and a reduction of Napoleon's despotism into trivial irritation ["a nuisance"]) that will, in one interpretation of the passage, characterize his support of Mussolini "wrecked for an error" in CXVI as well, and of himself, whose fragments, his poem, "lie about him" in that canto. The self-defense is not mere churlishness, though; the point is that in *Drafts & Fragments* Pound explores more deeply than before how all language, and by extension *The Cantos* that would absorb all language, can distort its referents, including himself. As he told the Italian interviewer

Grazia Livi as late as 1963, "I can't get at the kernel of my thoughts any more with words."[1]

If *Drafts & Fragments'* first two cantos are preparations of such a palette, the remainder of the volume becomes a deepening engagement with the problem of this verbal abyss. "From CXII," derived from Rock's *The ²Muan-¹Bpo Ceremony or the Sacrifice to Heaven as Practised by the Na-khi,* is a sudden and powerful response, offering itself not in any sense as translation, for that would perpetuate the problem, but as direct quotation without the mediation of context or explanation. In CX the ceremony was invoked as a type of purification—in that case personal; in "From CXII," in the absence of any context outside of that provided by *The Cantos'* close, its significance is more difficult to assess. Though the passages are derived almost verbatim from portions of Rock's text (see app. 2), near the end of the fragment Pound adds "the firm voice amid pine wood," and later "the clear discourse" to Rock's descriptions of a temple and a "jade stream." There Rock describes how the springs of this Na-khi *paradiso terrestre* "flow through the city of Li-chiang"; Pound extracts "flow through" and redirects it through the Confucian tao, the single principle from which all other action in man and nature "flows through, holds . . . together, germinates" (*CA,* 15.2). The similarity between this Confucian description and Pound's early one of the image in *Gaudier-Brzeska* ("from which and through which and into which ideas are constantly rushing") is striking and suggests how when translating the *Analects* in St. Elizabeths he still saw that ideally language and action could engage. With these alterations from the Rock text that is otherwise so closely followed, Pound relocates purification in a verbal dimension and through the Confucian detour merges language with conduct (and, if CX is evidence enough at this point in the volume, his own). The sense is of a writer offering images of verbal coherence and purification for a life and a poem that now seemed to require them, of a desire both to assert the possibility of their return and to relinquish the poem in favor of the natural world in which they inhere.[2]

Before the apocalyptic point in "Notes for CXVII et seq." where he will lament more directly the loss of this center that would cohere word, referent, and life, Pound entertains the possibility that it might be located elsewhere—in the world that is "saved . . . for memory" (CXIII) "in thy mind's space," the mnemonic text of luminous recollection. If "no man can see his own end," one can at least recall in imagery that precedes language and can turn in meditation to the unwritten private trace of one's own past. Thus the emphasis in CXIII and CXIV on what has been "said" by geologist Raphael Pumpelly, H. D., an "old Countess," Sir Ian Hamilton, W. B. Yeats, an old priest, and Pound's ancestors, in a move from the logocentric to the melopoeic, to the Platonic ideal of the spoken word and, beyond that, the preverbal image itself, the "blue flash" that empowered the astonished Dante but escapes his twentieth-century successor. Yet if this is so, how hard it is to know the self behind the one that language apparently creates; and how difficult to transcend the self to understand another's, or for a reader to understand the writer, to "climb another's stair" as Dante conceives it (*Paradiso* 17.58) and Pound by quotation "(scala altrui)" in CXIII. Through this isolation Pound is placed at the end of his poem not in paradise but in hell, his mind "as Ixion, unstill, ever turning" the language into fragments that will do no more than lie about him.

Fenollosa's *The Chinese Written Character as a Medium for Poetry*, so crucial to *The Cantos'* gestation and an indelible influence throughout the poem, holds some early clues to the poetics that will generate the semiotic paradise Pound strives for at its close as well. The argument in *The Chinese Written Character* that has large consequences here is that the Chinese ideogrammic sign structures are "a vivid shorthand picture of the operations of nature" (*CWCMP*, 8) and Western grammatical structures are not. Nature is a "vast storehouse of forces" (29), not a deposit of nouns (or forms) separate from verbs (or power), and the Chinese ideogrammic language recognizes this by not separating noun and verb, form and power, as Western language and thought do, but instead making them coincident: "The eye sees the noun and the verb as one: things in motion, motion in things, and so the Chinese conception tends to represent them" (10). Thus Chinese language preserves nature's energy, whereas Western language, with its appreciation of noun-form over verb-power, breaks it apart. Fenollosa also argues that in nature the continual transference of power that makes things take the form that they do is instantaneous, not bounded by time: "The type of sentence in nature is a flash of lightning. It passes between two terms, a cloud and the earth. No unit of natural process can be less than this" (12). As in nature, so in writing, there could really "be no complete sentence (according to this definition) save one which it would take all time to pronounce" (11). And in its synchronic quality, it could recreate nature's "sentences" that are a "flash of lightning," a transference of power: it could create "the blue flash and the moments" of "Notes for CXVII et seq." fragment no. 1.

The attraction of the semiotics of the Chinese ideogram for Pound was that it closed the gap between sign and referent by not separating the categories of form and power which are inherently coincident in nature: it built a "bridge over worlds." "In the algebraic figure and in the spoken word," Fenollosa writes, "there is no natural connection between thing and sign: all depends upon sheer convention. But the Chinese method follows natural suggestion" (CWCMP, 8). Pound saw in this the possibility of creating a "sign" that is not a displacement of the "thing" (to use either his or Fenollosa's terminology) that is its subject. With the erasure of this gap comes the erasure of origin, as well—a concept that "brings us close to nature" (19), for nature, too, perpetuates itself from multiple origins that are processes rather than beginnings. It also brings us close to a paradise, in which there are no origins, but only an eternal becoming. This identity of poetic language with nature, this merging of the two through poetry's incorporation of nature's structures, was a dimension of *The Cantos'* envisioned paradise from its inception and was to participate in the poem's close.[3] In the early collection's "115" and the first fragment of "Notes for CXVII et seq.," Pound offers an elegy on the failure to create this, largely through the reference to the *Paradiso*'s "flash" that remains elusive to him. In its place, he indicates nature's own language, the speaking wind, as the only utterance that, due to its originary status, can merge nature and speech.

> Do not move
>   Let the wind speak
>   That is Paradise
> The petals are almost still.
> The beauty of thought has not entered them.
>   That is, it has as but a flash in far darkness—
>
>   ("115")

In its replacement of human speech by nature's, and its erasure of the gap between signifier and referent, the passage draws on Plotinus's description of heaven in *Enneads* 4.3.1: "There all is pure, every being is, as it were, an eye, nothing is concealed or sophisticated, there is no need of speech, everything is seen and known." Its version in *Drafts & Fragments'* eventual "From CXV" is the Noh-like "pale flare over marshes / where the salt hay whispers to tide's change," whose images from *Kakitsubata,* the play in which the central character writes acrostics of the kind that Pound attempts in CX, show Pound abandoning linear Western grammar for a more ideogrammic language.

In *The Chinese Written Character* Pound saw a time-proven method for activating his apparent theory of the image, of creating a sign that was not merely a conventional representation of its subject. Like nature, the Poundian image was apparently to have no single point of origin to which it attempts to return and in this way hoped to be a repetition, with a difference, of an origin that is itself a repetition with a difference—just as objects in nature, as *The Chinese Written Character* argues, compose a matrix visible because of the differences between them.[4] From this perspective nature becomes the revelation of the forces that differentiate, and so for Pound should the image that will generate *The Cantos;* hence his (previously Upward's) later metaphor of the "rose in the steel dust" reveals the electromagnetic forces that raise the pattern of a rose into relief. Canto I is contained by this concept, for it is a translation of the *Nekuia,* which is itself a scripted version of an oral utterance whose origin is unknown. And within it is a different Odysseus, who is repeating a descent to the underworld for which there is no first time, only perpetual reenactments: "'A second time? why? man of ill star, / Facing the sunless dead and this joyless region?'"

Yet *The Cantos* denies this rupture of the signified's power by continually positing a world of immutable verities external to their linguistic formulation. Not so incidentally, this permits the poem's eventual appreciation of fascism as a truth that resists any interrogation or criticism, an ominous culmination of the paradoxical definition of the image as "the word beyond formulated language" that Pound offers so comfortably in *Gaudier-Brzeska.* Though the *Nekuia* that underlies Canto I is chosen for its ancient and originless status, its blind and prophetic figure of Tiresias, its "authorship" by the "poor old . . . blind, / blind as a bat" Homer, and its descent into the darkness of the underworld that will be replayed many times in the poem are early emblems of "the wisdom in blindness"[5] that directly contests the imagistic, pictorial, and visual program of both *Gaudier-Brzeska* and *The Chinese Written Character.*

The paradisal character and concluding position of *Drafts & Frag-*

ments cause Fenollosa's concepts to assume a more crucial and problematic status, however. It is here that Pound becomes most concerned about whether he has been able to absorb them into *The Cantos,* and whether he can sustain them through this final volume. In this way, the end of *The Cantos* is assisted by a revaluation of its own semiotic principles, for the concepts in Fenollosa's study, if sustained through *Drafts & Fragments,* create difficulties for ending the poem. How, for example, does an "endless sentence" stop? How is the gap between thing and sign closed when a Western readership understands only the very conventions that force the displacement? If the long poem increasingly draws upon itself, as *The Cantos* does in *Drafts & Fragments,* how can it remain synchronic? If *Drafts & Fragments'* revaluation of *The Cantos* is inseparable from a revaluation of the writer who created it, how can Pound sustain his impartiality? To employ Fenollosa's concepts through *Drafts & Fragments* is to erase the possibility of *The Cantos'* termination; to drop them is either to question the foundation of *The Cantos,* or to relinquish the ideal of utterance for which it strives. *Drafts & Fragments* faces these dilemmas that have remained latent in *The Cantos* from its inception, which I will suggest in the next chapter are concealed for most of the poem by its supposed approval of the vorticist principles of perpetuation and *paideuma,* which its various teleological narratives, including that of fascism, abuse instead of use.

In its exploration of the vorticist principle that begins with its first poem, *The Cantos* originally asked the reader to recognize the invalidity of a mimetic reading of the image, to reconsider the assumption that a text seeks to recuperate an external reality. The poem is not to be a transparent window onto an extratextual referent, but a group of images or signs that, in their own contiguity, create a self-contained design uninhibited either by a mimetic impulse or by the subjectivity of the poet—a design whose dynamics would be the same as nature's, and therefore self-perpetuating. This point, contained within Pound's theory of the image by 1913, is but the first step in a process whereby the poem will not subvert all reading strategies, and question the status of an extratextual reality, but will offer through vorticism and the Poundian image an alternative to such a mimetic strategy. The intention of vorticism is to show, through breaks in the mimetic process, that a new poetic language is necessary in order to make us see our world again, to defamiliarize it into a sudden radiance. This is one of the impulses behind the tremendous emphasis in *The Cantos* on light and perception,[6] and also on the inscription of previous texts that have fulfilled that intention in different ways, such as Dante's *Paradiso.* Vorticism does not assert the fictionality or ephemerality of an external reality such as nature; it posits that poetry, if organized along the principles of nature instead of the hierarchical principles of mimesis, will in effect bridge the otherwise inevitable gap between itself and that reality. In Pound's description of the image in *Gaudier-Brzeska* he writes of neutralizing the idea's traditional supremacy over the image: instead of being chosen to "back up some creed or some system of ethics or economics," the image is used because the poet "sees it or feels it," and any "age-old traditional meaning" that emerges from its use is tangential (*GB,* 86). In place of a representational poetry, then, is to be a poetry that celebrates its own units of composition, its images, and the energy in the design or style that is produced by their relationship with one another. Having admitted that, "you let in the jungle, you let in nature and truth and abundance and cubism and Kandinsky, and the lot of us" (*GB,* 85).[7]

To Fenollosa, the Chinese ideogram let in nature by following "the objective lines of relations in nature herself" (*CWCMP,* 22). The passage in Fenollosa's study that describes how it does this (and possibly one that attracted Pound to the offer of editing the book) spoke of the way in which ideogrammic script "passed over from the *seen to the unseen* by exactly the same process which all ancient races employed. This process is metaphor, the use of material images to suggest immaterial relations" (emphasis added). The influence of this phrase on Pound's verse is powerful; its recognition of "material images" as the source for metaphor is contained in his concept of *phanopoeia,* and the argument that attention to this existed in the poetry of "ancient races" is a confirmation of the insights in *Spirit of Romance* and influences his poetry from "The Tree" to *Drafts & Fragments,* where it makes an auspicious reappearance at the end of CX, introducing the theme of vision and its problematic inscription that will permeate the volume:

> The marble form in the pine wood,
> The shrine *seen and not seen*[8]
> From the roots of sequoias   (Emphasis added)

Fenollosa describes this transaction that the Chinese character performs as a "*bridge* whereby to cross from the minor truth of *the seen* to the major truth of *the unseen*" (CWCMP, 22; emphasis added), a word employed again at the end of *Drafts & Fragments* in "Notes for CXVII et seq.": "To have heard the farfalla gasping / as toward a bridge over worlds."

These passages, which introduce and end *The Cantos'* final movement as Pound saw it in its proofs stage, display its frequent conflation of the personal and the poetic. They evoke Pound's encounter with the margin between the visible and the ineffable, while reconsidering the capacity of the long poem to accomplish that through its employment of the principles of ideogrammic script. The patterns of nature to which Pound saw *The Cantos* corresponding seem no longer to exist as an analogy for the language of the long vorticist poem but are instead a pattern receding into isolation, from which the poem has been separated. The long poem, through the breadth of its own horizons, has always sacrificed itself to the lure of reflecting and magnifying the patterns of nature, to "wreathing / A flowery band to bind us to the earth," as Keats writes, preventing a natural thing of beauty from passing into nothingness. It is "Neath *this* altar now [that Keats's] Endymion lies" (CX/779), with the pun in the final word of the line revealing the long poem's deviation from its own mandate to emulate nature's truth. This suspicion on Pound's part of the gulf between *The Cantos'* language and the analogy of nature's diverse structure (Giordano Bruno's "diversa natura" in CXIV) assists in its termination in *Drafts & Fragments*. It is articulated in the difficult "From CXV" as the separation between the poem's "blown husk that is finished" and the constantly self-renewing nature that speaks to itself eternally, outlasting the poet who translates it—"but the light sings eternal"—and his language that would inscribe it. It also underlies Pound's growing interpretation of his own failure to articulate a patterned order from within an otherwise chaotic natural world; increasingly, in *Drafts & Fragments*, *The Cantos* is regarded as a "maze" and "a tangle," a "hall of mirrors," a labyrinth whose edges are obscured by the intricacies of its own design, and by the self-interrogation that begins in CX.[9]

By CXVI, however, the poetry more directly and self-consciously addresses these issues. For one thing, it contains a recognition of *The Cantos'* persistent undoing of sight by the ideal of transcendent blindness and reverses it with the claim, in homage again to Dante, that "the verb is 'see,' not 'walk on.'" Too, its lament that *The Cantos* is a "tangle of works unfinished" contains Pound's despair over his poem being understood, or its teachings employed, by his audience. In *Guide to Kulchur* Pound had written that "we should read for power. Man reading shd. be man intensely alive. The book shd. be a ball of light in one's hand" (*GK, 55*). Even if Pound has written such a text ("I have brought the great ball of crystal") no one can hold or understand it ("who can lift it?"), burdened as it is by complexity and the weight of a relentless intertextuality. The original vehicle in the metaphor of *The Cantos* as Homeric sea maintains its vitality and endurance— "Came Neptunus / his mind leaping / like dolphins"—yet Pound's poem, "the record / the palimpsest," is no more than "a little light / in great darkness— / cuniculi." The scene returns us to the opening of CX as well, where the "sea-wake" and the clear design in the Torcello mosaic are "as a dolphin on sea-brink," a vision of natural exuberance that exists happily "without [the] tyranny" of *Verkehr*, of (if we employ another of *Verkehr's* meanings) communication itself, which is artificial.

In CXVI, the vision of poetic transparency and of the successful long poem, the joyous "leaping" that "the human mind has attained," is interrupted by the thought of another tyranny, Mussolini's:

> To make Cosmos—
> To achieve the possible—
> Muss., wrecked for an error

Characteristic both of the indeterminacy in Pound's verse and of his ambivalent response to his own life now, the last line in the passage can be read in two mutually exclusive ways. If Mussolini is its subject, he was "wrecked for an error," and probably the error of not adhering closely enough to the Confucian ideal of the "unwobbling pivot." Pound suggested as much to Huntington Cairns in a 1949 letter, which censured Mussolini "for not 'working in centre'"—for failing to observe the Confucian principle of balancing at the still center or pivot— and criticizing Il Duce's policies for "plunging into the swamp instead of improving FROM the centre."[10] Yet Pound's censuring of Mussolini (though not of fascism itself) immediately after the war became quite severe, and the rather mild idea that Mussolini simply committed "an error" does not fit so easily here.[11] Another possible reading of the line is that Mussolini *is* the error that has "wrecked" something, which we might interpret (taking a cue from later in CXVI: "Tho' my errors and wrecks lie about me") as *The Cantos* itself and, implicated in that, Pound's life. If so, "the record / the palimpsest" is the text that will offer an alternative interpretation of Pound, extracting him from the association with a failed fascism and recalling that his *Cantos* has drawn "from the air a live tradition," the great ball of crystal that he will go on to disparage a few lines later.

Hence Pound "cannot make it flow thru." The "it" is the "Charity" of the previous line, fundamental to Dante (as *caritas*) and to Thomas Hardy, who like Pound "lived on after the era, [and] came to his final 'Surview' . . . 'That the greatest of things is Charity'" (*GK*, 290). It is also coherence in *The Cantos,* the "gold thread" that he hopes to trace through an otherwise labyrinthine pattern. Yet "flow thru" equates the poem with the private Pound, again via the Confucian reference to tao, the principle that "flows through, holds . . . together, germinates" an individual's actions. There is some measure of self-recognition here, of understanding that the poem's deviation from authoritative closure into fragmented dispersal, and Pound's journey from personal relevance to being "no use to anyone," are not unrelated. When he writes of having "lost my center / fighting the world" in "Notes for CXVII et seq.," then, he conflates the private and the poetic, suggesting that the deviation from his most intimate convictions has coincided with the poem's move to error and insignificance. If, for Pound, to be useful is to write a tale of the tribe that the tribe can understand, can "lift," he longs for the Noh "rushlight" that will "lead back to [the] splendour" of an earlier poetic simplicity and directness, reflective of an individual who has achieved and maintained such a center.

Thus the quotation from his 1910 "Larks at Allègre" in *The Spirit of Romance* in the last fragment of "Notes for CXVII et seq."—"'es laissa cader' / so high toward the sun and then falling, / 'de joi sas alas'"—representative of an early (and translated) poetry that, as Kathryne Lindberg points out, is predeconstructive and pre-Nietzschean[12] and hence does not contain the problematic image dynamics that *The Cantos* eventually reveals. The ideogram for splendor is composed of the radicals for light, feathers, and song bird—the very images that close the volume in the last "Notes for CXVII et seq." fragment in the form of Bernart's lark—signifying the state to which Pound desires to return, the splendor of poetic limpidity represented for him by the textual subjects of *The Spirit of Romance*. This is not to say that the paradise he had contemplated for his *Cantos* cannot exist, for "it coheres all right / even if my notes do not cohere." Instead, he is explicit in his point that his poem distorts a paradise that exists outside the realm of linguistic translation, that he can "see again," or reencounter, only by abandoning *The Cantos* for silence and observation, where the circle, to invoke Dante once more, can be seen, though it remains untranslatable. The eventually published fragment dedicating *The Cantos* to Olga Rudge is pertinent here, for it asserts, in its envisioned terminal position as an ode to strength and endurance, the inevitable distance between the self and the language that refers to it: "Her name was Courage / & is written Olga."

Chapter 5

Choosing Blindness: Vorticism and the Narrative of Fascism

Is this the end of it? I have seen no one who can see his errors and then go into his own mind and demand justice on them in precise, just, discriminating words.
                    —Confucius, *Analects* 34, trans. Pound

In his 1914 essay "The Prose Tradition in Verse" Pound invoked Remy de Gourmont's description of the writers who "think only husks and shells of the thoughts that have been already lived over by others" (*LE,* 371). It finds its way into Pound's indictment of his weaker contemporaries in Canto VII, first published in 1921:

> Thin husks I had known as men,
> Dry casques of departed locusts
>   speaking a shell of speech...
> Propped between chairs and table...
> Words like the locust-shells, moved by no inner being;
>   A dryness calling for death
>
>   (26)

The passage carries overtones of Eliot's *Waste Land* (and a prediction of *The Hollow Men*), merging the aridity of poetry at the time with a larger cultural poverty that he hopes to repair. Near the close of Canto VII the Easter Rebellion's Desmond Fitzgerald (so Pound tells us in the typescript's margin), imprisoned, then released to become an Irish minister and ardent critic of capitalism, is invoked as "The live man, out of lands and prisons" who "shakes the dry pods, / Probes for old wills and friendships." For Pound in the late 1950s, imprisoned, then re-

115

leased, yet not ministerial but marginalized, the ironic parallels hover. He had believed that he was being taken from Italy to America to be heard by Truman in 1945, that his voice was crucial to the health of the country; instead, excerpts from his recent *Pisan Cantos* were used as proof of his insanity.[1] Fifteen years later in "From CXV," the voice that is Canto VII's "dryness calling for death," writing "shells of the thoughts that have been already lived over by others," is his own, a *Kakitsubata*-like apparition of a previous self, a "blown husk that is finished." And the passage may extend beyond the personal reference to include *The Cantos* itself. Diminished by "From CXV" to a "pale flare," *The Cantos* had originally been placed by Pound in the vanguard of artistic experiment and radical form, along with "Picasso / or Lewis," harbingers of "great flares, new form." Now Pound regards the poem more like Canto VII's reduction of Homer's Helen to a museum piece (surrounded by "glass, / A petrefaction of air"), or a house of facades ("Shell of the older house. / Brown-yellow wood, and the no colour plaster, / Dry professorial talk . . . ").

Yet if, like a blown husk, *The Cantos* is "finished," it is so in contradictory terms—either in the sense of being ruined and exhausted, or in the more desired sense of being deliberately closed. Pound's response here to *The Cantos* is ambiguous, neither fully approving nor disparaging; he remains somewhat curious, if anything, as to why it has not achieved an unequivocal termination. ("And of man seeking good, / doing evil": no answer to that conundrum either.) In the language of "From CXV," Pound has been "diverted" from his "green time," when, such as in Canto VII, he scorned "the husk of talk" about Helen's beauty and envisioned *The Cantos* as a poem that would make the past immediate and powerful. If the equation between poet and text is drawn in "From CXV," then the text too has been diverted during its own green time—the metaphor of nature and growth suggesting again a latent energy, the "intelligence" that makes a cherry tree out of a cherry stone, and that "brings us close to nature"—by "asperities" that the pressure of making "it cohere" now raises into prominence.

After Pound's experience with Fenollosa's *Chinese Written Character* he involved himself with vorticism, a delineation of "patterned energy" in art that seemed to have affinities with nature's, such as the helical structure of galaxies observed by astronomers at the turn of the century. Vorticism was an ecstatic celebration of energy indifferent to the distinction between its creative and destructive versions, permitting Pound to think of it as "intelligence and knowledge of life, of the whole of it" (*LEP,* 74) at the same time that Lewis saw it as the way to "shatter the visible world to bits."[2] The capacity for energy to be used in either direction would of course not be lost on nuclear physicists of this century, apparent in CXV's opening lines that comment on this ambivalence that becomes paralysis—"The scientists are in terror / and the European mind stops / Wyndham Lewis chose blindness / rather than have his mind stop"—recalling again Canto VII's condemnation of "stillness" and "tall indifference." The opening of "From CXV" refers to an operation available to Lewis that offered a good chance of curing his encroaching blindness; he ran the risk of having his mind impaired by the procedure, however, and eventually chose to sacrifice sight for insight, and not to undergo the treatment. As with so much else in this canto, the last line here is heavily multivalent, playing on blindness in equal measure as an ocular and a moral dysfunction, a sign that Pound increasingly believed at this late point in his life that his own metaphoric blindness had stopped him from emerging from his own inflexible certainties. And considering the poetics of vorticism that brought Lewis and Pound together, the apparent testament to Lewis's stoicism is also invested with a criticism of his blindness to the consequences of vorticism's exuberant amorality. In this sense, *The Cantos'* evolving reverence for blindness under the guise of insight, which began with the figures of Homer and Tiresias, is now reexamined with a greater skepticism and care in *Drafts & Fragments* ("to 'see again,' /the verb is 'see,'") and with an eye toward the eventual political consequences of ignoring how power and energy are employed and expressed. And Canto VII's easy privileging of motion over stillness is now complicated in "From CXV" by the fact that it is blindness, with its own ominous significance, that replaces stasis.[3]

For Lewis and Pound (and more so for Pound) vorticism's capacity to be extended into a political analogue quickly contributed to an eventual embrace of fascism. In his 1926 *The Art of Being Ruled* Lewis argued that the artist required "the most powerful and stable authority that can be devised,"[4] the fascism that became for Pound by 1933 the cultural equivalent of "DIRECT action" (*J/M,* 70). Its strong central authority conveniently realized the patterned energy and underlying order that permeated vorticist art, and vorticism's apparent reciprocity with nature lent fascism a kind of supramoral legitimacy. Pound's encouragement and support of so many literary successes in the 1920s particularly, suggested his literary judgment was astute, and as Redman argues, the confidence he gained through that easily "extended... to the political sphere" in the 1930s.[5] The analogy probably did more to fragment the already disassembling vorticists than anything else, eliciting Eliot's assertion of "the priority of ethics over politics" in *Criterion* in 1933,[6] and Pound's equally strong defensiveness that would not relax until near the end of his life, where his thoughts return to Eliot and Lewis in *Drafts & Fragments*. Yet the "asperities" ("From CXV") that diverted Pound are not just these early personal conflicts. If the subject of "From CXV" is both Pound himself and *The Cantos*, the diversion is the imported narrative of fascism that begins relentlessly to complicate and distort the poem's vorticist celebration of energy, eventually prejudicing it against its own poetics, and generating Pound's desire in CXVI to return to an earlier poetic and personal splendor—represented by *The Spirit of Romance* through Dante, Bernart, and Camoens, and by Noh drama, the Gaudier-Brzeska memoir, and the first cantos—before fascism assumed its more menacing symmetry with its anti-Semitism beginning in 1935, and its bloody engagements in Abyssinia in 1935–36, Spain in 1936–39, and then the Second World War.

This is not to suggest that Pound renounces his fascism in *Drafts & Fragments,* for the whole debate is complicated by the subtleties of fascism's historical versions, by its swift internal evolution, and by its many compromises to the shifting political contexts of the time through which it was manifested. Though he was apparently incapable of registering these complexities, and of locating himself at a specific point within them, he does begin to recognize in *Drafts & Fragments* how his early interpretation of fascism as a political analogy to vorticism has compromised his poem, and to see it as a "will toward *order*" (*J/M,* 99), an example of how ineptly political pragmatism might be judged by aesthetic standards, ideas to which he naively clung through fascism's more harmful versions and then, after the war, beyond its own political relevance. That "CXX"—a most likely candidate for Pound's expression of political and racial remorse—cannot be invoked as Pound's renunciation of fascism is evident not only in his ambivalence toward the lines, and in his refusal to publish them. When he asks "the gods" to "forgive what I have made" in the first collection's "115," he echoes Daniele Varé's 1949 memoir *The Two Imposters,* where, in a section titled "The Dream Shattered," Mussolini's error is interpreted as pride, "the sin that the gods never forgive."[7] Varé, Italy's ambassador to the United States during Mussolini's leadership, was like Pound in the 1940s and 1950s a supporter of fascism as a corrective to Communism, and he would blame Mussolini in *The Two Impostors* for its later disintegration as a viable political system in Italy into excess and destruction. When Pound asks for forgiveness from the gods in these lines, he is not necessarily distancing himself from fascism, as he had interpreted it, at all; he is hoping to avoid the judgment brought to bear on Mussolini and to remedy his own blindness to fascism's eventual implications, its "terrible dialectic... [of an early] attempt to create/recover an experience of community [and its later] all-consuming, paranoid fascination with the ENEMY,"[8] to "see again," in CXVI's phrasing, where he and his poem diverted from an earlier optimism for fusing the poetic and the political, and an earlier delight in paradisal language.

It may be that Paolo Pasolini was correct when he recognized Pound's fascism as being "archaic," a nostalgic exaltation of "the laws of the peasant world and the cultural unity of a lord and his vassals,"[9] and that any relevance and practicality in its vision essentially vanished with Mussolini's alignment with Hitler. The "enormous tragedy of the peasant's bent shoulders," opening the *Pisan Cantos* and following the suppressed LXXII and LXXIII, remains as a carefully ambiguous testimony to that now debased vision. Pound's sense of himself in 1960 as "the last American living the tragedy of Europe" (*RP*, 244) is part of this nostalgia for an almost troubadourian, highly idealized community of love and a powerfully expressive land-based class (represented in the later cantos by the Na-khi, one suspects) and reveals his outdated, now shattered, anticipation that such a community could be revived in Europe through fascism. For Pound this "pride" has been revealed through what he has "made," through the poem that began around the time Gaudier-Brzeska sought an end to "arrogance, self-esteem, pride" (*GB*, 27) but that paradoxically came to indulge in an exclusive obsession.

In his 1916 memoir of Gaudier-Brzeska, and in his edition of Fenollosa's Noh plays of the same year, Pound had wondered whether vorticism's potential could be unleashed to generate the verbal energy necessary to sustain the mysterious design of the modern long poem.

I am often asked whether there can be a long imagiste or vorticist poem. The Japanese, who evolved the hokku, evolved also the Noh plays. In the best "Noh" the whole play may consist of one image. I mean, it is gathered about one image. Its unity consists in one image, enforced by movement and music. I see nothing against a long vorticist poem. (*GB*, 94)

Pound had described the image as a "node" two pages earlier in *Gaudier-Brzeska*, as a point or "cluster" of energy admitting, channeling, and emitting ideas: its effect was concentrated and local. In *Gaudier-Brzeska*, Pound speculates on the possibility of transfering that notion of the image to a long poem without sacrificing either the image's local intensity or the poem's inclusiveness.[10] This act of exploring is central to Pound's description of vorticism in *Gaudier-Brzeska* ("But let me go on with my own branch of vorticism, about which I can probably speak with greater clarity. All poetic language is the language of exploration" [*GB*, 88]). It is also central to *The Cantos*. Canto I is characterized by many types of exploration and is created out of the rubble of an earlier beginning, the three Ur-Cantos. For Pound, their weakness was their unsteady mimicry of Browning, whose own long poem *Sordello* was both a model and a foe for the new long poem *The Cantos*. The composition of *The Cantos* really begins when Pound discards the Ur-Cantos' Browningesque influence for the exploratory Canto I, which, free of imitative restraint, embarks on a journey into the uncharted poetics of vorticism. This ascent from the Ur-Cantos to Canto I is perhaps the first indication of the poem's heuristic nature, for in the process Pound discovers many of the poetic principles that will generate and shape *The Cantos*.

Canto I, whose content in part is the propitiatory rite Odysseus performs in order to receive guidance for the next stage of his journey, is also the poem's ceremonial beginning that gathers much of the "intelligence" that will inform its own future. Canto I seems to be a translation of the *Nekuia*, book 11 of the Odyssey, apparently the oldest section of the poem. Yet there are several discrepancies between Pound's version and Homer's that inevitably call this interpretation into question. For one thing, there are many omissions in Pound's version, and, for another, there are some curious additions or ruptures "out of Homer" like the one nine lines from the canto's end:

And he strong with the blood, said then: "Odysseus
"Shalt return through spiteful Neptune, over dark seas,
"Lose all companions." And then Anticlea came.
Lie quiet Divus. I mean, that is Andreas Divus,
In officina Wecheli, 1538, out of Homer.
And he sailed, by Sirens and thence outward and away
And unto Circe.   (Emphasis added)

The Andreas Divus mentioned in the fourth line of this passage was himself a translator of the *Odyssey;* his edition was published in 1538 in Paris in the workshop of Wechelus, who appears in the fifth line. Divus's text, too, contained discrepancies, such as the replacement of διογενές, meaning "sprung from Zeus" by δίγονος, meaning "double," which Pound would rework into English as "A second time" in his Canto I.[11] Yet another alteration in Pound's text begins immediately after the two interspliced lines about Divus, for Odysseus does not journey "by Sirens and thence ... unto Circe," but the reverse. Daniel Pearlman is the first to recognize this fact,[12] though his allegorical explanation of it (that "Pound is presenting images of the feminine in ascending order of desirability," from the Sirens to Circe to Aphrodite) can be augmented somewhat. Its significance is not in its miniature enactment of the forthcoming structure of *The Cantos* (the "'chopped seas' ... of the first xxx cantos," to Circe "the presiding goddess of the middle cantos," to Penelope of the later ones),[13] nor in its ascendence through increasingly beneficent visions of the feminine that *The Cantos* may or may not reveal on a larger scale. These allegorical readings, though plausible, assume that if *The Cantos* employed the material of previous texts like the *Divine Comedy* and the *Odyssey,* it must necessarily employ their structures as well. This assumption partly creates Pound's difficulties in terminating *The Cantos,* for it emphasizes a closural pattern that the poem's vorticist method would resist. The larger significance of this change is that it recognizes a principle of poetic discourse: it reveals that the canto is not a translation but a verbal location that differentiates at the same time that it recuperates. While Canto I may be read as a design for *The Cantos'* overall structure, it is also an investigation of poetic semiotics; *The Cantos'* structure and termination will be a consequence of their dynamics, rather than a simple allegorical inflation of the local narratives its initial poem contains.

But why begin *The Cantos* with the semblance of a translation at all? The answer to this question inevitably contributes to an interpretation of *The Cantos'* method and meaning. One possible answer, with which Pound seemed to agree, is that the translations call attention to their sources (among the earliest texts we have), and that Canto I is thus reintroducing the primitive power of poetry into a contemporary context, providing the translations, in other words, with a didactic purpose. Another is that Pound is locating his poetic models for *The Cantos,* whose epic structures and concerns will be reflected in his poem; the translations, in this sense, guide our reading.[14] Yet the Greek word that is corrupted in the Divus translation (and Divus himself may have been misled by an already corrupt Renaissance text) offers a fortuitous chance for another reading. That which "springs from Zeus' head," like Athena, has a single origin, whereas that which is "a second time" is (in Williams's *Paterson* phrase) a repetition with a difference, like Pound's opening canto. Canto I's status as a retranslation is designed to illuminate how poetry always participates in that act. *The Cantos'* method would become an exploration of this concept, that a poem is not of single but of multiple origin, which can never be fully recuperated, and whose task is not to recuperate. It is not coincidental that *The Cantos'* "first" poem is predicated upon this principle, for the undoing of its primary location by all the earlier texts that are its heritage—Divus's translation, the Renaissance Latin he worked from, the Greek that predated it, the Homeric utterance that was perpetuated and altered in its own retelling, the hidden enigmatic voice we call Homer, and the Anglo-Saxon line they are rendered through—questions the concept of beginnings, and thus of structural boundaries altogether, including endings.[15] In the process, it urges us to reevaluate our understanding of history, to recognize that empirical truth is known to us only through the mediation of the voices that relate it, which we call history. Ironically, this education of reading that Canto I affords will undermine the authority of Pound's later pronouncements on politics and race, which cannot, ultimately, withstand the skepticism the poem has already engendered in its attentive readers.

It was only after several years of poetry writing that involved translations of Romance languages, after watching Yeats deal with Noh translations, and after editing Fenollosa's investigation of translation—*The Chinese Written Character*—that Pound would see how the act of translating, once revealed, could become the subject of a poem, as it does in Canto I. But *The Cantos'* identity is created by taking the process a step further, by calling attention to its status as a translation with an endless heritage. This erases any possibility of single origin, makes explicit the fact of its multiple origin, and disseminates meaning indefinitely, thereby complicating the possibility of *The Cantos*' termination. Closely related to this is the fact that these disseminations generate a poem so apparently nondetermined that its poet, conveniently obscured by the mediations of texts, can and will exert enormous ideological control over it in order to direct its structure.

The multiple origin and exploration that were raised into prominence by the Canto I retranslation have consequences for the structure of *The Cantos*. They refuse to privilege the convention of narrative linearity in the poem (a negation undone, however, by the sequential numbering of its cantos, to which the reader inevitably assigns a linearity), since the poem was always only the visible point in a system without known beginning or end. Like the good epic Pound rather hoped it would be, *The Cantos* began in medias res, after its multiple textual origins; but rather differently, by having no preconceived telos beyond the writing of a long vorticist poem, it had at this early stage no future Ithaca to which a narrative, or an ethos of heroism, led. *The Cantos*' implicit ethos was vorticism, and thus the poem perpetuated that point of convergence between past and future—it remained in medias res—giving Pound tremendous freedom from structural restraint while writing it, and in the process ensuring that nothing was excluded "merely because it didn't fit" (RP, 222) into some planned narrative sequence.

Employing the vorticist method does not undermine order in a poem, however: it simply invalidates certain traditionally accessible structures (just as it denies a more conventional role for the image) and replaces them with others that emerge as the poem gains in length. Canto I had been a repetition with a difference from a previous host of texts, a response to an inherited subject. In its metamorphic focus, Canto II sustains this pattern. It is not only a retranslated response to a previous host of texts—among them Ovid's *Metamorphoses* and Arthur Golding's translation of it—but also the discovery that immutable truths can take various forms. They can be "seen, and half-seen" as Pound writes there, implying that the truth may escape full recognition but still be registered, in the depths of the psyche to which he descends near the end of CX; there he will alter that short phrase ("The marble form in the pine wood / The shrine seen and *not* seen"; emphasis added) and offer an ironic recognition of how a shrine such as fascism, invoked through the Brancusi-Mussolini reference, may also escape understanding entirely.

Sometime between 1925 and 1928[16] Pound began reading the work of anthropologist Leo Frobenius, who had arrived, through his studies of African tribal rites and artistic expression, at the concept of paideuma—what Pound would later translate in *Guide to Kulchur* as "the tangle or complex of the inrooted ideas of any period" and redefine for his own purposes as "the gristly roots of ideas that are in action" (*GK*, 58).[17] The consequences of the paideuma concept for *The Cantos* were large. The vorticist image itself was an idea in action, not ephemeral but tangible, thought become visible. The dual direction of the poem, back toward multiple origins and forward in exploration, was incorporated in the notions of prehistorical "roots" and their continual revelation "in action." These became confirmations of Pound's vorticist method, which itself had been in action for over a decade. Most important was the word *tangle:* it suggested the multiple origins, irreducible and interrelated concepts embedded in the psyche of a civilization, that were contiguous, in hypostasis, not hierarchical. Just as Frobenius saw the revelation of a culture's "inrooted ideas" in its primitive paintings, so did Pound see them in his civilization's artistic achievements, which were acts, explorations.

These concepts helped confirm Pound's poetic method, by giving it license to move in the territories of anthropology, archeology, history, and primarily politics, for in paideuma was the reflection of a culture's political and economic nature in its artistic one, and the reverse. The connection was simplistic and naive, applicable (possibly) to "the Renaissance court at, say, Urbino" but not to "more complex cultures except at the highest level of abstraction," as Redman cogently puts it.[18] Paideuma supplied the poem with its mandate to sustain the frequently obscuring play among its many informants,[19] helping to rhetorically blind its readers, but through its simplistic equation it also easily cohered the aesthetic with the political in a most reductive manner. In the first three cantos that education concerns the semiotic concepts of language and translation; but as the poem's length and obscurity gathers, it increasingly concerns Pound's own political and economic interests, made more persuasive and agreeable by the poem's apparent privileging of the fragment over the whole, of heuristic incompletion over authoritarian form.

The Cantos has always suffered the charge of obscurity and, no matter how many determined scholars continue to explicate its references, no doubt always will. One of the problems with the strategy of simplifying the poem for the innocent reader by explicating references is this very notion of multiple origins: to list a single source for each reference is to misconstrue and reduce the structure of the poem, and its burgeoning energy of vorticism, whose sources are always multiple, and invariably incapable of secure exegesis. To misconstrue this is to distort the poem in such a way as to make it difficult and laborious to read, to make the poem even more obscure. The multiplicity of origins, too, becomes one of the poem's obscuring factors, but it is a productive factor without which the poem cannot exist. Another contributing factor to all of this was Pound's encyclopedic knowledge, the product of extensive reading, itself the product of an irrepressible curiosity. Coupled with a poetic structure that can absorb limitless matter, the result is an exponential increase in verbal phenomena, cut through by the opposing energies of exploration and multiple origins, invaded by the power of metamorphosis—which generates a large part of the excitement of reading the poem, and a variety of options and expectations for its close.

The idea of multiple origins that manifested itself in Pound's vortex and Frobenius's "tangle" further complicated any possibility of closure in *The Cantos*. The presence of multiplicity in the poem creates a dialectic among its limitless sources, perpetuating the poem beyond resolution at any one point. In fact, it makes the perpetual deferral of resolution one of *The Cantos'* structural principles. For this reason Pound saw "fragments" as the units of composition in *The Cantos'* structure in 1927. The term addressed the irresolvable energies that crisscross the poem and recognized each canto's participation in their conflict. In this sense, the fragment was not the remnant of a larger whole that it hoped to recuperate, but the structural block bearing the pressure of a self-interfering process that had never acquiesced to wholeness. The fragment militates against "the myth of comprehensiveness implicit in the closure of poetic or narrative form," as Christine Froula writes, and signifies "a recognition of all that has been left out, lost, or effaced,"[20] or at least Pound hopes it will sustain that impression. Its nature is both an admission of incompletion and an apparent denial of any attraction to structural unity that would mar its sympathy with the flux and indeterminacy of history.

There is another level on which conflict existed that created not obscurity so much as a perpetuation of the poem through indeterminacy. *The Cantos'* indebtedness to Dante's *Divine Comedy*, Confucianism, Social Credit, and the fascist vision of Ecbatan, whose teleologies cross the nonlinear nature of *The Cantos'* vorticism, created a dialectic between method and textual informants that would remain equally irresolvable. The realization of these—so crucial to *The Cantos'* paradise envisioned at various points in its composition—is consistently deferred by the poem's vorticist method of narrative fragmentation. In trying to account for the stamina of readers' interest in *The Cantos*, through an opaque text and a problematic racial and political didacticism, it is interesting to see how this tension between closural and nonclosural energies creates its own brand of poetic suspense, to which readers, editors, and Pound responded in *Drafts & Fragments* in various ways. *Drafts & Fragments* would become in large part the location where Pound no longer attempts to arbitrate between these contrary urges toward and away from closure, where he exchanges any impetus previously held in the poem toward closure, an impetus supplied by *The Cantos'* use of these teleological narratives, for an appeal to the anticlosural vorticist properties it initially held.[21]

The fabulae of these narratives had informed the poem, somewhat more neutrally than we usually think, from its early stages, outside the context of teleological allegory. Critics until recently have tended to read Canto I's Homeric, Dantean, and Confucian influences as indications that *The Cantos* requires a similarly teleologic structure, a reading symptomatic of *Paterson's* "dream of the whole poem." Yet Pound was not initially attracted to the *Divine Comedy* for its pattern of ascent but for the subordination of its linear narrative to the informing and generative image of the circle. And Confucius's texts originally attracted Pound by their emphasis on the relationship between speech and action; only later in the poem did that relationship become arbitrated by the ulterior narrative of fascism, whose exemplary Confucian protagonist was Mussolini, and whose social paradise was the totalitarian state. Pound merged these separate narratives within the totalizing structure of the fascist dream in the 1930s because he saw Confucius, Dante, and Homer sharing with Mussolini what Pound termed (via Cavalcanti) "DIRECTION OF THE WILL. And if the reader will blow the fog off his brain and think for a few minutes or a few stray half-hours he will find this phrase brings us ultimately both to Confucius and to Dante" (*J/M*, 15–16). Typical of Pound's rationalization, this group to which Mussolini belonged was not only morally but even artistically superior. In 1933 Pound declared that Mussolini was an artist: "Take him as anything save the artist and you will get muddled in contradictions" (*J/M*, 33–34). The equation pushes Frobenius's connection between the aesthetic and the political to an extreme, for in the politician now inheres the very artistic figure that is a measure of the state. Once that equation is secured in Pound's mind in 1931, when he writes *Jefferson and/or Mussolini*, he can and will go on to rationalize Mussolini's eventual dissent from his earlier more attractive socialism as the inevitable unpredictability of the artist.[22]

When Pound first incorporated Confucianism, as he saw it, into his poem, it was not with a view toward its teleologic aspect so much as its example of a pattern of recurrence. Confucius terminates the canto in which he first appears by deferring the resolution of a teleological process: "The blossoms of the apricot / blow from the east to the west, / And I have tried to keep them from falling" (XIII/60).[23] In Canto XIII, drawn from the *Ta Hio*, Pound synchronizes Neoplatonism and Confucianism by means of Kung's inner order radiating out to the concentric social spheres of family and "dominion." Canto XLIX, though, witnesses a very different employment of Confucian thought; there, it is implicated in the fascist dream that Pound had embraced by the 1930s. The *Jefferson and/or Mussolini* economic program of creating a debt-free state is fused with a Confucian "dimension of stillness" and under the guise of sympathy for peasants[24] is revealed instead as a means of "power over wild beasts." It is worth noting, in addition, that an earlier moment of Confucian "stillness" in Canto XXXVI that was not encumbered by a fascist teleology is accompanied by an arrogant scorn for readers who do not comprehend the poem's growing obscurity.[25] When the "ply over ply" of Confucianism and fascism occurs, it is misread by the beguiled reader as a figment of his or her own misunderstanding.

Although vorticist indeterminacy was originally commensurate with the project of the long poem whose close was unforeseeable, it is challenged as *The Cantos* absorbs the teleological narratives that request completion. Of these, the narrative of fascism is the most powerful because the poem is the least prepared for it, because in its political form it thwarts the very fragmentation and indeterminacy that vorticism permits in art.

"Whether in politics, culture, or society," as Casillo writes in *The Genealogy of Demons,* "Pound envisions Italian Fascism as aspiring toward a totalitarian completeness and unity, toward organic harmony, hierarchy, and proportion,"[26] an excessive inflation of the characteristics that Pound's original vorticism troubled and even challenged at the level of poetic form, and that he reverses at the many points in *Drafts & Fragments,* where hierarchy is undone and margins ("the salt hay whispers to tide's change") are dissolved. Dissolving the differences that any hierarchical system solidified has consequences for Pound's anti-Semitism as well, which was based on a racist misreading of usury, "the name which Pound gives to indistinction itself."[27] The swamp, *The Cantos'* symbol of all that is undifferentiated, luxuriant, and infectious, was Pound's constant invocation of the Jew, and in "From CXV"'s Whitmanesque trope of the indistinct margin between water and land is Pound's faint acknowledgment of the "diversion" of anti-Semitism as well.

Like *Drafts & Fragments,* the *Pisan Cantos* envisions a paradise, though its is the Fascist state, whose overthrow is the burden and tragedy of the peasant's shoulders ("The enormous tragedy of the dream in the peasant's bent / shoulders") in its opening lines. Mussolini's Salò Republic, erected in the wake of that tragedy, was at Gardone on Lake Garda, the site of much of CX's imagery and composition. To Pound in Canto LXXIV the goal of Mussolini's political program merges imagistically with Dante's paradise, and Mussolini himself becomes the subject of Confucius's definition of "the superior man" who follows what is right and just in *The Analects.* The canto is not guided by a sense of the error of fascism, but by the tragedy of its demise. Its fate, and ultimately Mussolini's, begins a reflection on the fates of several other "resisters" who reappear in CX and elsewhere in *Drafts & Fragments:* Bunting, Upward, "Uncle George" Tinkham, Joseph Wadsworth.[28] Rationalizing this is Pound's belief in the natural intelligence that permeates the world, which appears in the canto mostly through texts such as Erigena's *De Divisione Naturae,* Confucius's *Analects,* and Dante's *Paradiso* that achieve a vision of paradisal beauty. The emerging narrative of fascism's destruction is thus redeemed by other texts that record and sustain a belief in divine purpose, in the process salvaging fascism from criticism and placing it in the context of man's continual blindness to what, according to the text of nature, is right. Thus the *spezzato* paradise shall be reconstructed, and *The Cantos* will move "out of hell" through the temporarily disrupted "orderly Dantescan rising" to a vision of recurrent beauty symbolized by the rose in the steel dust.

Aphrodite, *The Cantos*' symbolic crossing of poetic form and vision required by the vorticist method that is otherwise potentially indeterminate, is replaced in Canto LXXXI by Pound's affirmation of fascism, which will now supply form: her (in)sight, "careless or unaware it had not the / whole tent's room," defers in that canto to

> What thou lovest well remains,
> > the rest is dross
> What thou lov'st well shall not be reft from thee
> What thou lov'st well is thy true heritage
> Whose world, or mine or theirs
> > or is it of none?
> First came the seen, then thus the palpable
> > Elysium, though it were in the halls of hell
>
> > > > (520–21)

When Pound writes, late in the composition of *Drafts & Fragments,* that he no longer knows what he loves,

> M'amour, m'amour
> > what do I love and
> > > where are you?
> That I lost my center
> > fighting the world.
> The dreams clash
> > and are shattered—
> and that I tried to make a paradiso
> > > terrestre
> > > ("Notes for CXVII et seq.")

he is voicing a despair that is deepened by its Pisan reference, where what Pound loves and calls his poem's "true heritage" is its fascism, as Jerome McGann points out, not "some ideal of love."[29] The Canto LXXXI passage, so enshrouded in intertextual humility and reverence (echoes of Chaucer's line "Subdue thyself, and others thee shall hear" follow the passage, of Jonson's "Have you seen but a bright lily grow, / Before rude hands have touched it?" precede it) does not yield this interpretation easily, either to the reader or, more significantly, to Pound at the time. By "Notes for CXVII et seq.," though, the confusion over an object for his love is more than a reference to his tangled personal relationships with Olga Rudge, Marcella Spann, and Dorothy Pound. It is simultaneously a confusion over a "lost ... center," possibly the Confucian center within tao, but also the diverted vorticist poetics of *The Cantos.* What is "bound by love in one volume" for Dante at the culmination of the *Paradiso* into a vision of "the universal form" is a "clash" of "dreams" for Pound, whose reference to Varé's "The Dream Shattered" in *The Two Impostors* suggests that fascism as he and so many others first conceived it held the potential to cohere.

Thus the final "Notes for CXVII et seq." fragment is imbued with Dantean imagery, drawn from *Purgatorio* 10.124–25: "Do you not perceive that we are worms born to form the angelic butterfly [farfalla] that soars to judgement without defence? Why does your mind float so high ... ?":

> Two mice and a moth my guides—
> To have heard the farfalla gasping
>   as toward a bridge over worlds.

The "gasp" of the farfalla in Pound's line is reminiscent of Dante "panting like one spent" in *Inferno* 34 when leaving the gravitational pull of Satan's realm—the place of darkness from which he seeks escape into the light of paradise—and the "bridge over worlds" toward which they (and Dante) strive travels from this place in the earth to the base of Mount Purgatory.[30] Nature's inexorable processes, *The Cantos'* original model, then reappear in the monarch butterfly (the "king wings") in migration

> That the kings meet in their island,
>   where no food is after flight from the pole.
> Milkweed the sustenance
>   as to enter arcanum

in company with the fragment's invocation of poetic simplicity, "The Larks at Allègre" from *The Spirit of Romance,* and alongside the 1929 bankruptcy ("faillite") of the printing house of "Francois Bernouard, Paris," a victim of the economic problems Pound hoped fascism later would solve. The lark itself in Pound's early translation flies "so high toward the sun and then fall[s]," but the reference now is as much to a kind of Icarus/Pound, who escapes from the labyrinth—in Pound's case the "diverted" *Cantos*—only to suffer for his aspiration to write the poem at all.

Drafts & Fragments is thus a point where *The Cantos'* original premises, attenuated and magnified by its own structure, are reencountered against the unnatural pressure of a narrative termination. Though *The Cantos* began as an exploration of the potential to write "a long imagiste or vorticist poem," it becomes by *Drafts & Fragments* a response to its own discovery that the poem has practiced a teleological mandate beneath an early poetics that it has only imperfectly, if not deceptively, employed. Now, instead of a poem whose very images would merge with nature's structures, Pound comments upon how his *Cantos* has generated its own meanings that are far from a neutral manifestation of nature's impassive and inexorable forces. However, Pound does not repudiate his earlier fascism so completely in *Drafts & Fragments*—if that happens at all, it takes the form of his later silence, which is as much a result of puzzlement and self-contradiction that cannot be resolved in *The Cantos,* as it is of any remorse. The return to splendor he desires near the volume's termination, while partly a trope for a prefascist stage in *The Cantos* and in his *ouevre*, simultaneously recalls one of the most stridently fascist points in the poem, the previously suppressed Canto LXXII, in which an Italian girl leads Canadian soldiers to their deaths: "What splendour!" Pound writes of the deed, "what fine lads wear the black!" The words "What splendour!" will reappear in Pound's translation of Sophocles' *Trachiniae* at a point in the text that celebrates coherence, implying again that in *Drafts & Fragments* Pound is not disparaging the political ideology of fascism outside *The Cantos* so much as resenting how his blindness to its eventually terrifying form diverts the poem's earlier principles. It suggests that the act of terminating *The Cantos* generates Pound's assessment of the contradictions that now prevent the options of coherence and closure, and that he begins to overcome the urge that has dominated him for years to vindicate and rationalize the poem's engagement with politics. But the question of Pound's fascism and anti-Semitism remains much more complex than any simple renunciation will permit. Pound can regret aspects of fascism that superseded its more idealistic beginnings, but with *The Cantos* as witness he cannot unwrite his frequent celebration of it, but only explore its activity and "see again" what preceded it in the poem.[31] Any individual coherence at the intimate level of personal understanding and self-recognition is inextricably bound to the now imploding *Cantos,* and he can no more reunify his own fragmentary contradictions and paradoxes than he can his poem's.

Chapter 6

The Mirrored Self: The *Trachiniae* and a Lost Center

In the "search for oneself," in the search for "sincere self-expression," one gropes, one finds some seeming verity. One says "I am" this, that, or the other, and with the words scarcely uttered one ceases to be that thing.

—*Gaudier-Brzeska: A Memoir*

Surely I never looked like that? How would you know? What's this "you" that you might resemble or not resemble? Where would you find it on what morphological or expressive plane? Where is your real body? You're the only one who can't see yourself except in reflections, in images.

—Roland Barthes, *Roland Barthes par lui-même*

The publication history of *Drafts & Fragments,* and its poems' frequent moments of ambivalence and contradiction, point to the difficulty Pound experienced in designing an end to his *Cantos.* They suggest that the volume represents neither failed closure nor foreseen open-endedness, but instead an expression of the irresolvable conflicts permeating Pound's poem and his self-perception that combined to help generate its abandonment. Perhaps in response to this, the final cantos still contain traces of the dream of closure that would provide it with coherence and completion, "like the double arch of a window / Or some great colonnade." Vestiges of the architecture of closure also appear in the quiet house of CX, and in several other places in the volume: in the "pyramid" and "lifting and folding brightness" of CXIII, the "great ball of crystal" and "great acorn of light" in CXVI, and in the "bridge over worlds" of the volume's final lines.

Not even the closural image of the double arch in the first "Notes for CXVII et seq." fragment escapes its own betrayal of coherence, however. Underlying it is Pound's recognition of the elusiveness of closure, and of its perils, for the image invokes its first appearance in

Canto IV, a canto where Actaeon is devoured by his own hounds for his presumptuous desire. This reversal of the self from master to victim in the Actaeon myth is ironically replayed here at the end of *The Cantos* as Pound's defeat by the dynamics of his own poem, and by the notoriety that makes him such an imperiled figure. The subversive thrust of the image, in fact, is even more extreme, since it also centers Canto IV's multiple scenes of mythic and troubadour villainy, culminating in suicide, and resonates with that part of the Na-khi *Romance* intertext in CX:

> Et ter flebiliter, Ityn, Ityn!
> And she went toward the window, and cast her down,
> . . . .
> And she went toward the window,
>   the slim white stone bar
> Making a double arch;
> Firm even fingers held to the firm pale stone;
> Swung for a moment
>
>   (IV/13)

If the double arch in the first "Notes for CXVII et seq." fragment raises the question of closure, then, it also conflates it with Pound's personal tensions at the time—the troubadour suicide scene, a consequence of love's repression, combining here with the sexual betrayals in the Philomela myth that end in inarticulate silence and death.

    The personal and the textual combine almost relentlessly at this apocalyptic point late in *The Cantos,* offering a more complex, and ultimately truer, insight into Pound's self-reflections. Canto II's opening ("Hang it all, Robert Browning / there can be but one 'Sordello'") conflated the textual and personal as well, pondering the difficult interplay of a text, its referent, and its reader's interpretation. But the poet in question there was Browning, not Pound, the text in question Browning's *Sordello,* the referent Sordello the troubadour poet, the interpretation Pound's reading of Browning's poem, which may or may not diverge from Browning's intention, and from the referent. In that passage Pound alerted the reader to the various metamorphoses that occur between a referent, an inscription of it in language, and a reading of the inscription.[1] By the end of *Drafts & Fragments,* the meditation on Sordello's fate has become internalized, and it is Pound, his poem, and its interpretation by him that, like the Maent of "Near Perigord" ("a shifting change, / A broken bundle of mirrors"), now vie for some kind of coherence that cannot be achieved.

Beyond *The Cantos*, however, a rather more idealized image of Pound as tragic hero prevailed.[2] It placed him in a Dantescan narrative of exile caused by public and political misinterpretation, a narrative that reinforced some readers' view of the poem's ostensibly disappointing close as a consequence of entirely external, not intrinsic, conditions, and permitted him (and others, if one is to believe him) to cast himself in the heroic capacity of "the last American living the tragedy of Europe."[3] Those who knew him and wrote of his deliberate "silence" after 1961, and particularly of his later admissions that *The Cantos* was a "mess," "gibberish," "stupidity and ignorance all the way through,"[4] declared a puzzled disbelief in Pound's opinion and implied that some kind of geriatric depression occasioned his pessimistic view of his poem and life. Pound may have interpreted the situation more keenly when he spoke to Hall in 1960 of awakening from the "long sleep" like Rip Van Winkle; although he used the image to refer to his incarceration in St. Elizabeths, which separated him from the world of human affairs that went on without him, the long sleep applies as well to his long deflection of the implications of his political and social ideologies, which he was suppressing even from himself, though not altogether successfully.

Pound's eventual release from St. Elizabeths was the result of many influences—legal, artistic, political, medical—but as Robert Frost stated it to the court on the day of the announcement, the real reason was that "Ezra Pound is not too dangerous to go free in his wife's care, and too insane ever to be tried—a very nice distinction."[5] Though the state had been technically satisfied, its decision merely sustained the unresolved nature of Pound's views, not only legally but personally as well. In 1958 he was confirming his anti-Semitism; a decade later he was regretting it to Allen Ginsberg as a "stupid and suburban prejudice,"[6] and confused gestures of fascist allegiance and abhorrence were made in the intervening years. The adoration he received from so many during the St. Elizabeths period, in fact, deflected the kind of poetic and personal self-examination that emerges in *Drafts & Fragments*. Those years saw him at the center of a political and artistic controversy that raised his visibility and strengthened rather than undermined his commitment to the fascism that helped imprison him, and to his racial prejudice. Copious letters of the time attest to Pound's pervasive anti-

Semitism, and the 1960 volume *Impact: Essays on Ignorance and the Decline of American Civilization,* which reprinted many of his earlier essays and whose editing he oversaw, retains their connection between that decline, "semitic insanity," and "schizophrenia."[7]

Yet the origins of what would later stimulate a revisionist urge in his last cantos were present, though they went undetected beneath the diversions of the time. The attention to the private sphere, delayed through much of the previous two volumes, would awaken him in *Drafts & Fragments* to some of the errors of his earlier beliefs, allowing the elderly and introspective Pound to reconsider *The Cantos'* politics and racial assertions, and ultimately to regard them as imprecise reflections of a deeper self he now seeks yet barely recognizes.[8] While completing the first collection of post-*Thrones* cantos in November 1959, less than two years after invoking himself ("Aloof / 1 Jan '58") at the end of Canto C, he begins to distance himself from his earlier political views, writing Laughlin that he "has forgotten what or which politics he ever had. Certainly has none now."[9] It is notable that the absence of any sustained work on *The Cantos* in the following decade occurs alongside Pound's spoken confession in the 1960s of his earlier racial and political errors, as if he can only discard them by discarding the poem that contained and even generated them, making its last volume the crucial point where *The Cantos* exchanges political and racial certainty for ambivalence and confusion, on the threshold of the silence that would follow. What Pound termed "the certainty of the greatest uncertainty. . . . my doubt" emerges as the theme of the 1963 Livi interview, in fact, thwarting her best attempts to avoid "too abstract a conversation" (and enraging her American translator, who thought the interview a "smear of perhaps the greatest literary personality of our century").[10] If a faint revision of anti-Semitism does occur in *Drafts & Fragments,* it is in the image of Pound's own ephemeral and insubstantial "heimat" in "From CXV," through which he now associates the traditional homelessness and alienation of the Jewish people with himself. Yet the phrasing of Pound's famous statement in 1968 concerning his "stupid and suburban prejudice," while apparently corroborating the "From CXV" image, suggests that he is as uneasy with the conformity of anti-Semitism, its "suburban" aspect, as he is with its racial intolerance, a conformity that he has always abhorred in the artist, who should occupy a vorticist center of energy in society, and not lose that individuality to disappear into its distant and uniform margins, to "drift to the periphery," as he put it in his 1968 interview with Paolo Pasolini.[11] Pound is perhaps a most extreme example of that view, and the diversion of fascism that came to dominate the latter half of his working life was a symptom of his "need to be at the center or vortex of any new movement,"[12] a naive, dramatic display of ideological commitment and endurance.

The alternative of preserving the self against his own many versions of indistinction and marginality—in verbal terms the blurring of metaphor and of imprecise language; in political ones the conformity of Communism; in racial ones the Jew—simultaneously requires cohering its various dimensions of poet, lover, husband, father, political and economic essayist, among so many others. To find their common source, in Confucian terms their tao, can mean tracing their appearance through a family paideuma to their reorganization in him, as Pound does in the family history that appears as early as the Connecticut Charter typescript and that dominates the middle of CXIV. But it can also mean recognizing how that genetic equation, in its sum in the individual, is contentious and unstable—a "genealogy of demons" coauthored ("are *we* to write...?") with "fear," its own "father of cruelty." The reference may simply be to Pound's belief that demonology is a society's scare tactic to control its younger generation. Its culmination to the long "tribù" history suggests its deeper relevance to Pound, however, whose fragmented sense of self has been accelerated by the demons of conscience that now trouble his *Cantos'* paradise.

The Pisan Cantos display in rich variety the provisional versions of Pound's self-perception. There, suddenly emerging from behind the diaries and letters of Jefferson and Adams in Cantos LII–LXXI, Pound struggles to locate himself within a complex array of literary and historical identities, oscillating fitfully between the Elpenor "of no fortune and with a name to come" and the more familiar persona of Odysseus, now in Canto LXXIV "a man on whom the sun has gone down." One of the images he chooses substitutes for identity a combination of insignificance, anonymity, and ruin—"a lone ant from a broken ant-hill / from the wreckage of Europe"—which paradoxically (or, perhaps, therefore) maintains the fragile role of a communicating self—"ego scriptor." Here is where Upward's suicide is invoked, where the "solitude of Mt. Taishan" is broken only by the shades in the *Nekuia*, where the residue of Pound's tradition, modern poetry, offers fragile resistance to destruction and death. What emerges by the end of the volume is not a resolute voice so much as a stereotype of fatigue and age, "an old man" in Canto LXXXIII who, having "no one to converse with," wants simply the anonymity of "rest," an escape from the self. If the Pisan poems drew "Pound" out from behind *The Cantos'* many voices, it kept him obscured and indistinct.

But outside the poem the encounter proceeded somewhat differently. Immediately after the publication of the *Pisan Cantos,* Pound translated Sophocles' *Elektra* and *Trachiniae,* which combine to represent perhaps the clearest illustration of his delayed but nonetheless vivid encounter with the personal that the Pisan poems tentatively began—the *Elektra* displaying his political and ethical self-perceptions in ways that he would eventually discard. Pound called his 1949 collaborative transla-tion of the *Elektra* with Rudd Fleming "provisional," and he never returned to the text to complete it. As its 1989 editor Richard Reid informs us, Pound "and his collaborator intended to make major revi-sions, especially of the choral lyrics. But these were not to be."[13] Of the two Sophocles plays he translated, the *Elektra* figured much less promi-nently as a source in Pound's subsequent cantos as well, and together the absence of poetic influence and the incomplete nature of the project imply the *Elektra*'s diminishing appropriateness for him, even his effec-tive rejection of it, after translating it. The same cannot be said of the *Trachiniae,* which would serve as a delayed catalyst for introspection, and as a poetic source particularly in *Drafts & Fragments.*

Pound clearly identifies with his bristling and unrepentant Elektra in 1949, however, shortly after his trial and at the beginning of his incarceration at St. Elizabeths. One of her conflicts is with the prudent yet ethically unattractive advice of her sister Chrysothemis, who warns against the revenge Elektra seeks for their father's murder with what becomes a virtual refrain in the play, "dont go up against the people in power." Pound's Chrysothemis is petulant and nagging, echoing in satirically shrill tones his version of his own critics. "All I know is that if you dont quit bawling / they'll shut you up where you'll never see daylight / in some black jail outside the country," she tells Elektra, completing her assessment of the situation with a smug "do stop to think, and dont blame me / when it's too late." Clytemnestra is an unrepentant murderer, essentially one-dimensional (Pound allowing her only an impoverished version of the paradoxical and complicated moti-

vations Sophocles explores), verging on a caricature of unreflective ego-
tism and self-delusion. Perhaps the clearest sign of how Pound arranges
the characters into an unequivocal testament to justice and revenge,
though, appears in the illuminating stereotype of Aegisthus, extracted
from Sophocles' mixture of guilt and imperiousness to become a sim-
pleminded, effete antagonist, directed to speak in a "rather sissy voice,
even a slight lisp." Pound concentrates upon him an unpleasant mixture
of homophobia and disgust and strands him as an unbelievable and
easy target of Elektra and Orestes' hate.

Other ways of allegorizing the *Elektra*'s connection with Pound
hover. He may have been attracted to a narrative in which a daughter
uncompromisingly defends her father's actions and memory, for instance, adding a further set of reflections to the somewhat incomplete
Elektra/Pound mirror. Yet another emerges in the figure of Orestes, an
exile who returns to abolish his enemies, and to declare triumphantly
to the sputtering Aegisthus, "Haven't you ever learned / that the DEAD
dont DIE." Reid senses the influence of Pound's suppressed Canto
LXXII here, where the Italian girl sacrifices herself for her country; we
might also see in it an echo of Pound's defensive and tenacious commitment to his fascism in 1949. To him at the time, any act of repentance,
or of reconsideration, was tantamount to cowardice, the sin that
Elektra seems most anxious to avoid when she tells her sister that "it's
just awful the way you take her part / and forget [Agamem-
non].... Need we add cowardice to all the rest of this filth?" (In a
footnote in the *Trachiniae* translated a year later, Pound would recall
this statement as the *Elektra*'s "key phrase.") Under Pound's treatment
Chrysothemis's advice to Elektra to bow to the authority of Clytemnestra and Aegisthus is transparently weak, and we are repeatedly told to
admire Elektra's refusal to capitulate to it, to applaud Orestes' mocking
reappearance from his own ashes (the rumors of his death, and Pound's
ignominy, greatly exaggerated), and to equate reconsideration with
cowardice. Despite Reid's energetic defense of the *Elektra*'s irresolution
in his introduction, it remains quite clearly resolved in the direction of
singular retributive justice, stoicism, and bravery. Although it is true,
as Reid offers, that Pound may have chosen Sophocles' play and not
the trilogy for a translation because "to a poet for whom the future is
very much in doubt, and a trial by jury obviated, Sophocles could well
prove the safer bet" (*Elektra*, xiii), an equally likely inference is that

Pound recognized an allegory for his own situation when he saw one and was not available at the time to the alternative of recurring conflict and pursuit that Euripides' version, for instance, would involve.

It would be in *Rock-Drill*, however, that Pound would resurrect the play to consider, however temporarily, the alternative of residual and unresolved conflict that had terminated so authoritatively in the *Elektra*. In Canto XC, first published in 1955, Elektra is invoked through the epithet Sophocles originally supplies her, ignored by Pound in the play but translated by him now as "the dark shade of courage... / bowed still with the wrongs of Aegisthus," in the process reinterpreting her as a haunted figure now suffering within the moral dilemma of her act, another restless shade in the Hades of Canto I. And why "bowed with the wrongs of Aegisthus," and not of Clytemnestra? Is it Pound's faint recognition of the man's role in the fragmentation of the "House of Atreus," of how it is not just the consequence of his one-dimensional Clytemnestra, of how a man hovers behind the fragmentation of a "quiet house"? The trace is faint, and one can only surmise—but Canto XC remains as Pound's deepest exploration of Dantean justice and love and was written in the year of Pound's first acquaintance with the spiritual wisdom of the Na-khi.

The revisionist character of *Drafts & Fragments*, absent in the *Elektra* translation of 1949 but tentatively visible by Canto XC of 1955, is predicted more clearly in his 1950 translation of Sophocles' *Trachiniae*, a text that would hold a remarkable legitimacy for *Drafts & Fragments*' drama of attempted self-perception. In translating the *Trachiniae* Pound wanted "to see what would happen to a Greek play, given that same medium and the hope of its being performed by the [Noh] Minorou company," as he told Hall in 1960 (*RP*, 224). The translation would prompt more than the *Trachiniae*, however; it would play a role in the reassessment within *Drafts & Fragments*' poems that he would begin to write later in the decade. Pound's interest in the play, that is, operated within two contexts whose similarity, not entirely apparent to him in 1950, became clearer when writing the poems. While it originally appealed to Pound's reading of his own situation at the time, when a paradise was resisting inscription in *Drafts & Fragments* it also seemed applicable to the situation of his *Cantos*.

The Sophoclean Herakles is in many ways an original creation, loosely drawn from tradition but substantially altered to promote a tragic dramatic form. Works prior to Sophocles', like Euripides' *Alces-*

tis and Pindar's first Nemean ode, had concentrated on the hero's ability to overcome the most severe obstacles with unruffled composure and had prophecied his old age as peaceful and happy. In the *Trachiniae,* however, Herakles has completed the last of his twelve labors and acts not in the context of heroic action but in its tragic aftermath. He first appears on a stretcher, borne by others, wild with pain, almost incoherent with frustrated rage, incapable of remedying or avenging his agony. Ordinarily independent of his family's haven, he is suddenly desperate for his son's assistance; accustomed to a world that supplied his needs at the behest of his power, he longs for a condition of rest and peace that, alone, he cannot effect. The situation is an ironic fulfillment of the Dodonian oracle and of his father Zeus's prophecy. The oracle had stated that after the twelve years of his labors Herakles would either be happy, rested, and in peace, or that he would die. Zeus had prophesied that no "living" being would kill Herakles. Herakles interprets them together to mean that he will live a long and pleasant life after his labors. Instead, as he recognizes late in the *Trachiniae,* they signify that someone will successfully design his murder and die before it occurs. Years earlier the centaur Nessus, who had raped Herakles' wife and was dying by Herakles' hand, had given her a potion of his blood ostensibly to sustain her husband's love for her. Hearing now that Herakles loves another woman, she innocently soaks a robe in Nessus's blood and sends it to him; as the centaur originally intended, however, it slowly kills him.

In Sophocles' dramatic world of the *Trachiniae* (and, more dimly, in that of the *Elektra*) is a prototype for CX's bewilderment over the "twist" from love to hate and CXVI's perception of irreversible "error," all presided over by CXIII's "Pater Helios," whose own Sophoclean parallel is Zeus, Herakles' father and omnipotent creator of his destiny, whom the chorus invokes. The *Trachiniae* cosmos emerges frequently in CXIII in particular, first with the Helios figure of the opening four lines (and in the translation Pound calls his Herakles the "vitality" of the sun), and then with the Θρῆνος that signals Herakles' appearance in the play. The following line, "Mortal praise has no sound in her ears" (786), though from Dante, recalls Herakles' destruction on Fate's wheel also, for the passion he once exhibited in his earlier glory is now his downfall. Pound reinforces the Heraklean references later in the same canto with "apples from Hesperides," and by condensing Sophocles' battle metaphor of the fighting bull (whose horns clash with its competitor's while the female waits anxiously for the outcome) with Remy de Gourmont's example of the bull whose attraction to the female is caused by "a force exterior to the individual although included in his organism":

> And the bull by the force that is in him—
> not lord of it,
> mastered.
>
> (789)

Richard Seiburth describes the subject of this point in Gourmont's *Physique de l'Amour* as "the inexorable tyranny of the sexual instinct";[14] as such it joins with *Drafts & Fragments*' rebellion against various tyrannies, in CX ("I am all for Verkehr without tyranny"), and then in the response to the tyranny of *The Cantos*' narrative of fascism. In Pound's own "grumpiness / malvagità" (and the DH1 "116" typescript's "Charity is what I've got— / damn it") is some of Herakles' bad temper, softened in his *Women of Trachis* from Sophocles' passage of mortal agony to a wry irritability:

> Get away,
> let me lie quiet, for the last time
> aaah. What you doin' trying to turn me over,
> Let me alone. Blast it.
>
> (WT, 54)

Sophocles' original passage, though, has Herakles lamenting the fact that he is roused from unconsciousness back into his suffering. Pound's translation avoids this, nine years before composing *Drafts & Fragments,* because the web of political and personal confusions that generate much of the volume is not yet a significant, or accessible, issue for him. He replaces Sophocles' passage with the irrascibility of a testy old man, mixed with the echo of Andreas Divus, who was told to "lie quiet" in Canto I, with whom Pound, having offered his own epic translation in the form of *The Cantos,* feels some affinity. In *Drafts & Fragments,* though, Pound extends the implications of the original *Trachiniae* passage into his own situation. Now, it is the misreading of the oracle and Zeus's prophecy, occasioning Herakles' present impotence and reassessment and generating the play's final tragic calm of anagnorisis, that evokes Pound's relationship to his own poetic labors, his misreading of them, and their subsequent reappraisal. "No man can see his own end / The Gods have not returned," reminiscent of Hyllus's description of the humility Herakles learns by the play's end ("Of what is to come, nothing is seen"), is Pound's comment on the mystery that shrouds everyone's fate. It also invokes his early poem "The Return"— "See, they return; ah, see the tentative / Movements, and the slow feet"—CXIII's ambiguous vision now replacing the earlier poem's more confident one.

If the *Trachiniae* is relevant to Pound's personal situation at St. Elizabeths when translating it in 1950 therefore, it acquires a new significance in relation to *The Cantos* by 1959. When Pound footnoted Herakles' sudden recognition of the truth of the oracle and Zeus's prophecy as "the key phrase" of *Women of Trachis,*

> Time lives and it's going on now.
> I am released from trouble.
> I thought it meant life in comfort.
> It doesn't. It means I die.
> For amid the dead there is no work in service.
> Come at it that way, my boy, what
> SPLENDOUR,
>   IT ALL COHERES
>
> (WT, 49–50)

he was doing so in the context of his own imprisonment. Herakles sees how the two predictions are fulfilled, and that his present suffering merges with a divine coherence. During the translation of the *Trachiniae* Pound sees in Herakles' vision a significance that transcends and redeems his own incarceration, then in its fifth year and showing no sign of terminating. His belief in the publicly unrecognized validity of his *Cantos* to the tribe was still as strong as ever, and his fascist dream had so far resisted any efforts since his Pisan experience to reform him or his poem. (His reworked "what you doin' trying to turn me over" in the *Trachiniae* might reveal, in this context, his powerful antipathy to a reassessment of his politics and his *Cantos*.) In CXVI however, whose language is inextricable from the context of *The Cantos'* banishment from its intended paradise, the "key phrase" assumes another relevance. Herakles recognizes his own misreading of the Dodonian oracle and Zeus's prophecy and overcomes that misreading to release himself from agony, gathering a splendor of coherence around his last days. The oracular pronouncement that Pound longs to realize in *The Cantos* is his own—for the poem's coherence—and he laments his inability to fulfill it in CXVI: "Tho' my errors and wrecks lie about me. / And I am not a demigod, / I cannot make it cohere." CXVI is replete with images of the labyrinth ("cuniculi," "a tangle," "Ariadne," "to affirm the gold thread") by which he now describes his *Cantos*. The mythical demigod Herakles ultimately triumphs over Daedalus the labyrinth maker, as Sophocles' hero defeats his own entrapment in a fate apparently too large for his comprehension. The Sophoclean figure's potential status as a model for Pound's triumph over the exigencies of his personal situation (of physical and emotional imprisonment, and the object of jealousy) is compromised by his failure to defeat the poem's labyrinthine self-contradictions that thwart any hope of a paradisal close.

After the legal distractions of the St. Elizabeths years and the adoration that sustained his fascist and anti-Semitic rhetoric, *Drafts & Fragments* would contain a more muted and candid self-revaluation, likely assisted by this rereading of the Heraklean persona in *Women of Trachis*. The process of self-redefinition is evident elsewhere too, particularly in Pound's writings and publications during the period. With the exception of *Rock-Drill* (published in 1955) and *Thrones* (1959) his output, though copious, is mainly retrospective: the first collected edition of *The Cantos* in 1948 (it had appeared before only in its separate volumes), two editions of his earlier poetry; reprints of *Patria Mia* (from 1912), of his various translations (the latest from 1919), of his literary essays (including nothing later than 1922), of his Gaudier-Brzeska study (originally published in 1916), of *Pavannes and Divagations* (collected from earlier writings), of *A Lume Spento* (from 1908), of *Indiscretions* (from 1923). His shorter publications of the period share this retrospection. They include letters to W. B. Yeats from the 1930s, selections from *ABC of Reading,* and extracts from letters in the 1920s. Together with the first appearance of studies of his life and work (Charles Norman's *The Case of Ezra Pound* appeared in 1948, Hugh Kenner's *The Poetry of Ezra Pound* in 1951) it seemed that a maelstrom of texts was interpreting the self and its creations, separately, into various constructs among, or in spite of, whose plenitude he would try to locate his own self-reflection, a self that would make sense to him.[15]

The Cantos had always surged forward through a deflection of the self caused by the creation of various personae, crucial in transcending the subjective restrictions of the lyric.[16] *The Cantos'* method of speaking through the mediation of earlier texts, practiced in earlier poems like "Near Perigord" and *Hugh Selwyn Mauberley: Life and Contacts,* is one way in which it subverted the possibility of real presence, replacing it with a provisional one that simultaneously released the poem from any apparent authority. This liberating strategy replaces it with a network of competing and mutually effacing voices that undermine authoritative perception and knowledge, and creates the perpetually inflating sphere of textual sources and references in *The Cantos.* Nearly every one of its volumes introduces a new voice and new time in history, beginning with classical Greece and then Renaissance Italy, and moving through Oriental and American myth and politics, Confucianism, the Founding Fathers, and fascist Italy, to the Byzantine socioeconomic worlds of *Rock-Drill* and *Thrones.* With each of these epochs comes a circle of narrative perspectives disallowing the reduction of life to artifact, asserting truth, and the notion of self, to be unceasingly mutable and indeterminate.

In the midst of this complex and chaotic interplay, any possible notion by the narrating self *of* itself is repeatedly erased in the face of ever new visions, and knowledge. This process begins as early as Canto II, where what is "seen"—"wine-red algae," "wave-tinge," "water-shift"—is also only "half-seen" by the previously authoritative ("I have seen what I have seen"), but mystified, observer Acoetes. His partial vision is then replaced by So-shu, who

> churned in the sea, So-shu also,
> using the long moon for a churn-stick...
> Lithe turning of water,
> sinews of Poseidon
>
> (9)

So-shu (the second century B.C. Chinese poet Ssu-ma Hsiang-ju) supposedly drowned in a drunken attempt to embrace the reflection of the moon in the water. For Pound the significance is in the equation of misperception with effaced self, located in the figure of the poet. This is a prediction of the opening of Canto III, in which the "I" of the poem, sitting in Venice "on the Dogana's steps" too poor to pay for a gondola ride, has only a rhetorical presence; he exists only by virtue

of the many texts, the "words, tags, and quotations," that he combines
into a perception. "Gods float in the azure air" is the perception, yet
its subsequent unfolding is so intertextually mediated, so multiple and
untraceable in its origins, as to be a merely postulated presence "within
a complex field of cultural discourse":[17]

> Gods float in the azure air,
> Bright gods and Tuscan, back before dew was shed.
> Light: and the first light, before ever dew was fallen.
> Panisks, and from the oak, dryas,
> And from the apple, maelid,
> Through all the wood, and the leaves are full of voices
> A-whisper, and the clouds bowe over the lake,
> And there are gods upon them,
> And in the water, the almond-white swimmers,
> The silvery water glazes the upturned nipple,
> As Poggio has remarked.
>
> (III/11)

This effacement of the self, here in the guise of escape from a howling
and impoverished present (itself mediated by time: "I sat") would
gradually become so complete, yet simultaneously so convenient a
transmitter of the illusion of impartiality, that *Drafts & Fragments*
would be torn by an awakening desire to reclaim that original "lost
center" and to perpetuate its dispersal. Its opening canto recalls Canto
II's metamorphosed Daphne, and the female imagery of Canto III's
start, and culminates in a darkened rendering of Acoetes' speculative
half-vision:

> Over water bluer than midnight
> where the winter olive is taken
> Here are earth's breasts mirroured
> and all Euridices,
> Laurel bark sheathing the fugitive,
> . . . .
> A wind of darkness hurls against forest
> the candle flickers
> is faint
> Lux enim—
> versus this tempest.
> The marble form in the pine wood,
> The shrine seen and not seen

In Cantos II and III the imagery is employed as a remnant of its earlier existence (in Ovid's, and then Golding's, *Metamorphoses*), and as Pound's recollection of an extremely mediated and conflated reading (of Poggio's letter to Niccolò de'Niccoli, and of Catullus).[18] In CX the texts being recalled include Cantos II and III, partly because the Italian scene that presents itself to Pound in 1959 is reminiscent of the Canto III location (Italy's Lago di Garda, relevant, for the Pound of 1916, to Catullus and, for the Pound of 1959, to the site of Mussolini's Salò Republic) but also because in his encounter with the fractured self he inevitably recalls the earliest location of its concealment. The indebtedness of CX to earlier cantos predicts quite forcefully the aspect of *Drafts & Fragments* that is so involved in its terminating role: the text that becomes its frequent referent is *The Cantos* itself, and the authorial "Pound" that emerges in the last cantos is not only the creator but also the reflected product of its aspirations and its shortcomings, a new actor in the history the poem included. "Nomina sunt consequentia rerum" announces Pound's Elektra in 1949—words are the consequence of things. A decade later Pound might have more perceptively reversed the statement—things are the consequence of words.

As the composition of *The Cantos* moved through time so did its poet, and by the Pisan sequence one of the selves that speaks is apparently Pound, occasioned by physical isolation and the deprivation of external texts (poetic, historical, political, or otherwise) that he was forced to endure. By that point however, over four hundred pages and seventy-three cantos into the poem, "Pound" is really no more than a composite of the many elusive selves that have already populated it. Even there, with the opportunity for self-examination and revelation, he registers himself through the various personae whose provisionality the poem's length has overturned into authority: the voyaging Odysseus and the imprisoned Elpenor are the fundamental voices, but Pope, Baudelaire, John Heydon, and Ovid supply others. Even the most explicitly introspective passage of the volume—"Pull down thy vanity, / Paquin pull down!"—is rhetorically invaded by an earlier Jonsonian voice to address, by implication, a self that is neither fully exposed, nor fully present, to itself.

The personae of the *Pisan Cantos* bring with them a clearly defined audience to which the poetry is directed. One member of this audience is the indefatigable Aphrodite, whose affection the poet hopes to rekindle through humility after the "steady crescendo of raucous arrogance" manifested in the preceding volume.[19] His vision of her is explicit and detailed, certain in its extravagant use of simile ("Δρυάς, your eyes are like the clouds over Taishan" [LXXXIII/530]). Another member is the reader who Pound suspects has not suffered the hardship nor gained the knowledge that he has at the end of his Pisan experience, and thus many passages in the volume reflect a seemingly chastened individual guiding and cautioning ("Nor can who has passed a month in the death cells /believe in capital punishment" [LXXXIII/530]). In contrast to the mediated voice of the Pisan sequence, Drafts & Fragments culminates with Pound attempting to speak to or with himself, and being incapable of locating that previously mediated and obscured self now. If Drafts & Fragments recognizes the undifferentiated and complex, the consequences for a previously assertive and independent individuality are apocalyptic. "Notes for CXVII et seq."'s "M'amour, m'amour / what do I love and / where are you?" among its intertextual echoes of Canto LXXIV's "what thou lovest well remains" reference to fascism, vainly searches for the self that remains after its dissipation, for a way to gather the scattered limbs of Pound and cohere him again. Here, most graphically, and in unprecedented fashion, he relinquishes the didactic tone so frequent in the three preceding volumes, directed toward those whom he has attempted to educate concerning myth and tradition throughout The Cantos, and writes more privately, creating the volume's hushed anxiety that no coherent self (such as LXXXIII's "old man") remains. Through the French/Provençal "M'amour" we also hear an echo of the troubadour, addressing the eternally elusive object of desire, and again of The Spirit of Romance as the emotional paradise for the urge to reencounter a prefascist site of love—"that terzo / third heaven, / that Venere" (CXVI/796)—and poetic limpidity.

Focusing upon the self as subject is an activity new to the previously mediating and heavily intertextual poetry that scattered it beyond recognition. It is assisted, though, by Pound's release from St. Elizabeths into a world vastly different from the one he had so confidently participated in thirteen years before. It prevents the continuum that The Cantos had to that point sustained, requiring Pound to regard himself outside the symbolic political and economic narratives through which he had previously defined himself and had been defined, just as the Sophoclean Herakles is suddenly helpless in a world much altered from the one that recognized his labors. Hence the various reminiscential passages in *Drafts & Fragments* that view the personal past now from a distance, as a ruin upon which a fragmented and unstable self is shored, and the final lament over the lost center. The eventual version of "From CXV," composed when the shape of the volume began to emerge for Pound (and, we might speculate, after he began to see that his own *Cantos* had been a vessel of the self all along), fitfully recognizes the objects of memory as always having been the poet's residence. "Meiner Heimat" is Pound's geographical homeland, his poem, and his memory—that place where the inhabitants of the past walk, against a two-dimensional "cardboard" backdrop of the present. Notably "the dead walk*ed* / and the living *were* made of cardboard," indicating not only how the past has erased the present, but how both have consequently been reduced to caricature, despite the mandate of his *Cantos* to keep history alive and not reduce it to artifact. The lines are in part an ironic recognition of how he has silenced any possibility of a present self through the mediations of time and pre-texts, and that he is now virtually unknowable as anything but an ephemeral linguistic creation, the "Pound" who remains foreign to himself around 1960 and who, partly for this very reason, is variously redefined yet again through the editorial revisions of his *Cantos'* close.

The Cantos has always employed memory as part of its energy, and its thrust has been to replace the present with the past, to render the past alive in the present through language. Myths were a way of doing this, Pound believed; his use of them, of the *Odyssey,* of Browning's *Sordello,* which rekindled the past through the poetic utterance of a persona, his earlier retranslation of "The Seafarer," of Catullus's *Propertius* before *The Cantos'* genesis, of Sophocles' *Trachiniae* and Confucius's *Analects* just before writing the *Drafts & Fragments* cantos all reflect his continual attempts to efface the present with the past by conserving and reviving its language. From the inception of *The Cantos* Pound had been influenced by texts that unearthed the past, and the self, through utterance. Telemachus learns of his past and ultimately of himself through the narratives of Nestor and Menelaos, Odysseus through the narrative of Eumaios, Dante through the narratives of all who speak to him in hell; this is one of the reasons the texts containing these characters were models for *The Cantos.* Pound had carried with him, from *The Spirit of Romance,* an interest in writers who considered this relationship, and later, around the time of *The Cantos'* beginnings, Alan Upward became one of these; he wrote eloquently on the coincidence of language and memory, particularly in *The New Word:*

> [A word] is a magic *crystal,* and by looking long into it, you will see wonderful meanings come and go. It will change colour like an opal while you gaze, reflecting the thoughts in your own mind. It is a most chameleon-like *ball.* It has this deeper magic that it will show you, not only the thoughts you knew about before, but other thoughts you did not know of, old, drowned thoughts, hereditary thoughts; it will awaken the slumbering ancestral ghosts that haunt the brain; you will remember things you used to know and feel long, long ago. (Emphasis added)[20]

The fact that Upward's imagery is employed in CXVI suggests that the passage significantly informs the process of reappraisal that winds through *Drafts & Fragments.* The urgency behind the CXVI question— "I have brought the great ball of crystal; / who can lift it?"—permeates these cantos in a variety of ways, for it contains the troubling undertones of Upward's message that a word shows "other thoughts you did not know of, old, drowned thoughts, hereditary thoughts; it will awaken the slumbering ancestral ghosts that haunt the brain," the genealogy of demons, we might say, of CXIV. The composition of *Drafts & Fragments* generates precisely this, tracing for Pound an imaginary or postulated self exterior to, and prior to, his poem, which he now can neither articulate nor recognize. "Tho' [my] errors and wrecks lie about me," Pound writes, in the sense of their having failed, but also of their being deceptive and distorting, he nevertheless can do no more than note that distortion and cannot make any coherent and true self "flow thru."

The suppressed self that is sought in *Drafts & Fragments* leads to a revaluation of *The Cantos,* and the reverse is true as well, for the reassessment of *The Cantos* that the volume's composition generates leads to a painful and incomplete exposure of the self. Together they create an inescapable contraction of the poem that assists in its close. The final fragments of the volume contain the clearest expression of this: the imminent attainment of the volume's opening image of the quiet house has disintegrated through the cantos and canto fragments that follow, and even the hopeful gesture of "darkness shattered" in

CXIII that these fragments were intended to achieve is inverted to become a memory of the shattered dreams of the poet's paradise for *The Cantos*. With the shattered past dreams for *The Cantos*' paradise come the shattered hopes of the poet who sought forgiveness in the first collection "115" for the "errors" that the poem, and the life of the poet who made it, have contained. Aside from its association, through Varé, with fascism, "shattered" at *The Cantos*' end also recalls *The Cantos*' beginning, in which Elpenor, hopeful of home, instead "shattered the nape-nerve [and] . . . sought Avernus." In the second "Notes for CXVII et seq." fragment ("That I lost my center / fighting the world. / The dreams clash / and are shattered") Pound perceives himself more in terms of the transitory Elpenor who, unburied, unnamed, unresolved, seeks a Noh-like reconciliation with his anguished soul, and whose memory at all depends upon Odysseus's inscription of his name on his grave. His reappearance here in *The Cantos* quietly replaces the voice of Odysseus achieving his *nostos,* or for that matter Dante his paradise or Confucius his tao, and displays Pound's recognition of his own fractured identity, and its consequences of doubt and uncertainty. The self that remains, devoid of texts to arbitrate and manipulate, and of narratives to resolve, is perilously close to the two-dimensional rhetorical facades it previously disguised itself with, and thus it counts itself among "the living [that] were made of cardboard," the degradation of self-caricature that remains after he has been stripped of the many selves that hid a now irrecoverable center.

Perhaps in the difficult writing and hesitant publication of *The Cantos*' terminus we can see Pound wrestling with and discarding the many selves that hold the imaginary possibility of eventual coherence, itself as much an ideological dream as the telic narrative of fascism was for part of the poem. Remaining is an elegy on the illusory unity with which he declines to artificially suture it, on the closed and unified, and an admission of the heteroclite and irresolvable selves that have been traced through *The Cantos*' own creation, and through its imperfect paradise of flawed words and stubborn sounds. Just as vividly, *Drafts & Fragments*' significance is in its poet's direct encounter with doubt and uncertainty, and his recognition of how the paradisal vision remains "flitting and fading at will," to the point where the incoherence of poetic language is exchanged for silence. Perhaps then, in their fashion, the poems and the tangled pattern of their reception and production characterize not just the irresolvable enterprise of closing *The Can-*

tos but of closing one dimension of an inner life, a place in its own right of "constantly increasing, indefinitely spreading complexity,"[21] defying the patterns and expectations of others, and even of oneself. *Drafts & Fragments* contains many reminiscences, and Pound's 1915 translation of Rihaku's "Exile's Letter"—"What is the use of talking, and there is no end of / talking. / There is no end of things in the heart"—flickers among them.

Afterword: "To 'See Again'"

"The test of a writer," Pound wrote to Harriet Monroe in 1915, when *The Cantos* was in its earliest gestational stage, "is his ability . . . to stay concentrated till he gets to the end of his poem, whether it is two lines or two hundred" (*LEP*, 49). A poet's worth, in other words, was in direct proportion to his verbal stamina. Given the year, it is perhaps not coincidental that Pound suddenly connected the issue of a poet's ability with the unimpeded achievement of his poem's close, for the equation would inevitably celebrate as the most crucial testing ground the long poem he was just beginning. It is an early hint of the importance that the writing of *Drafts & Fragments* would hold for him over forty years later; its "success" or "failure" in making *The Cantos* cohere would retroactively judge both the poem's validity and his own ability to pass the masterly test of poetic concentration. Over three decades later, the fact that neither the months in the gorilla cage nor the years in St. Elizabeths deflected him from the task of writing *The Cantos* corroborated the stamina of its purpose, and his worth, for him. Indeed, his defensive grip throughout those years on fascism in *The Cantos* was in part an inability to confess that the poem could lose the focus, the center, with which he had started it decades before.

Throughout the composition of *The Cantos* Pound had been able to defend those ideologies of the poem as provisional statements in a fluctuating text that never sought to manifest "the accomplished," but that instead evoked "a man hurling himself at an indomitable chaos, and yanking and hauling as much of it as possible into some sort of order" (*LE*, 396). Contesting that, however, was the poem's mandate not simply to record the indomitable chaos of the empirical world, but to recognize how within that chaos lay an eternal beauty "as free of accident as any of the philosophical demands of a 'Paradiso' can make

153

it" (*LE*, 444) that becomes specifically manifested in the poem politically and racially. Such beauty is not in an object but the result of a manner of seeing the object. It is an intelligence that Pound notes the Platonists call the *nous*, "the sea crystalline and enduring... the bright as it were molten glass that envelops us, full of light" (*GK*, 44), and Aristoteleans call "intuitive in a special way" permitting "one to 'see' that two straight lines can't enclose a surface, and that the triangle is the simplest possible polygon" (*GK*, 327). Such beauty, in other words, is perceptible to those who see it, and hidden from those who do not.

This rather privileged intelligence of vision (not unlike Dante's *semplice lume*), which *The Cantos* attempted to emulate, inhibited by two world wars, a frequently uncomprehending public, and by Pound's imprisonment and committal, was in his view free by 1958 to permeate *The Cantos'* paradise. Pound suspected that if any impediments to writing that paradise remained they were merely "superficial" (*RP*, 241), the world's misguided sense of its own decline. What Pound either did not suspect or could not admit was that the remaining impediments were more accurately the result of the poem's repressed contradiction between a vorticist indeterminacy and Pound's will for mastery that sympathized with the poem's evolving fascist narrative, for "passing the test," which the task of writing paradise would raise out of an earlier obscurity into a painful and finally silencing visibility for him.

Well before *Drafts & Fragments'* composition it appeared evident that one could *write* "a long vorticist poem," particularly if that vorticism were used to shield the fact of an overdetermined text. The more difficult question by 1959 was whether one could end it. Several impediments within the poem arose to challenge Pound's desire to do that. One, latent in *The Cantos* from its inception, was the true vorticist mandate of perpetual motion, a result of its multiple origin, its heuristic nature, and the erasure of termination inherent in its elementary particle, the Poundian image. Another, sheltered beneath the guise of a vorticist democratic urge to "leave nothing out simply because it didn't fit" was Pound's selection of various narratives whose closure in *The Cantos* could only occur in direct defiance of the history for which the poem so ardently proclaimed itself a vessel. The recurrence of Ecbatan was not realized through fascism, and Western economic ills were not remedied by an anti-Semitic reading of Social Credit. Neither, on a more personal level, did Coke's *Institutes* ultimately contain the relevance to Pound's own situation that he hoped it would. If it had,

Pound's belief in the "repeat in history" would have found some meagre confirmation; since they did not, he was left either to proclaim his insupportable contentions to what would have been an increasingly sceptical readership, or to review ("See again") or reread his poem to locate where it went wrong.

The always unstable, or only vaguely demarcated, boundary between reader and writer has persisted through *The Cantos* from its first poem, where Pound's retranslation of the *Nekuia* is both a reading and a writing of it. At the beginning of *The Cantos* this is a productive and generative conflation, but it undergoes an ironic transformation in *Drafts & Fragments,* where the subject of reading and writing is the poem itself, and not a complementary text external to it.[1] Added to the exhaustive conflict between closural and nonclosural urges, then, is the displacement of the poet from an author's into a reader's relationship with the poem, a further contributing factor to *The Cantos*' termination before some point of secure resolution. In this sense *The Cantos* has a kind of poetic half-life, beyond which it is read as much as written, and thereby self-absorbs into a silence that is not initially an intended closural strategy. Here, we might return to Poe's argument in "The Poetic Principle" that "the long poem is a contradiction in terms," that it is merely a succession of lyric poems with no indigenous structure of its own. Certainly *Drafts & Fragments,* through its various readings and rereadings, can be read as a lyric palinode to the long poem of which it is a part. Its fragmentary nature is a lyric response to its own failed gesture of verbal inclusiveness. Its prepublished existence temporarily maintained a lyric privacy that is only overheard by chance. And its lyrical intensity replaces the didactic ideologies that increasingly manipulate the pre–*Drafts & Fragments* cantos. In these various ways, the internal counterstructure of *The Cantos* resembles that of the lyric; it points out the lyric's self-undoing by providing a verbal location, a "hall of mirrors," large enough to expose it.[2]

Modern long poem is a term fraught with such difficulties as to be almost impractical. Does its domain include poems before *The Cantos* but after Browning's *Sordello* (to use a not entirely arbitrary early boundary)? is the "poetic sequence" to be considered a part of it? what about *Leaves of Grass*? or Dickinson's *Fascicles*? is the vorticist long poem a special case? are *The Waste Land* and *Four Quartets* to be considered? how long is "long"? Most of these questions test the ade-

quacy of the label, not the validity of the texts, which remain intact
no matter what we call them. Nevertheless, poets such as Pound,
William Carlos Williams, Charles Olson, David Jones, Kenneth
Rexroth, Hart Crane, Basil Bunting, Hugh MacDiarmid, Robert Lowell
(and many others whose words have suffered the disappearance that
Drafts & Fragments barely escaped) have tried to write one. The reason
is both personal and poetic; the Romantic desire to achieve a Miltonic
status defers in the modern poets to a curiosity to test the strength of
their revolutionary poetics on the magnified field of the long poem. As
Pound would write in *Guide to Kulchur*, "Ideas are true as they go into
action" (*GK*, 188), and what more visible field of action was available
to them all than the long poem?

Ironically, the enaction of the poetic idea had the potential to reveal
not only its truth but its deficiencies, a troublesome thought that
nagged Pound into writing that the "component of error in an idea
shows in its working out" less than a page later in *Guide to Kulchur*,
and that would return to haunt him in *Drafts & Fragments*. It would
haunt Williams in book 5 of *Paterson* too, articulated in his painful
sense that the poem, metaphorized as the river,

> "has returned to its beginnings"
> and backward
>   (and forward)
> it tortures itself within me
>   until time has been washed finally under:
>   and
>   "I knew all (or enough)
> it became me."

In 1968, two years before his death, it would also cause Olson, while
clarifying the mandate of the last volume of *Maximus—The Maximus
Poems: Volume Three*—which was to "write a Republic / in gloom on
Watch-House Point," to regard his long poem as having been the test
site for his rhythm and image theories:

> from rhythm to
> image, and image is knowing, and
> knowing, Confucius says, brings one
> to the goal: *nothing is possible without
> doing it. It is where the test lies,* malgre

all the thought and all the pell-mell of
proposing it. Or thinking it out or living it
ahead of time.   (Emphasis added)

and to admit, in the last thirty-six lines he wrote for the poem, that its
destiny is now to reside in the imagination without the intervention of
language:

> Nasturtium
> is still my flower   but I am a poet
> who now more thinks   than writes, my
> nose-gay

It is an insight, bound within the territory of the poem's close, that is
not unlike that contained in Pound's first collection "115": "Do not
move / Let the wind speak / that is paradise." Olson, like Pound in
Drafts & Fragments, had already perceived that his poem revealed him
in spite of its objectivist poetics, and so he too lamented its distortion
of its maker:[3]

> It is not I,
> even if the life appeared
> biographical

And, in the shadow of this separation between self and poem, he writes
of his poem's withdrawal from the harbor that was its point of genesis
541 pages earlier:

> I am once more writing
> in the light at
>   the bridge
> the air again
>   cleared   the moon once more
>   in its piece missing
>   free in the sky & the harbor
>   all free   and orange too
>   as with no more reason than
>   thirst or another desire I
> with out wish & full of
>   love, leave it to
>   itself
>   & tell you I have————?

Born of the separation is the labyrinth of the self, reduced to mapping a "personal preserve" that remains to be explored, whose emergence culminates in the distraction of structure, and the displacement of attention:

> wholly absorbed
> into my own conduits to
> an inner nature or subterranean lake
> the depths or bounds of which I more and more
> explore and know more
> of, in that sense that other
>   than that all else
> closes out and I tend further to fall into
> the Beloved Lake and I am blinder from
> spending time as insistently in and on
> this personal preserve from which
> what I do do emerges more well-known than
> other ways and other outside places which
> don't give as much and distract me from
> keeping my attentions as clear

For Olson, as for Pound, the emergence of a "blinder" self "more and more" taunted the premises of the poem and acted as an ironic counterpoint to its objectivist poetics; *Maximus*'s termination occurs not simply as a result of the poet's untimely death, but also in response to this internal subversion.

Like Pound's *Drafts & Fragments,* the poems and sequence of the final volume of Olson's *Maximus* were arranged by others, who were told what the first and last poems of the volume were to be, but nothing else.[4] Unlike in *Drafts & Fragments'* case, however, the sense of urgency to publish the "last" poems was absent, replaced by the careful editorial project that was undertaken by Butterick and Boer upon Olson's death at the beginning of 1970 and that lasted five years. One of the consequences of this is the attention to the sequence of composition of the final *Maximus* poems; their order in the volume is, as well as can be ascertained after a detailed study of the available manuscripts, the sequence of composition—a difficult editorial task somewhat facilitated by Olson's attempts at ordering his poems in anticipation of his own death. The problem was compounded by the alternating urges for and away from closure during the complete poem's composition. In volume 1, very close to the beginning of the poem in 1950, the choice

of "facts" that will become the poem will be "dealt with, as the sea is
. . . [by] ear"; by 1954, five years before the completion of what became
the first collected volume of *Maximus,* Olson was searching for the
poem's close, expressed in the unpublished manuscripts of three poems—"Max X," "Max Y," and "Max Z." The last title shared the
words "& end of the problem!"[5] Fifteen years later, Olson was still
expressing contrary desires for the poem. Although he told his literary
executor, Boer, what the last poem was to be (presumably the playful
3.229: "my wife my car my color and myself"), he was simultaneously
hoping he would live "ten more years to complete his work."[6] The
implication, as in Pound's request to include the poem honoring Olga
Rudge at the end of *The Cantos* (fulfilled in the 1986 printing), is that
although 3.229 was to be the final poem of *Maximus,* Olson still intended to compose more of *Maximus* before this poem terminated the
sequence. A close was envisioned, that is, but it was occurring earlier
than he desired, and outside his control. In the end, Olson's words
near the beginning of the poem echo with an ironic validity:

> one loves only form,
> and form only comes
> into existence when
> the thing is born

The passage seems to anticipate and answer the question in "Notes for
CXVII et seq." fragment no. 2 that animates so much of *Drafts &
Fragments*—"what do I love and / where are you?" For both Pound
and Olson, form would be created through its deferral, and realized
only retroactively in their long poems' tendency to reveal their makers,
and to self-absorb into a silence that is read as an ending. The premises
of projective verse that sought to purge "the lyrical interference of the
individual as ego" and that, in the words of Robert Creeley, "clears us
from the usual sense of . . . relaxing to an 'end,'" were subverted within
the poem they bred.[7]

Well before the poems in *The Maximus Poems: Volume Three* were
composed, Olson had contradicted the assumption that his poem was
a product of Pound's experiment with form in *The Cantos.* As annoy-
able and bombastic as Pound could occasionally be (and possibly by
influence there too), Olson asserted that his own poetic theories were
the more sophisticated, and wholly separate from Pound's, or Wil-

liams's for that matter: "My interest is not in *The Cantos,*" he told one interviewer in 1970,[8] and in *Projective Verse* itself he yawned at the impetus behind his recent predecessors' work: "Pound and Williams were variously involved in a movement which got called 'objectivism.' But that word was then used in some sort of necessary quarrel, I take it, with 'subjectivism.' It is now too late to be bothered with the latter."[9] While his self-conscious distancing from *The Cantos* signals its influence, more crucial is the fact that even the attempt to renounce *The Cantos* as a model could not prevent his *Maximus* from encountering the same fate.

Paterson's identity, too, was created in deliberate opposition to *The Cantos*'. Williams had always written under the shadow of his former university friend and detested the fact that his work was regarded as a product of Pound's, as a secondary affiliation that would not have existed had Pound not articulated the poetics of imagism and vorticism in the early years of each writer's development. As he wrote to Laughlin in 1940,

> Ezra is an important poet, we must forgive him his stupidities; I do, no matter how much he riles me. But I prefer not to have to do with him in any way. He wants to patronize me. Don't tell me this isn't so, for I know better. His letters are insults, the mewings of an 8th-grade teacher. That's where he thinks I exist in relation to his catastrophic knowledge of affairs, his blinding judgments of contemporary values. In one sense he is quite right to protect himself as he does. But my perceptions overtook him twenty years ago—not however my accomplishments. When I have finished, if I can go on to the finish, there'll be another measuring. (*SLW*, 192)

In 1940 book 1 of *Paterson* was still six years away. Williams had composed the shorter poem "Paterson" in 1926, however, and the intervening twenty years allowed him to regard the production of *The Cantos*' first seventy-one poems as "a pre-composition . . . which when later (perhaps) packed and realized in living, breathing stuff will (in its changed form) be the thing" (*SLW*, 135). Williams's entry into the struggle of the long poem's composition caused *The Cantos* to become an adversary, not a model, though. In 1947, before the publication of *The Pisan Cantos,* he wrote to Robert McAlmon that *The Cantos* up to that point did not:

increase Pound's reputation or are [sic] likely to increase it. There are good passages here and there in everything he writes but, to me, it seems woefully repetitious—I can't find a new departure anywhere or any new lead in construction or enlightenment. I'd be interested to get your slant. Pretty sad stuff to me. (SLW, 254)

Somehow The Cantos had not become "the thing" Williams had thought it would, and so his Paterson arose in part as an antidote to Pound's effort, a long poem "designed not so much to apply Pound's lesson ... but rather to contest the fundamental priorities, the entire hierarchy of values" The Cantos contained.[10] As with Olson's Maximus, however, the dynamics of Paterson's close would reveal a curious affiliation instead; the lesson of Pound's text was to be that the long poem inescapably designs its own self-contesting structure, to which the unwilling Cantos and its reluctant progeny would submit.

For Williams, as for Olson and for Pound, the long poem loomed as the final testing ground for a poetics that had already been articulated repeatedly in essays and shorter poems. Paterson began in the wake of its own poetic precepts, as an exploration and confirmation of them. In 1943, at the time that he was composing the introduction to The Wedge that he termed "an explanation of my poetic creed ... for all time,"[11] he was writing to Laughlin that Paterson "is crying to be written" (SLW, 214). The letter, in fact, contains the various forces of origin in miniature: a deliberate dismissal of Pound (and Eliot), the sense that the long poem will validate his own poetics and, finally, the deferral of form that dominates The Cantos and Maximus: "Order is what is discovered after the fact, not a little piss pot for us all to urinate into—and call ourselves satisfied" (SLW, 214). Paterson, too, was to discover the long poem's structure through the exploration of its informing poetics; a structure that, despite Williams's claim, did have a predetermined form and which, furthermore, was perpetuated beyond its envisioned close by the irresolvable struggle between a telic narrative and a poetic theory that resisted termination.

The telic narrative is expressed in Williams's preface to the poem's first book, written in 1946. Its intention is to disperse linear narrative structure throughout the field of action of a metaphor—"a man in himself is a city"—but the imagery is that of predetermined sequence:

Paterson is a long poem in four parts—that a man in himself is a city, *beginning, seeking, achieving and concluding* his life in ways which the various aspects of a city may embody—if imaginatively conceived—any city, all the details of which may be made to voice his most intimate convictions. (Emphasis added)

The dash after the opening assertion is an odd one, a convenient seam that hides the unresolved relationship between structure and argument that lies at the core of the poem's eventual unstable termination. Does "that a man in himself is a city" refer to what *Paterson is,* or to what its argument is, or to an informing metaphor for the "four parts"? If the "long poem" is about a man/city beginning, seeking, achieving and concluding his/its life, then a linear narrative already exists, to which "all the details" will be subservient. Possibly this contest between a preconceived linear narrative and the belief that "order is what is dis- covered after the fact" contributed to Williams's struggle to write the poem during its early stages: "I want to work at it but I shy away whenever I sit down to work. It's maddening but I have the hardest time to make myself stick to it. In spite of which I have done a hundred pages or so—it ought to be nearly finished by now. I hope I finish it soon" (*SLW*, 216).

After book 4 had been completed in 1951, Williams saw the poem in terms of two opposed dynamics—its "story" and its "language" (*SLW*, 304)—dynamics whose conflict was responsible for the poem's continuation beyond its planned termination into a fifth and incomplete sixth books. The "language" was the means by which to "break through to the actual" (*SLW*, 324), an "awakening of letters" out of the repose of "rehash, repetition ... paraphrase," the poetics that had dominated his work for years. Contrary to this was the poem's linear four-part structure, which took "the actual" and wrenched it into form. It is not surprising, therefore, to see book 5 begin with a repudiation of predetermined form—"not prophecy! NOT prophecy! / but the thing itself!"—and to voice a reappraisal that involves the abandonment of its past self:

> calling
> for its own murder
> Paterson, from the air
> above the low range of its hills

                              across the river
             on a rock-ridge
                         has returned to the old scenes
                                  to witness
             What has happened

What had happened was that the poem had eluded the control of its
maker, moving beyond an enactment of its own early precepts to a
repudiation of them, and that Williams was now beginning to recognize
that situation.[12] So long as *Paterson* remained in a state of genesis,
deferring the revelation of its errors in its working out, it was compara-
tively free of self-consciousness. In a letter to Wallace Stevens in 1944,
in fact, he could identify his poem only in terms of prebeginning, of
precepts: "I'm . . . gradually maneuvering a mass of material I have been
collecting over the years into the *Introduction (all there will be of it)*
to the *impossible* poem *Paterson*" (*SLW*, 230; emphasis added).

Once the impossible poem *Paterson* reached its preordained end, it
had already produced the dynamics for its continuation. In a sense,
books 1 to 4 were "impossible" because they comprised not the poem
but the poem's perpetual beginning, a stage that could not be sustained
indefinitely, and that eventually led to its own undoing by its emergence
into two subsequent books that act as a palinode to it. The end of
book 4 repudiates itself as the original point of termination by denying
the "conclusion" of the river/poem's path—"I warn you, the sea is *not*
our home"—and by envisioning itself in terms of its own suicide:

             Murder.
                   —you cannot believe
             that it can begin again, again, here
             again   .   here
             Waken from a dream, this dream of
             the whole poem   .   sea-bound,
                         rises, a sea of blood
             —the sea that sucks in all rivers,
                                          dazzled, led
             by the salmon and the shad
             Turn back I warn you
                         (October 10, 1950)
             from the shark, that snaps
             at its own trailing guts

For Williams, as for Pound, this self-absorption of the poem marked its "failure" to fulfill its early narrative design. He writes to Marianne Moore in 1951, during the decade between the appearance of books 4 and 5, that "if the vaunted purpose of my poem seems to fall apart at the end—it's rather frequent that one has to admit an essential failure. At times there is no other way to assert the truth than by stating our failure to achieve it" (*SLW*, 304), in a language predicting Pound's "To confess wrong without losing rightness" in CXVI. And in 1952, when he senses the inevitable continuation of his poem beyond its original boundary, his appreciation of Pound reawakens, as if he sees in *The Cantos'* own internal struggle the identical forces that are at work in *Paterson:* "Maybe there'll be a 5th book of *Paterson*," he writes to Robert Lowell, "Pound has helped at the beginning and has, it must be said, not weakened. Both Pound and Eliot have been faithful artists, both have refused to weaken" (*SLW*, 312–13).

Paterson's book 5 is then a refusal to abdicate the struggle for "a unity" (as he terms it in the introduction), to weaken in his struggle with the poem whose structure has overtaken his own desire for its design. He alerts the reader to a mandate that the poem has revealed over the composition of its first four books—"I have been forced to realize that there can be no end to such a story as I have envisioned with the terms which I had laid down for myself"—and so rebegins a struggle to continue the poem until the merging of narrative and poetics occurs. It would become a struggle that eventually exhausted *Paterson*, as it did *The Cantos*, pictured in the penultimate book's central image of the ouroboros ("a snake with its tail in / its mouth")—signalling both eternity and self-devouring exhaustion—and in an abandoned final volume that both laments the defeating weight of its own medium—"Words are the burden of poems, poems are made of /words"—and that, in its last lines, celebrates the irresistible attraction of a narrative and its teller:

> I delivered her
> > of 13 children
> before she came around
> > she was vulgar
> but fiercely loyal to me
> > she had a friend
> > > Mrs. Carmody
> an Irish woman

who could tell a story
when she'd a bit taken

Pound initially hoped that through the *Drafts & Fragments* poems *The Cantos* would achieve a greater limpidity and end its obscurity through an exegetical elaboration and clarification. Pound's eventual concept of ending, in this respect, is really of revelation, of "see[ing] again," as CXVI declares, what the poem has concealed and suppressed beneath the poetics it was to test from the Gaudier-Brzeska memoir onward. As in the examples of *Paterson* and *Maximus*'s last stages, though, we finally observe in *Drafts & Fragments* Pound recognizing the trace of a previous misreading or diversion, sometimes willful, sometimes innocent, that had urged *The Cantos* toward an impossible conclusion.

In their separate ways, *Maximus, Paterson,* and *The Cantos* were all the "impossible" poems for their poets that Williams declared his to be, since each sustained itself through an aesthetic that could not sustain the narrative that each long poem bred. In 1918, at the time of *The Cantos'* genesis, Pound had written that

artists who discover anything make ... detours and must, in the course of things ... push certain experiments beyond the right curve of their art. This is not so much the doom as the function of all "revolutionary" or experimental art, and I think *master*work is usually the result of the return from such *excess*. One does not know, simply does not know, the true curve until one has pushed one's method beyond it. Until then it is merely a frontier, not a chosen route. (*LE,* 321; emphasis added)

The statement is a prediction of *The Cantos'* temporary overthrow of vorticist indeterminacy by its telic narratives; but it also describes how the poem will, in its late self-rereading, become truly revolutionary, returning from political excess to an unresolved and complicated self-scrutiny. The revolution is ironic not only because it occurs in spite of Pound's temporary masterful desire to totalize the poem in accordance with its fascist dream for a *paradiso terrestre,* but because Pound's fascist and Social Credit ideologies, so "excessive" in *The Cantos,* were intended to erase usurious excess. The inherent ambiguity of usury as a concept emerges through the poem's own ironic structure, therefore, recalling Pound's puzzlement with it in "Addendum for C" that he suppresses until 1968 from the politically more confident period around 1941: "All other sins are open, / Usura alone not understood." If a hundredth canto was originally to supply a close, that very canto's addendum in *Drafts & Fragments* contemplates the paradox of usury as both an object of the poem's criticism and an aspect of its character.[13]

This militation by the long poem against the designs of its poet is fascinating in *Paterson* and *Maximus* because their poets keep a careful vigil on the progress of *The Cantos* yet still do not avoid its fate of self-interrogation for their poems. Perhaps Pound's is the most interesting of these cases because we see his poem's supremacy as an ironic repudiation of his own political agenda. The spectacle of a man "hurling himself at an indomitable chaos" is more vivid in Pound's case because that contest can be allegorized as a battle between Pound's poetics and his own ideological urges. Yet those ideological urges are, in their latent form, possibly the genesis of the desire to write a long poem that can sufficiently test them, for *The Cantos'* composition begins during the decade that marks his "passage from aesthete to politically engaged poet."[14] Pound's writing of *The Cantos* reflects the confrontation and conflict upon which he thrived—whether in the aestheticized form of vorticism's frictional "ply over ply," or of a narrative's teleology against vorticism's indeterminacy. In the process *The Cantos* becomes the ideal medium for the contesting urges of art and economic politics, and it lends him a substantial foe whose overthrow would attest to his narrative's undeniable validity, and to his superior endurance. The opposite, *Drafts & Fragments* tells us, is what actually happens.

The undoing of the epic poet's traditional mastery of the narrative code is not the only inversion that *Drafts & Fragments, Paterson 5*, and *The Maximus Poems: Volume Three* perform; the fact of his usurpation by the poems troubles other previously stable relationships as well. The removed and elevated status of the poet over the reader is not reversed, but it is neutralized in a manner that changes the nature of the poems' endings from the intentions of their poets. Each poet leaves the apparently impartial transcendence of his poem to become its reader, and that reading, as provisional as all readings, is what we read—and occasionally rewrite—as an end. Though provisionality was central to the "poetics of indeterminacy" that generated each long poem, Pound was uneasy with the disempowered place it finally afforded him, Williams fought it by continuing his attempt to master his poem beyond its proposed termination, and Olson continually predicted closural points to reclaim his authority.

Involved in this inversion of previously stable relationships, though sometimes unwillingly, are the poems' editors, who must assume an authority that the poet has for so many reasons relinquished. In the cases of *Drafts & Fragments, The Maximus Poems: Volume Three,* and *Paterson 6,* where the poets' declining health augmented the problems, the editors were in some ways no more privileged in their access to intentions than any other close readers of the texts and could not have known the crisis of rereading, so central to the nature of each final section, that was subverting those intentions anyway. These relationships, previously so hierarchical, recombine into a lateral network in which all readings—the poet's, the editor's, and the "reader's"—participate and occasionally compete in the final text's creation and production.

This traditional supremacy of poet over text is another order that is revolutionized in the final stages of these poems. Though Pound contests "symmetrical form" as an impediment to rendering a fluctuating world,[15] *The Cantos* succumbs to a formal unity that supplants self-deception with self-interrogation. There were precedents for this kind of subverting pattern in the history of the long poem after Dante's *Divine Comedy,* but they were poems that Pound ignored or repudiated for one reason or another: Milton's *Paradise Lost,*[16] Spenser's *Faerie Queene,* Pope's *Dunciad,* Wordsworth's *Prelude,* Keats's *Hyperion: A Fragment.* Pound placed himself in the heroic role of the poet who "stagger[s] as he can" in the face of the command to "all mankind . . . never again to attempt a poem of any length" (*LEP,* 180), yet he does not explain where that command comes from. In fact, though he sees it as the incapacity of the "malleable mud" of humanity to read an extended "masterwork," the command is really the lesson of the long poem's history that finality is inevitably to be placed "beyond the poem's horizon." As copious and encyclopedic a reader as Pound was, his history of reading was conveniently exclusive and, when not, frequently blind to its own self-contradictions.

Pound's new and disempowered place in the traditional writer-text-reader hierarchy in *Drafts & Fragments* asserts the multiply originating poetry that *The Cantos,* through its display of retranslation in its early poems, had explored at the outset. It is perhaps a testament to the vision of that relationship *The Cantos* originally contained, and also a reflection of what the real consequences of that vision, if pushed to its extreme, are for its poet. The apocalyptic moment of seeing again in *Drafts & Fragments* is also, for Pound, the moment of reacquaintance with the earlier *Cantos* written when the negotiation between poetry and politics was just beginning for him. In *Drafts & Fragments* he emerges as a reader questioning the eventual balance in that relationship, conscious of how his own political narrative gradually attempted to master the poem against its original, less authoritarian, personality.

Ultimately, the poem's reminiscence upon its emergent totalitarianism generates Pound's private backward glance; he encounters, in the isolation of composing his last poems, "that further terror" of which he wrote in Canto LXXXII. The context at Pisa was his sudden physical incarceration; in *Drafts & Fragments* the incarceration is poetic and personal. Pound's reminiscence, in *Drafts & Fragments*' interrogation of *The Cantos,* is at least not evasive but, in keeping with his life and writing, confrontational. Pound sensed the failure of his vision of coherence for his poem and himself strongly enough not to attempt to master the threat of its revelation in its final cantos. Their refusal to resolve is the success of its poetics in weakening the tenacity of its closural dynamic; and the spectacle of Pound reading "Pound" is the consequence of that particular failure, and a partial redemption, at least, of *The Cantos*' lost paradise.

Appendixes

Appendix 1

Magazine, Journal, and Volume Publications of *Drafts & Fragments* Cantos

In the spring of 1962 *Threshold* printed the first page of the first collection "115" version (minus four lines) titled "Fragment from Canto 115" (*Threshold* 17 [spring? 1962]: 20; see chap. 2, fig. 4). This edition of *Threshold* was guest edited by Professor Roger McHugh of University College Dublin. He asked *Threshold*'s editor, Desmond O'Grady, who was living in Rome in 1961, if O'Grady would contact Pound about offering some poetry for the journal. Either Pound or Mary de Rachewiltz gave O'Grady the fragment, O'Grady sent it to McHugh, and McHugh published it in *Threshold* the next year (Desmond O'Grady, letter to the author, 1 November 1991). Four months later *Paris Review* carried the DH2 version (*Paris Review* 28 [summer–fall 1962]: 13–14). The *Paris Review* selections were made by Hall and Plimpton from the transcripts in Hall's possession.

Between 1962 and 1966 Laughlin sent selections (apparently chosen from the material sent to him by Hall) to five different magazines. In the autumn of 1962 *Poetry* printed "From Canto CXIII," which follows a portion of the DH2 version (*Poetry* 101 [October–November 1962]: 13–14), and *Agenda* published "From Canto CXI," an exact copy of the DH1 version, in the spring of 1963 (*Agenda* 2, nos. 11–12 [March–April 1963]: 1–2). A few months later *National Review* carried a page titled "Mindscapes," which contained various fragments of five untitled cantos (*National Review* 15, no. 10 [September 1963]: 197). The first two passages are from portions of CX. The third passage is comprised of the last thirteen lines of "From CXII." Seventeen lines from the first collection "115" form the fourth passage (to become the first fragment of *Drafts & Fragments'* "Notes for CXVII et seq."). The final "Mindscapes" passage, also seventeen lines, is from the page of insertions in DH2: the "Ambracia" lines and the "blown husk" lines (see chap. 2, n. 26). This is another curious choice, because two versions of a canto 115 had already been published, the second of which contained these lines, suggesting that Pound was not determining the choice of passages to be published.

These passages were reprinted in *Agenda* in December 1965 in a special issue honoring Pound's eightieth birthday. In *Agenda* the passages have numerical headings that conform to the cantos of which they will be a part in *Drafts & Fragments*. The final *National Review* entry is headed "From CXV"—a strange choice for a title, since Pound had already designated the "Ambracia" lines for CXIV in the DH2 group, and since no version of a canto 115 included the lines. The implication again seems to be that Pound was not overseeing the choices. *Agenda* in the fall of 1965 also printed "From Canto 115," which, with the exception of some accidentals, is a replica of the DH2 "115" and very close to *Drafts & Fragments'* version (*Agenda* 4, no. 2 [October–November 1965]: 3).

In the same year, in time for Pound's eightieth birthday, Guy Davenport printed eighty copies of CX, having obtained the original from Laughlin, who obtained his from Hall: it is identical to the DH2 CX that retained "at Torcello / Alma Patrona." Ten copies were numbered, and none were distributed except by Pound himself to friends. In the spring of 1966 parts of a slightly earlier CX were reprinted, along with the DH2 canto 116, in *Niagara Frontier Review* 1 (spring 1966): 29–36).

The lines that comprise the 1972 "CXX" were originally lines 23, 16, 17, 18, 24, and 25 (in that new order) of the *Threshold* "Fragment from Canto 115." The identical *Anonym* version, titled "Canto 120," is authored by "The Fox," *The Anonym Quarterly* 4 ([Summer?], 1969): 1, and reprinted in the *New York Times,* 26 November 1972, A42.

Not surprisingly, the volume publication history of *Drafts & Fragments* eventually follows a convoluted path of imprecise reference and description. The first publication is the pirated one, *Cantos 110–116* (New York: Fuck You Press, 1967). The first authorized publication is James Laughlin's *Drafts & Fragments of Cantos CX–CXVII* (New York:

New Directions, 1969). In the same year, the collaborative New York: New Directions/Iowa City: Stone Wall Press limited edition appeared, whose contents are identical to its immediate predecessor. Faber and Faber of London publishes the first English edition in 1970, whose contents are also identical to the New Directions 1969 edition, and in that year the Faber and Faber/Stone Wall Press edition appears as well.

The first inclusion of a *Drafts & Fragments* volume in *The Cantos* is in the New Directions 1970 volume, the first printing of the third American collected edition. Its third printing in 1972 (the second printing appeared in 1971) is actually a new edition; though it repeats the *Drafts & Fragments of Cantos CX–CXVII* title for its final volume, it includes a "CXX" on its last page. Faber and Faber publishes *Drafts & Fragments of Cantos CX–CXVII* in its fourth English collected edition of 1976, whose contents are essentially identical to the New Directions 1970 *Cantos* with the notable exception that no CXX appears at the end. Peter du Sautoy writes a letter in the *Times Literary Supplement* (cf. chap. 2, n. 46) in that year, explaining the decision. New Directions publishes an eighth printing of its 1970 edition in 1981, but this too is more properly a new edition, repositioning "CXX" as the third fragment of "Notes for CXVII et seq." (displacing what was previously the third fragment into the fourth and final spot) and introducing "Fragment (1966)" at the end. A tenth "printing" appears in 1986, carrying the previously absent Cantos LXXII and LXXIII between the updated "Notes for CXVII et seq." and "Fragment (1966)." In 1989 an eleventh "printing" follows, which situates Cantos LXXII and LXXIII in their numerical sequence in the *Pisan Cantos* and otherwise maintains the alterations of the tenth printing. A twelfth printing in 1991 is the same.

Appendix 2

"From CXII" and Joseph Rock's *The ²Muan-¹Bpo Ceremony or the Sacrifice to Heaven as Practised by the Na-khi*

"From CXII," excerpted from the early CX typescript that begins "Thy quiet house at Torcello / Alma Astarte" (EPAB Box 71, Folder 2756), comprises passages from Joseph Rock's *The ²Muan-¹Bpo Ceremony or the Sacrifice to Heaven as Practised by the Na-khi* (Monumenta Serica 8 [Peking: Catholic University Press, 1948]). In chapter 1 I discuss the specific and various attractions the article had for Pound while writing *The Cantos'* last three volumes, and in chapter 4 I speculate as to why Pound departed from Rock's text in "From CXII" in small but crucial ways. The sequence of the passages in "From CXII" follows their sequence in Rock's article.

Pound:	. . . owl and wagtail and huo³-hu², the fire fox
Rock:	the . . . black vulture with the white head and . . . the *owl* were ch'ou [infested with evil impurities], the form rid itself of ch'ou on the horizon, the latter in the cave of a cliff (24).
	[In three footnotes to the above Rock mentions *Strix nivipotens*, *Wagtail motacilla alba Hodgsonii*, and *Huo³-hu²* or *fire-fox*, each of which appears either in "From CXII" or in the early CX typescript].
Pound:	amrta, that is nectar
Rock:	Amrta . . . [used to chase away evil impurities] is nectar,

175

the food of the gods, the potion that confers immortality (27n).

Pound: white wind, white dew

Rock: [The chief of the gods'] breath caused a magic whereupon *white wind* and *white dew* came forth, the two caused a magic (or had intercourse) and a white lake and white foam were born; after three nights there was born an egg and from it came forth [the celestial female] (39n).

Pound: From her breath were the goddesses
^{2}La ^{2}mun ^{3}mi

Rock: After three nights [the celestial female] caused a magic and *from her breath* there came forth 13 brilliant ... Goddesses. ^{2}La-^{2}mun is the Tibetan Lha-mo, to which the Na-khi add the word *mi* or female (39n).

Pound: If we did not perform ^{2}Ndaw ^{1}bpo
nothing is solid

Rock: *If we do not perform* ^{2}Ndaw ^{1}bpö [sacrifice to the Earth], *all that we have accomplished will not be real;* if ^{2}Muan ^{1}bpo is not performed we will not attain perfection like the others (41).

Pound: Agility, that is from the juniper

Rock: The family's livestock, grain, riches, honor, worthiness, beauty, courage, *agility,* and long life *are due to the Juniper* (42).

Pound: rice grows and the land is invisible

Rock: When *rice* is transplanted into the fields and it grows so that *the ground is invisible,* this is due to O-ma-ha [descendants of Ngaw], so therefore we perform Ch'u-bpa (ba) to them (45).

Pound: By the pomegranate water,
in the clear air
over Li Chiang

Rock: One specific area where Nagas [spirits] inhabiting springs are propitiated is a beautiful spot with many springs ... the springs themselves are called Ssi ... ie. *pomegranate water, and are five li north of Li-chiang* (65n).

Pound: many spirits are at the foot of
                      Hsiang Shan

Rock: Another place where Nagas inhabiting springs are pro-
pitiated has *many springs* which issue *at the foot of the Hsiang Shan,* or Elephant Mountain, immediately north of Li-chiang (65n).

Pound: By the temple pool, Lung Wang's
                  the clear discourse
                  as Jade Stream

$$玉\quad \text{Yü}^4$$
$$河\quad \text{ho}^2$$

Rock: Referring to the same area as above. A Lung-wang Miao ... or Dragon King *Temple,* has been built there with a large *pond* with sacred fish. The springs are called Ngu-lu gyi, and their waters *flow through* the city of Li-chiang as the Yu ho or *Jade Stream* (65n).
[Note how Pound connects Rock's "flow through" with the Confucian notion of "flowing through ... ger-minating," and thus has in mind his own desire for limpidity of verse and coherent form for *The Cantos.*]

Pound: Artemisia
[This is mentioned throuhout Rock's text. It is a long slender bamboo (Arundinaria Faberi) with which the winnowing tray is made.]

Pound: Winnowed in fate's tray
     neath
                 luna

Rock: [In a discussion of a ceremony that begins "Before the sun has risen" and thus "'*neath / luna*" is a "picture of a large *winnowing tray* made of the small bamboo called mun" (67).
[Pound's retranslation of the early morning ceremony into "'neath / luna" is another example of the coinci-dence he sees between "Rock's world" and the world already inscribed in *The Cantos.* In this case, Rock's description recalls Dante's "All 'neath the moon is For-tuna's."]

Notes

Introduction

1. Respectively, Michael Andre Bernstein, *The Tale of the Tribe: Ezra Pound and the Modern Verse Epic* (Princeton: Princeton University Press, 1980), 125; Massimo Bacigalupo, *The Forméd Trace: The Later Poetry of Ezra Pound* (New York: Columbia University Press, 1980), 489; Leon Surette, *A Light from Eleusis: A Study of Ezra Pound's Cantos* (London: Oxford University Press, 1979), 260; James J. Wilhelm, *The Later Cantos of Ezra Pound* (New York: Walker, 1977), 168.

2. Respectively, Wilhelm, *Later Cantos,* 168; Benjamin Sankey, *A Companion to William Carlos Williams' "Paterson"* (Berkeley and Los Angeles: University of California Press, 1971), 213.

3. Barbara Herrnstein-Smith, *Poetic Closure: A Study of How Poems End* (Chicago: University of Chicago Press, 1974). She suggests that one reason for "minimal closural effects" in a poem can be that the "last allusions are . . . to unstable events" (210).

4. Marjorie Perloff, *The Poetics of Indeterminacy: Rimbaud to Cage* (Princeton: Princeton University Press, 1981).

5. Robert Casillo, *The Genealogy of Demons: Anti-Semitism, Fascism, and the Myths of Ezra Pound* (Evanston, Ill.: Northwestern University Press, 1988), 325.

6. Noel Stock, *The Life of Ezra Pound* (New York: Pantheon Books, 1970), 460. In his revised version of 1982 Stock did not change the wording. Stock's critical response to *The Cantos* contains in miniature the tensions pervading the universal appraisal of the poem; while his biography of Pound contains this kind of sympathy, in his earlier *Reading "The Cantos": A Study of Meaning in Ezra Pound* (London: Routledge and Kegan Paul, 1967) he believes that:

we are unlikely most of the time to have any idea what [*The Cantos*] is about unless we locate the precise subject he was turning over in his mind at the time of composition. . . . Pound is no visionary poet peering into the heart of things, or the depths of the spirit. Of these he knows little, and this at second hand. (194)

If Stock's two books contain the contradictory responses that the poem elicits within its history of readership, Pound's obituary in the *Times of London* (2 November 1972) combines them into one puzzled testament. Amid a five-column discussion whose key adjective for Pound is "impenetrable" it asserts both his "staunchness and loyalty as a friend" and his "lack of piety and respect for the feelings of others." And the post–St. Elizabeths cantos are "in their digressiveness very much an old man's ramblings."

Chapter 1

1. Harry Meacham, *The Caged Panther: Ezra Pound at St. Elizabeths* (New York: Twayne, 1967), 141.

2. Richard Pevear, "Notes on *The Cantos* of Ezra Pound," in *Ezra Pound: A Collection of Criticism,* ed. Grace Schulman (New York: McGraw-Hill, 1974), 135.

3. Pound's explanation of the title is confusing, however. In the interview with Hall he says that the "thrones in Dante's *Paradiso* are for the spirits of the people who have been responsible for good government. The thrones in *The Cantos* are an attempt to move out from egoism to establish some definition of an order possible or at any rate conceivable on earth" (*RP*, 242). The *Paradiso* contains two thrones, however: those for God and the Blessed in canto 5, and those of the angelic hierarchy that delivers divine judgment in canto 28.

4. Christine Froula, *To Write Paradise: Style and Error in Pound's Cantos* (New Haven: Yale University Press, 1984), 18.

5. *The Divine Comedy of Dante Alighieri,* trans. Charles Sinclair, 3 vols. (New York: Oxford University Press, 1979). All subsequent translations from *The Divine Comedy* are from this edition.

6. As he said to Hall in 1960, "One can't follow the Dantesquan cosmos in an age of experiment" (*RP*, 242).

7. Ronald Bush, *The Genesis of Ezra Pound's Cantos* (Princeton: Princeton University Press, 1976), 19.

8. Pound to Felix E. Schelling, 8–9 July 1922 (*LEP*, 180). Pound continues on to say that:

I *have to* get down all the colours or elements I want for the poem. Some perhaps too enigmatically and abbreviatedly. I hope, heaven help me, to bring them into some sort of design and architecture later.

9. Baccigalupo, in *Forméd Trace,* is probably the most vociferous critic of the density of *Thrones:* among some "remarkable poetic breakthroughs" (336) he reads in it "tracts of sorry weariness" (334) and passages containing "the rough outline of some idea, perhaps evocative, certainly undeveloped" (333).

10. Chang Yao-hsin, "Pound's *Cantos* and Confucianism," in *Ezra Pound: The Legacy of Kulchur,* ed. Marcel Smith and William A. Ulmer (Tuscaloosa: University of Alabama Press, 1988). He shows how Pound employed a Li Po poem translated in Amy Lowell's *Fir-Flower Tablets,* titled "On Hearing the Buddhist Priest of Shu Play His Table Lute" (92–93). Li Po will be invoked in *Drafts & Fragments* as well.

11. Tim Redman, *Ezra Pound and Italian Fascism* (Cambridge: Cambridge University Press, 1991).

12. Redman, *Ezra Pound and Italian Fascism,* 198.

13. As early as 1953, Pound told Guy Davenport, after writing Canto LXXXIV, that he would surpass his earlier prediction of a Canto C close: "The poet looks forward to what is coming next in the poem, not backward to what has been accomplished. . . . My *Paradiso* will have no St Dominic or Augustine, but will be a *Paradiso* just the same, moving toward final coherence." Quoted in Humphrey Carpenter, *A Serious Character: The Life of Ezra Pound* (London: Faber and Faber, 1988), 812.

14. Wilhelm, *Later Cantos,* 49.

15. Carroll F. Terrell, "The Na-Khi Documents I," *Paideuma* 3, no. 1 (spring 1974), 94.

16. In *The ²Muan-¹Bpo Ceremony or the Sacrifice to Heaven as Practised by the Na-khi,* Monumenta Serica 8 (Peking: Catholic University Press, 1948), Rock states that he

was forced to ship [the original research papers] by boat (because of Japanese bombing). They left Calcutta . . . for the U.S.A. Alas, the steamer never reached its destination. . . . It was torpedoed by a Japanese submarine, and twelve years of work were sent with it to the bottom of the Arabian Sea. That I felt the loss keenly I need not waste time to tell. (2)

17. In one of his broadcasts Pound questioned the size of his audience at the time: "I was wonerin' if anybody listened to what I said on Rome Radio." Quoted in *Ezra Pound Speaking: Radio Speeches of World War II,* ed. Leonard W. Doob (Westport, Connecticut: Greenwood Press, 1978), xii.

18. See Conrad L. Rushing, "'Mere Words': The Trial of Ezra Pound," *Critical Inquiry* 14, no. 1 (autumn 1987): 111–33. He notes that a previous court deciding on a similar charge ruled that while "'the mere utterance of disloyal sentiments is not treason...the communication of an idea, whether by speech or writing, is as much an act as is throwing a brick, though different muscles are used to achieve different effects.' What this told Pound and his lawyer was that in the field of radio propaganda 'mere words' was no defense. The words would be inquired into to determine the intent to betray—something a poet might expect" (130). Rushing also points out that had the then unpublished Cantos LXXII and LXXIII been uncovered, their words could have been used against Pound as well.

19. In "The End of *The Cantos*," in *Modern Critical Views: Ezra Pound,* ed. Harold Bloom (New York: Chelsea House, 1987), 33, Eva Hesse suggests that Pound means his own family as much as he means the Shang dynasty here: "Wearing the mask of Fa [the Shang dynasty's first ruler], he is speaking at this particular moment very much for himself." He is speaking *for* himself, though the reference is less determinate, it seems to me, than Hesse maintains. This indeterminacy becomes impossible for Pound to control as *The Cantos* progresses, thus complicating its close.

20. The similarities are striking between Dante's description of the landscape on the side of the summit of Mount Purgatory, which Pound quotes at length in *The Spirit of Romance* (139–40), and Rock's of the Tibetan countryside described throughout *The Ancient Na-khi Kingdom of Southwest China,* 2 vols., (Harvard-Yenching Institute Monograph Series, vols. 8–9, Cambridge: 1947) and suggest again how the *Divine Comedy*'s influence operated so powerfully on Pound even in the last stages of *Cantos* composition that the echoes of Dante's imagery helped recommend Rock's texts to him.

21. Curtis G. Pepper, "The Homesick Poet," *Newsweek* (21 March 1960): 130.

22. Dorothy Pound to Harry Meacham (no date) as quoted in Meacham, *Caged Panther,* 183. Pound wrote Hall that if the troubles he encountered in correcting the *Thrones* proofs were any indication, any further composition on *The Cantos* would be extremely difficult: "Heaven knows where I will be, and if anything more than fragments will be available.... The mess made of proofs for Thrones, due to my incapacity to attend to 'em, is no harBINGer for new composition, but one can hope." (7 January 1960, ULNH.)

23. Pepper, "The Homesick Poet," 131.

24. Meacham, *Caged Panther,* 183.

25. Ezra Pound, letter to Harry Meacham, 1 January 1960, as quoted in Meacham, *Caged Panther,* 185–86.

26. Donald Hall, letter to Harry Meacham (undated) as quoted in Meacham, *Caged Panther,* 188.

27. Ezra Pound, letter to James Laughlin, dated "1960," EPAB.

28. Ezra Pound to Norman Holmes Pearson, 5 December 1958, Beinecke Rare Book and Manuscript Library.

Chapter 2

1. Louis Montrose, "Renaissance Literary Studies and the Subject of History," *English Literary Renaissance* 16, no. 1 (1986): 8.

2. "Notebook #59, December 28, 1957–May 20, 1958." EPAB Box 71, Folder 2750. On the margin of a carbon of the typescript, sent to Norman Holmes Pearson on 22 January 1958, is the comment "Juzza a little one, before we git on to Linnaeus," as if it is a short transitional prelude to a paradisal stage of the poem.

3. EPAB Box 71, Folder 2757. The allusion is contained in the third and fourth lines, which refer to the reward made to Joseph W. Wadsworth for his deed:

> 20 shillings to Wadsworth
> "in resentment." Town house in Hartford.

Resentment here is used for its archaic meaning of "appreciation." These lines now rest in "Notes for CXI."

4. Ronald Bush, "'Unstill, Ever Turning': The Composition of Ezra Pound's *Drafts & Fragments,*" in *Ezra Pound and Europe,* ed. Richard Taylor and Claus Melchior (Amsterdam and Atlanta: Rodopi, 1993): 223-42. The Na-khi narrative is translated and annotated in Joseph Rock, *The Romance of the Ka-Ma-Gyu-Mi-Gkyi: A Na-khi Tribal Love Story Translated from Na-khi Pictograph Manuscripts* (Hanoi: Indo-China, 1939), rpt. from *Extrait du Bulletin de l'Ecole Francaise d'Extreme-Orient* 39, fasc. 1, 1939.

5. Bush locates the first trace of the *Drafts & Fragments* CX in an early Beinecke typescript (EPAB Box 71, Folder 2741), which describes in similar terms "the 'gaiety' and the 'exuberance' of the 'waves' in Venice" ("'Unstill, Ever Turning,'" 227). Bush was also the first to research manuscripts in Marcella Spann Booth's possession pertinent to the evolution of CX: "On an envelope marked 'Venice / 12 Nov '58,' Pound drafted lines beginning 'To thy quiet house @ Torcello' and ending 'what panache—.' And by 'December 10' he had made a typescript and carbon, on which he had among other things added the words 'paw flap / wave tap.'" (227)

6. EPAB Box 71, Folder 2756.

7. EPAB Box 71, Folder 2751.

8. Now in Marcella Spann Booth's possession, this sequence was located by Bush, who identifies it as the "proto-sequence version of *Drafts & Frag-*

ments" ("'Unstill, Ever Turning,'" 233). Marcella Spann sent the retyped version, which I call the "first collection," to Pound in August 1960 (now at EPAB Box 71, Folders 2752, 2760, 2765, 2767, 2770, 2773).

9. See Bush, "'Unstill, Ever Turning'" for a detailed description of the composition dates and circumstances of these cantos. As he discovered, a typescript of CX (now at the Houghton Library at Harvard) that Pound sent to Craig La Drière at the time suggests that Pound considered reducing CX to its first (Torcello) page, and heavily editing the early "CXI" to produce a canto of that number, the second in the sequence.

10. EPAB Box 71, Folder 2756.

11. As Bush has revealed, Dorothy Pound's diaries hold the key to the composition date: "Dorothy also writes in her Diary that Pound found a file of Wyndham Lewis letters, a discovery which seems to have spurred a striking new canto, '115,' which Pound wrote out in the notebook now in Marcella Spann Booth's possession" ("'Unstill, Ever Turning,'" 230).

12. EPAB Box 71, Folder 2773.

13. Pound retained three passages from this early "117," totalling six lines, in "Notes for CXI" and "From CXV":

> i.e., the power to issue currency.
>
> ("Notes for CXI")

> Wyndham Lewis chose blindness,
>
> rather than have his mind stop
> ("From CXV")

> in meine Heimat
>
> ~~Kam-ich weider~~
> where the dead walked & the living were
>
> made of card board
> ("From CXV")

14. Donald Hall, letter to Ezra Pound, 10 January 1960, ULNH. The material pertaining to Hall's *Paris Review* interview with Pound was given to that library in September 1986. In his chapter on Pound in *Remembering Poets,* Hall describes much of this material. Pound was reluctant at first to grant the interview, suspicious that he would not be paid for it. In a brief card to Hall on 9 December 1959: "I am, frankly, looking for people who will feed the producer, whereas they mainly want me to help them . . . time and again by the dozen. No doubt the supported think such an attitude very crass" (ULNH). That Pound wanted Hall to use material other than the new cantos is evident in several communications from him to Hall, including a note left outside the

door of Pound's apartment in Rome: "I will be back by 4:30 or sooner . . . You can go up and glance @ Versi Prosaici (unpublished) Bunting letters. Letters to Untermeyer. . . . of course we shd. talk before I turn you loose on the discarded fragments . . . but the chairs are comfortable. Only extracts, possible for use & abusive expressions shd be cancelled" (ULNH).

15. *Versi Prosaici* (Rome: Caltanissetta, 1959) was published in June. In a note at the end of the fifty-eight page volume Pound wrote that the poems were not part of *Thrones,* but that they might illuminate some of the refrains or themes for the ("kindly") reader: "Questi Versi Prosaici non appartengono ai Cantos (a Los Cantares) ma forse ne rischiareranno alcuni ritornelli a qualche lettore benevolo." The "Versi Prosaici" material Pound thought Hall might use was poetry left over from the Rome publication.

16. Three of these translations are introduced into the second (enlarged) edition of *EPT.* 1.31 is titled "By the Flat Cup," and 3.30 is titled "This Monument Will Outlast." The first in the triad is 1.11, titled "Ask Not Ungainly." Considering that in 1930 (in *Criterion* 9, no. 35 [30 January]) Pound described Horace as not only "bald-headed, pot-bellied, underbred, sycophantic, less poetic than any other great master of literature" but as the father of "about half the bad poetry in English" (217) whose emotion is no stronger than "might move one toward a particularly luscious oyster" (218) one wonders why he turned to him in the late 1950s. Most likely, in his desire to achieve a greater limpidity in his approaching *paradiso* Pound looked again to what he termed Horace's "order of words, and their cadence in a line measured by the duration of syllables" (219), which he argues in *The Criterion* had not been adequately translated into English. The translated odes might therefore have served equally as experiment, practice and, as is clear from the choices, personal relevance.

17. "Versi Prosaici," *Listen* 3, nos. 3–4 (spring 1960): 22. The material consisted of five lines. Pound's confusion over how *Listen* obtained it testifies to the extent to which, by this point in his life, his control over the release and publication of his own creations was not absolute. Either he forgot that he had sent it to *Listen,* or else someone at Brunnenburg sent it.

18. The DH1 and DH2 groups, sent by Pound to Hall, are in the Houghton Library at Harvard (with duplicates, from Pound's collection, now at EPAB), donated by Hall in April 1967. Together they comprise a twenty-two page typescript of Cantos CX–116 (eighteen pages of poetry, three duplicated pages, and a page headed "omissions, these pages 1–9"), with Pound's handwritten corrections. Hall's retypings are at ULNH. See Bush, " 'Unstill, Ever Turning,' " app. A for a complete description of the contents of DH1 and DH2.

19. Donald Hall, letter to James Laughlin, 2 April 1982, JLA.

20. Bush, " 'Unstill, Ever Turning,' " 227–29, has given the most authoritative account of this evolution.

21. It is difficult to give an exact date to the deletion. There are two copies of a first page for CX in the DH2 group. One contains the alteration from "Astarte" to "Patrona" and keeps "at Torcello." The other has "at Torcello" scissored out, and "Alma Astarte" crossed out. Guy Davenport's version of CX, published in the year of Pound's eightieth birthday (see app. 1), keeps the "at Torcello / Alma Patrona" phrase even though it had been deleted five years before in the one DH2 version. Laughlin sent the CX version to Davenport, however, and Hall must have sent Laughlin the CX that retained the phrase. The publication history, in this case, cannot confirm Pound's intentions by 1965. Certainly by 1968 the proofs for the New Directions *Drafts & Fragments* volume maintain the deletions, however.

22. Hall seems to have liked the "I have tried to write Paradise" lines very much and wrote to Pound when they were not included in DH1 "Is nothing of the vanity theme—or the personal passages—yet printable?" As quoted in Bush, "'Unstill, Ever Turning,'" 234.

23. Pound's evolving responses to portions of the interview with Hall that touch on politics and racism are a case in point. Hall asked Pound, "Doesn't the law of treason talk about 'giving aid and comfort to the enemy,' and isn't the enemy the country with whom we are at war?" Pound responds by saying, "I don't know whether I was doing any good or not, whether I was doing any harm. And I probably was. Oh, I was probably offside." In the margin of Hall's typescript, though, Pound questions the "And I probably was" statement: "Is this on tape? I don't think I said it?" (ULNH). And before seeing the proofs of the interview, Pound had written to Hall to have him include a passage debating his anti-Semitism: "And if any man, any individual man, can say he has had a bad deal from me because of race, creed, or colour, let him come out and state it with particulars. The Guide to Kulchur was dedicated to Basil Bunting and Louis Zukofsky, a Quaker and a Jew." Hall deleted "And I probably was" and added the Bunting and Zukofsky passage.

24. Donald Hall, letter to Ezra Pound, 21 May 1960, EPAB.

25. Bush details changes to the other poems in DH2 from the early collection and DH1 and observes Pound "removing the political material [from "112"] and leaving the ceremony of heaven Na khi material he did not absorb into Canto CX" ("'Unstill, Ever Turning,'" 235). Bush also shows how Pound "relocated the Lake Garda 'jealousy' material from proto-113 to the new Canto CX in order to further emphasize the somberness of the opening" (236-37).

26. DH2 also included a page of what seemed to be three passages that Pound was in the process of incorporating into the sequence. The first passage was introduced as being for "Canto/ 114/ or after. Thru the 12 houses" and contained ten lines that become the opening of *Drafts & Fragments*' CXIV. The second passage consisted of (*a*) lines from the last page of *Drafts &*

Fragments' CXIV (essentially from "Ambracia, / for the delicacy" to "ubi amor, ibi oculus," with the omission of *Drafts & Fragments*' "are we to write a genealogy of demons?"); (*b*) the lines "to all men for an instant? / beati / The sky leaded with elm-boughs / ..." which, with the exception of the last line, used in "Notes for CXVII et seq.," are not incorporated into *Drafts & Fragments;* and (*c*) lines 11–14 of *Drafts & Fragments*' "From CXV": "A blown husk that is finished / but the light sings eternal / a pale flare over marshes / where the salt hay whispers to tide's change." Beneath it Pound typed "This ends canto that precedes the one starting. CAME NEPTUNUS," a reference to CXVI.

27. James Laughlin, letter to Ezra Pound, 9 June 1960, EPAB.

28. Ezra Pound, letter to James Laughlin, 12 February 1965, EPAB. The typescript of the letter questions the exact date, but the year is correct.

29. Tom Clark, letter to the author, 26 October 1982.

30. Sanders misread Pound's longhand "Alma Patrona" (nourishing or bounteous female guardian) in the first line of the Hall typescript as "Alma Pulnuoa." Bacigalupo accepts Sanders's error and sees Pound's invocation of a white goddess (*Forméd Trace,* 461–62).

31. James Laughlin, letter to Robert Gales, 9 September 1968, JLA.

32. James Laughlin, letter to Robert Gales, 7 May 1968, JLA.

33. A case in point is Pound's response to Laughlin's query concerning the ideograms in "From Canto CXII" beneath "as Jade stream." Laughlin, in a letter of 26 June 1968 to Pound (JLA), asked a number of textual questions about the *Drafts & Fragments* typescripts. Pound, needing to conserve his energy by this point, wrote his answers in the margins of Laughlin's letter, and returned it to him. Beside Laughlin's question about the ideograms, Pound ambiguously draws them in and writes the word "delete." Laughlin, writing to the printer of the first authorized edition, Kim Merker, advises him to "put everything in" (27 June 1968, JLA).

34. In the winter of 1969 *Sumac* published "Notes for Canto CXI" and "Notes for a Later Canto" (*Sumac,* 1–2 [winter 1969]: 5–7). The latter title was Laughlin's choice: the poem itself in 1968 became the third fragment (now the fourth fragment) of "Notes for CXVII et seq."

35. Eva Hesse, letter to James Laughlin (no month), 1968, JLA.

36. Another example of this conviction involves Pound's line "Mozart, Linnaeus, Sulmona" in "From Canto CXV." Eva Hesse wrote to Laughlin that "Sulmona (place name) is [an] obvious error. The line should certainly read: Mozart, Linnaeus, Agassiz—the same three men whom Ezra places in Paradise in fragment CXII in the line: Mozart, Agassiz and Linnaeus." Laughlin wrote Pound that "Another didakt worries because it says here 'Mozart, Linnaeus, Sulmona' when somewhere earlier there is a line 'Mozart, Linnaeus, Agassiz.' Jas does not see why you have to say the same thing every time, but passes this

along for what it may be worth. 'Sulmona' is, I believe, a hamlet in the Abruzzi, with which EP may well have associations" (James Laughlin, letter to Ezra Pound, 26 June 1968, JLA). It is also the birthplace of Ovid and thus releases a constellation of significances, one of which is a reminder of the Ur-Cantos and Canto II, where *Metamorphoses* figured prominently; as such, it suggests how the writing of *The Cantos'* last poems recalled for Pound the process of writing the first.

37. James Laughlin, letter to Kim Merker, 27 June 1968, JLA.

38. James Laughlin, letter to Ezra Pound, 26 June 1968, JLA. Pound wrote his ambiguous "yes" response in the margin beside Laughlin's question.

39. James Laughlin, letter to Kim Merker, 27 June 1968, JLA.

40. James Laughlin, letter to Douglas D. Paige, 16 August 1968, JLA.

41. Charles Norman, *Ezra Pound: A Biography* (London: Macdonald, 1969), 465.

42. At the time of writing this, new material has arrived at the Beinecke Rare Book and Manuscript Library, including some that relates to a "Canto 120." It is presently uncatalogued, and not available for examination.

43. Scott Edwin Ewing, "Weighing a Pound of Flesh," *Bloomsbury Review* 6, no. 4 (March 1986): 23.

44. Gianfranco Ivancich, ed., *Ezra Pound in Italy: From "The Pisan Cantos"* (New York: Rizzoli, 1970).

45. Laughlin has no record of when or how he first saw a "CXX," and the decision to resituate it in the CXVII fragments for the 1986 *Cantos* was based on "what seemed appropriate" at the time. James Laughlin, letter to the author, 30 January 1989.

46. In a letter to Laughlin, 13 June 1973, William Cookson writes that "I had a letter from E.P. himself saying that no permission had been given to Antonym [*sic*]" (JLA).

Peter du Sautoy, chairman of Faber & Faber at the time, declined to print the poem in their 1975 edition of *The Cantos,* writing in the *Times Literary Supplement* in 1976 that

> the new edition of *The Cantos* which we have recently published consists of sheets of the American edition . . . published by New Directions. There is one small difference: the sheets we have used do not contain the "Canto 120" that appears in the New Directions edition as we did not feel certain that these lines were what Pound intended to come at the end of his long poem. We hope that it is a convenience to scholars that apart from this minor difference the two texts are now identical.
>
> As for Cantos 72 and 73, we shall include them if and when they are offered to us by Pound's literary trustees. (*London Times Literary Supplement,* 20 August 1976, 1032)

47. *New York Times,* 26 November 1972.

48. Froula, *To Write Paradise,* 175.

49. These five are the 1967 pirated edition, the 1968/9 New Directions edition (identical to the 1969 limited edition printed by Stone Wall Press), and the 1972, 1986, and 1989 editions in the New Directions *Cantos.* Although New Directions terms the last three "printings," and not editions, their substantial changes and additions to *Drafts & Fragments,* the addition of Cantos LXXII and LXXIII in 1986, the resituating of Cantos LXXII and LXXIII in 1989, and alterations in the *Pisan Cantos* in 1989, qualify them as editions.

50. Jerome J. McGann, *The Beauty of Inflections: Literary Investigations in Historical Method and Theory* (Oxford: Clarendon Press, 1985), 85.

51. See Barbara Eastman, *Ezra Pound's "Cantos": The Story of the Text* (Orono, Maine: National Poetry Foundation, 1979), 129–41 for a detailed account of these changes.

52. Eastman's 1979 *Ezra Pound's "Cantos"* was the first study to concentrate on the provisionality of the text's state. Froula in 1984 extends the findings through an intensive examination of Canto IV and writes that the "editorial difficulties have to do not only with the technical problems posed by the poem's highly complex textual history but, more important, with a perhaps unprecedented divergence between the author's intentions regarding his text and those which the policies of his editors have tended to project upon it" (*To Write Paradise,* 6). "Monolithic authority" is her term.

53. A more harmless example of a reader who felt that Pound had not "completed" *The Cantos* is Daniel Kaminsky, whose six-page *Canto the Last* (Cleveland: Pranayama Publications, 1976) is "an attempt to finish Ezra Pound's huge opus . . . now that he is gone" (2). It offers a grand finale, depicting a triumphant and coherent light "traveling into / ONE" after "the storm of violins," endlessly renewing itself with "pale promise in the east" (8).

54. Bernstein, *Tale of the Tribe,* 124.

55. Ronald Bush, "'Quiet, Not Scornful?' The Composition of *The Pisan Cantos,*" in *A Poem Including History: The Cantos of Ezra Pound,* ed. Lawrence Rainey (Ann Arbor: University of Michigan Press, forthcoming).

56. Jerome J. McGann, "Keats and the Historical Method in Literary Criticism," *Modern Language Notes* 94, no. 5 (December 1979): 993.

57. Balachandra Rajan, *The Form of the Unfinished: English Poetics from Spenser to Pound* (Princeton: Princeton University Press, 1985), 295.

Chapter 3

1. Daniel Cory, "Ezra Pound: A Memoir," *Encounter* 30, no. 5 (May 1968): 38.

2. As early as 1907, something of the same kind of private dialogue is outlined in the poem "In Durance," coupled with the notion of home:

> "Thee"? Oh, "Thee" is who cometh first
> Out of mine own soul-kin,
> For I am homesick after mine own kind
> And ordinary people touch me not.
>> And I am homesick
> After mine own kind that know, and feel
> And have some breath for beauty and the arts...

And in the first lines of the early "Thy quiet house at Torcello / Alma Astarte, / The crozier's curve runs in the wall" is a faint echo of the opening of "Canzon: Of Incense":

> Thy gracious ways,
>> O Lady of my heart, have
> O'er all my thought their golden glamour cast;

3. To add to the personal relevance of the bishop, the word has evolved from the Greek *episkopos* (one looking over), which also suggests the poet (scop) of the Old English epic.

4. Bacigalupo makes a similar point: "feathers are used to write with...[and] the wake which we are directed to attend is the written trace that the poet leaves behind, and which in fact is arranged here in wavelike fashion" (*Forméd Trace*, 463–64).

5. Toba Sojo (Kakūyu), *The Animal Frolic*, text by Velma Varner (New York: Putnam, 1954).

6. Pound spoke to Hall of what he termed the "Confucian side of Disney" (*RP*, 225).

7. This Odyssean quest, which will meet not only with the impediments of the long poem's composition throughout *The Cantos*, but also with the unforeseen lure of a fascist narrative, is reintroduced yet again in CXVI in a context that specifically recalls Tiresias's prediction in Canto I that Odysseus "'Shalt return through spiteful Neptune, over dark seas, / Lose all companions'" (5):

> Came Neptunus
>> his mind leaping
>>> like dolphins

The recollection of this passage in CXVI reveals Pound flirting with a circular close to *The Cantos*, but also the now personal relevance of the phrase "Lose all companions," many of whom appear in the various reminiscences of former friends and lovers throughout *Drafts & Fragments*.

8. Hesse writes that Pound "uses quite correctly the German term *Verkehr* for sexual intercourse, characteristically switching to a foreign language as is his wont whenever he wishes to record some intimate thought that readers are not supposed to grasp straight off" ("End of *The Cantos*," 36). However, the word's significance extends beyond the personal criticism of sexual intolerance to an interrogation of *The Cantos*. If the sexual reading is the only one, his reluctance to announce it is understandable; yet surely *The Cantos*' employment of foreign words is not simply a reflex of camouflage. He uses the word here because it contains a crucially multiple significance.

9. Rock, *Romance*, 2.

10. Rock, *Romance*, 3.

11. Helios first appears in Greek in Canto XV: he "blinds" Pound, who is waking from the nightmarish dream that is the canto.

12. Northrop Frye, introduction to *The Tempest*, in *William Shakespeare: The Complete Works*, ed. Alfred Harbage (Baltimore: Penguin, 1969), 1370.

13. Herrlee Glessner Creel, *Confucius: The Man and the Myth* (New York: John Day, 1949), 292.

14. Pound had written to George Santayana in December 1949 about his "respect for the kind of intelligence that enables the cherry-stone to make cherry; the grass seed to make grass." Santayana responded by considering the term "intelligence" in this particular context, and ultimately finding it appropriate: "it would be fussy to object to your word 'intelligence' to describe that potentiality in the cherry-stone; somehow it possesses a capacity to develop other cherries under favourable circumstances without getting anything wrong." Pound then questioned Santayana's belief in the unconsciousness of the intelligence (Cory, "A Memoir," 34).

15. Bush, *Genesis*, 100–101.

16. Charles Singleton, *Dante's "Commedia": Elements of Structure* (Baltimore: Johns Hopkins University Press, 1977), 27.

17. Pound refers to both Basil Bunting and Allen Upward in Canto LXXIV. Bunting, a great friend of Pound's to whom he dedicates *Guide to Kulchur*, resisted various attempts to be enlisted into the British army and was jailed six months for doing so. His book *Redimiculum Matellarum* was not understood, "to the shame of various critics" (LXXIV/431). Upward, author of *The Divine Mystery*, had always been a model of the intellectual resister for Pound, and his thought influenced *The Cantos*' notions of etymology, among so much else. *Drafts & Fragments* mentions several others, with whom Pound has hoped throughout *The Cantos* to populate his paradise: Wyndham Lewis, Mozart,

Linnaeus, Agassiz, Confucius, Dante, and so on. In most cases, *Drafts & Fragments* reluctantly points out their new inappropriateness, either because Pound had too enthusiastically embraced them before and now reconsiders, or because his new rereading of *The Cantos* negates the *paradiso terrestre* that once urged their usefulness. His reassessment still privileges the desire to merge art and clear observation, though, as implied by the conflation of "Mozart, Agassiz and Linnaeus" in CXIII, which Kathryne Lindberg calls "an illegitimate hybrid . . . of the various arts and sciences." *Reading Pound Reading,* (Oxford: Oxford University Press, 1988), 75. The disputed replacement of Linnaeus by Sulmona, Ovid's birthplace, in "From CXV" may signal Pound's reassessment of the hybrid's legitimacy himself.

18. "Uncle G" is George Holden Tinkham, a friend of Pound's and a Massachusetts member of the House of Representatives, who stands "like a statesman" in Canto LXXIV. "Lodge" is Henry Cabot Lodge; along with Philander Chase Knox he is "against world entanglement" in Canto LXXVIII. Each opposed the League of Nations, and at this point in *The Cantos* represents for Pound the patriotic source of his turn to fascism in the 1930s and 1940s.

19. The Quemoy-Matsu crisis began in 1954 when the Communist Chinese shelled these islands, which, because of their strategic location in the Taiwan Strait, protected Taiwan from military aggression. Although the public hoped for strong retaliation by the United States, President Eisenhower refused to intensify the conflict and risk nuclear war over the issue. Although the crisis lost momentum in 1955, it erupted anew in September 1958 when Chou-En-Lai's forces shelled the islands once more. At this point U.S. public hostility toward the Communists ran high, and debate over the degree of necessary U.S. involvement intensified. The U.S. Seventh Fleet was sent as a deterrent, and the crisis abated. Many, however, regarded it as a portent of war: "At stake is a free Pacific, not two little islands," warned the *Saturday Evening Post* on 18 October, and a *U.S. News* headline crowed, "Quemoy, one battle the reds lost" on 24 October. Pound may have had this incident in mind when telling Hall four months later that "it is difficult to write a paradiso when all the superficial indications are that you ought to write an apocalypse" (*RP,* 241). Pound was critical of sloughing off the incident as cold war "politics" too, calling attention instead to the human suffering ("600 more dead"), and implying that unstable individual ethics and principles were the primary cause, and politics only the symptom ("they call it politics").

20. The result, as Rajan points out, is one of indeterminacy "all the more evocative because Pound's phrase is a fragment of a previous text which was itself put forward as a salvaging of fragments. Are the fragments now to be regarded as shored against a ruined self? Or are they shored against a surrounding ruin . . . ?" (*Form of the Unfinished,* 293).

21. Jamilia Ismail, "'News of the Universe': ²Muan ¹Bpo and *The Cantos*," *Agenda* 9, nos. 2–3 (summer–fall 1971): 75.

22. Most speculation about whether Pound intended *anthesis* (sexual flowering) or *antithesis* (which appears in the typescripts but is contradicted by the Greek word he later adds in the proofs) suggests the former (see Eastman, *Ezra Pound's Cantos,* 138). I would think that Pound intended what he wrote in the typescripts, though, for Geryon in the passage presents the antithesis of himself, as Pound believes *The Cantos* lie about Pound. Too, the notion of locating truth by setting it against its opposite conforms to the dialogic nature of Confucius's texts and "universe," with Fenollosa's concept of nature, and with CXIV's "'You respect a good book, contradicting it— / the rest aren't worth powder.'" "Truth by sexual flowering" could relate to *Drafts & Fragments'* concern with sexual freedom. Hesse, arguing for this interpretation, writes that anthesis "is a clear reference to the heterogenesis of the anthomedusa" ("End of *The Cantos,*" 33). I find her argument for "anthesis" as one possible reading somewhat convincing (though do not share her enthusiastic sense of the clarity of the reference). Even she resorts to writing that this "is an oblique way of informing us that truth resides in full sexual flowering." The most crucial fact of this debate is that the indeterminacy of *The Cantos* permits either reading.

23. Wendy Stallard Flory, *The American Ezra Pound* (New Haven: Yale University Press, 1989), 175–76.

24. Flory, *American Ezra Pound,* 194.

25. Bush, *Genesis,* 110.

26. Mary de Rachewiltz's Italian translation of his Introduction to "*Noh*" or *Accomplishment,* titled *Introduzione ai No, con un dramma in un atto di Motokiyo: Kagekiyo* (Milan: All'Insegna del Pesce d'Oro, 1954).

Chapter 4

1. Grazia Livi, "Interview with Ezra Pound," *Epoca,* 24 March 1963, 45, reprinted in *City Lights Journal* 2 (1964): 37–46, trans. Jean McClean.

2. The inclusion of "Hsiang Shan" ("fragrant mountain") and "Lung Wang" ("dragon king")—icons of Taoism and Buddhism—may also reveal Pound's emerging acceptance of belief systems he previously rejected in *The Cantos.* As David Hsin-Fu Wand argues in "To The Summit of Tai Shan: Ezra Pound's Use of Chinese Mythology," *Paideuma* 3, no. 1 (spring 1974), "when Pound becomes totally absorbed in attaining his terrestrial paradise, he forgets even his bias against the Taoists and the Buddhists, to whom he is indebted for the vision of the 'Jade Stream' near Hsian Shan" (7).

3. Froula writes that from *The Cantos'* beginning Pound strives for "a 'paradisal' language of patterned continuities in which poetic idea and the

words, sounds, and rhythms that embody it reflect each other" (*To Write Paradise*, 33).

4. As Joseph N. Riddell writes, the Poundian image "repeats by weaving together or inscribing that which cannot be reduced to a singularity." "Decentering the Image: The 'Project' of American Poetics," in *The Question of Textuality: Strategies of Reading in Contemporary American Criticism*, ed. William V. Spanos et al. (Bloomington: Indiana University Press, 1982), 173–74.

5. Alan Durant, *Ezra Pound: Identity in Crisis: A Fundamental Reassessment of the Poet and His Work* (Sussex: Harvester Press, 1981), 176.

6. It is also a reason for the phrase "to 'see again,'" in CXVI; it literally states the premise of defamiliarization, and restates the Confucian maxim "make it new."

7. As Froula writes, "Pound's abstract poetics . . . is an 'interpretation of nature,' a mimetic formalism which celebrates not the particulars of the correspondence but the implication of enduring patterns" (*To Write Paradise*, 21).

8. A nice coincidence occurs between Pound's phrasing here and Wallace Stevens's in "An Ordinary Evening In New Haven" (xxviii). The source for each (through however many mediations) is probably Hebrews 11:1: "Now faith is the assurance of things hoped for, the conviction of things not seen." Stevens, appropriately (to our purposes) musing that "This endlessly elaborating poem / Displays the theory of poetry," writes of

> the intricate evasions of as,
> In things *seen and unseen, created from nothingness,*
> The heavens, the hells, the worlds, the longed-for lands. (Emphasis added)

For him, the "intricate evasions" of metaphor or metonymy are generative, weaving an endlessly elaborating poem that is both a characteristic of life and of text. The imperfection of language that creates its distance from the world sui generis is also "our paradise" of perpetual remaking. Pound, differently, is imprisoned in CX by the desire for a closural paradise that terminates remaking. Pound's language, and his medium of the long poem, Stevens might say, simply do not allow it. Or, as Stevens celebrates in "Like Decorations in a Nigger Cemetery," "The worlds that were and will be, death and day. / Nothing is final, he chants. No man shall see the end." In CXIII (influenced by his translation of Sophocles' *Trachiniae*) Pound casts a tragic shadow on the same concept: "The hells move in cycles, / No man can see his own end."

9. That "hall of mirrors" refers in part to *The Cantos* itself, and its failed merger of word and world, is suggested by a passage in the first collection's "114" where the phrase first appears:

> rumours, blown words under Li Chiang,
>> these words in the snow range,
> in the mirroured hall amid images,

10. Carpenter, *Serious Character*, 652.

11. As Carpenter writes, "In 1946, talking to Charles Olson, he even indulged in personal abuse, alleging that Pavolini had told him that 'he couldn't walk on the side of the street under M's Palazzo because of the stink of the boss!'" (*Serious Character*, 652).

12. Lindberg, *Reading Pound Reading*, 15.

Chapter 5

1. Carpenter, *Serious Character*, 718.

2. Wyndham Lewis, *Wyndham Lewis on Art*, ed. Walter Michel and C. J. Fox (New York: Funk and Wagnalls, 1969), 340.

3. Timothy Materer, "A Reading of 'From Canto CXV,'" *Paideuma* 2, no. 2 (fall 1973), suggests that the poem "may be read as a finished elegy for Wyndham Lewis rather than as a 'fragment'" (205). However, its fragmentary state is a direct result of Pound's conflicting responses to the issues of blindness and insight, and political awareness, that are raised in it. For the same reason, the fragment does not so simply "commemorate[ ] the lost leader of the Vortex, Wyndham Lewis" (207), but exchanges a nostalgic vision of him as such a hero for a more troubled image of him as a "diversion" from aesthetics into politics.

4. Wyndham Lewis, *The Art of Being Ruled* (New York: Harper and Brothers, 1926), 370.

5. Redman, *Ezra Pound and Italian Fascism*, 104.

6. Quoted by Timothy Materer in *Vortex: Pound, Eliot, and Lewis* (Ithaca, N.Y.: Cornell University Press, 1979), 49; originally from *Criterion* 13 (October 1933): 119.

7. Daniel Varé, *The Two Imposters* (London: John Murray, 1949), 246.

8. Burton Hatlen, "Ezra Pound and Fascism," in *Ezra Pound and History*, ed. Marianne Korn (Orono, Maine: National Poetry Foundation, 1985), 157–8.

9. Quoted in David Anderson, "Breaking the Silence: The Interview of Vanni Ronsisvalle and Pier Paolo Pasolini with Ezra Pound in 1968," *Paideuma* 10, no. 2 (fall 1981): 345. Anderson includes a portion of Pasolini's review of *Drafts & Fragments* from *Descrizioni di descrizioni* (Turin: Einaudi, 1979), 295–96.

10. Froula, in a different context, makes a similar distinction: "[Pound's] problem was now to extend the inherently brief Image into the desired long

poem, to maintain the virtues of an 'intensive' art in an extensive one" (*To Write Paradise*, 21).

11. The Divus reference is usually considered the first "splice" in the canto, but Pound's reworking of the Divus translation earlier in the canto is actually the first significant one. It is a minor quibble, but the consequences for a reading of *The Cantos* are large, as I argue here.

12. Daniel Pearlman, "Canto I as Microcosm," in *Ezra Pound: A Collection of Criticism,* ed. Grace Schulman (New York: McGraw-Hill, 1974), 146. Bacigalupo makes essentially the same point (*Forméd Trace,* 16).

13. Bacigalupo, *Forméd Trace,* 16.

14. Yet another interpretation is that Pound is "criticizing" the mediating texts that denude the "original flavor" of the *Nekuia* Pound is attempting to recover (Bacigalupo, *Forméd Trace,* 14). Yet the mediating texts serve many purposes central to the generation of *The Cantos,* as I go on to discuss.

15. Bacigalupo suggests that Pound is practicing a "poetics of translation or parody" whose purpose is "to manipulate and distort, intentionally or not, the texts of others" (*Forméd Trace,* 7). I am arguing that a reading of Canto I may go further than this, to see its purpose as exposing the retranslative dynamics of the poetic act.

16. Various writers suggest different years for Pound's meeting with, and reading of, Frobenius. In *The Pound Era* (Berkeley and Los Angeles: University of California Press, 1974), 507, Hugh Kenner writes that they first met in 1928. Carroll Terrell, in *A Companion to the Cantos of Ezra Pound,* 2 vols. (Berkeley and Los Angeles: University of California Press, 1980), 1:157, claims they met in 1927, and that Pound read Frobenius in the early 1930s.

17. It is interesting to see how Pound even describes Frobenius's work in terms of the vortex principle. He quotes Frobenius on rock drawings and then describes his power of perception: "'Where we found these rock drawings, there was always water within six feet of the surface.' That kind of research goes not only into past and forgotten life, but points to tomorrow's water supply. This is not **mere** utilitarianism, it is *a double charge, a sense of two sets of values and their relation*" (*GK,* 57; italics added, bold type Pound's emphasis).

18. Redman, *Ezra Pound and Italian Fascism,* 85.

19. As Lindberg points out, Pound "uses 'paideuma' in a number of contradictory senses, until it virtually marks the translative moments by which Pound hopes to renovate culture and cultural history (to 'make it new'). In this way, paideuma can mean anything from art's special truth to a good meal" (*Reading Pound Reading,* 195). Lindberg is persuasive in arguing for the self-contradictions inherent in the concept; I think it is also true that paideuma assisted Pound's manipulation of the theory of vorticism to cloud the teleological dimension of his *Cantos.*

20. Froula, *To Write Paradise,* 14.

21. This contradiction is reflected in the physical production of the early volumes of *The Cantos: A Draft of XVI Cantos* in 1925, and *A Draft of the Cantos XVII–XXVII* in 1928. As McGann points out, their finely wrought covers, reminiscent of "the work of William Morris and the whole tradition of decorated book production which was revived in the late nineteenth century," strive for an "ideal of finishedness and control," while the poetry they contain "says something very different." Jerome J. McGann, "*The Cantos* of Ezra Pound, the Truth in Contradiction," *Critical Inquiry* 15, no. 1 (autumn 1988): 9.

22. Or, as Redman argues, Pound "allowed himself to dismiss any apparent contradictions in Mussolini's political philosophy or actions with the excuse that he was an artist and not bound by ordinary rules of consistency" (*Ezra Pound and Italian Fascism,* 118).

23. These are among the lines initially reemployed in the first collection "115" and then erased, as if Pound recognizes that his poem has committed itself, in the interval between Canto XIII and *Drafts & Fragments,* to a teleological narrative that it can neither deny nor resolve.

24. The lines immediately before "the dimension of stillness. / And the power over wild beasts" are taken from a notebook of Fenollosa's, and probably recreate a song "sung by contented peasantry" (Terrell, *Companion,* 1:191).

25. See Peter Brooker, "The Lesson of Ezra Pound: An Essay in Poetry, Literary Ideology, and Politics," in *Ezra Pound: Tactics for Reading,* ed. Ian Bell (Totowa, N.J.: Vision Press, 1982), 26, who describes this moment in Canto XXXVI as "one of the most inaccessible sections of the poem," a convenient obscurity that Pound uses as a chance to turn against his reader, to "arrogantly jettison those who neither understand nor sympathize."

26. Casillo, *Genealogy,* 51.

27. Casillo, *Genealogy,* 221.

28. "Uncle G.," George Holden Tinkham, advocated the United States stay out of the League of Nations because it disapproved of Italy's invasion of Ethiopia. Incidentally, Pound's desire to see his own exile as analogous to Ch'u Yuan's faces difficulty here: Ch'u Yuan was exiled for opposing military aggression by his state.

29. Jerome McGann continues on, in his examination of this passage, to write that "the illusion that [Pound's] poetry—that any poetry?—is a matter of unadulterated beauty, is mere dross. Pound's text speaks a fuller truth than his mind was able to grasp" ("*Cantos* of Ezra Pound," 16).

30. The "worlds" to be bridged are those of language and reality, sign and referent as well, however, as I have argued—worlds that Pound believes the *Divine Comedy* has bridged, and his *Cantos* have not. The line "Two mice and

a moth my guides," which inaugurates the "farfalla" image, is partly a refer-ence to Remy de Gourmont's *Physique de l'amour* (1903), in which the sexual urge of the natural world is analyzed. There, Gourmont refers, in particular, to the peacock moth. See Richard Sieburth, *Instigations: Ezra Pound and Remy de Gourmont* (Cambridge: Harvard University Press, 1978), 155–56 for a very clear analysis of Pound's reading of Gourmont, and for a specific analysis of Gourmont's influence in the final fragment of "Notes for CXVII et seq."

31. Paolo Valesio, writing of how individuality within fascism is "an essen-tial contradiction . . . implicit in the morphology of its designation," considers how the "Italian citizen today can find his integrated individuality only in the wake of a total vindication of the past. If he derides that easily vanquished (but long-lived) dictatorship, if he laughs at that slightly pompous black cap—if he stoops to that, in an homage to the victorious empire that surrounds him, then it is at himself, at his historical self, that he is laughing, it is himself he degrades into a caricature." "The Beautiful Lie: Heroic Individuality and Fas-cism," in *Reconstructing Individualism: Autonomy, Individuality, and the Self in Western Thought,* ed. Thomas C. Heller et al. (Stanford: Stanford University Press, 1986), 171. Complicating matters for Pound was the fact that he partici-pated in Italian fascism without of course holding Italian citizenship, and thus, strictly speaking, outside of its historical legacy.

Chapter 6

1. Christine Brooke-Rose, in *A ZBC of Ezra Pound* (London: Faber and Faber, 1971), 41, counts six different Sordellos metamorphosed in this passage: the one Browning rewrites in his poem; Pound's; Sordello as he actually existed ("if we can get at him," writes Brooke-Rose); the Sordello that his own poetry reveals; Sordello in Dante's *Purgatorio;* and a "partly apocryphal" Sordello as retranslated by Pound from a biography of him that "stands in a manuscript in the Ambrosian library at Milan" (*LE,* 97). These facets of what becomes a kind of multiple personality cohere to make a seventh Sordello, whom we know only by virtue of this aleatory and idiosyncratic mixture; it is, in all its instability and ephemerality, still very much Pound's Sordello.

2. See, for instance, Peter Russell, "Ezra Pound: The Last Years," *Malahat Review* 29 (January 1974): 11–44, a memoir of his meetings with Pound in 1964. The recollections are helpful but hardly impartial, with Russell insisting somewhat defensively that "In all the time I knew him I never heard him talk specifically of Fascism and Fascists, or of Jews" (26). Daniel Cory also tries to counter any negative depiction of Pound and describes in some detail "a good turn he did me one day in September" ("Ezra Pound," 36). And Hesse main-tains that the last poems must be considered "in relation to the human tragedy

of their author's return to Italy in 1958" as a precondition for our understanding of them ("End of *The Cantos*," 25).

3. Pound used the expression in the Hall interview in 1960, and again in the interview with Grazia Livi three years later. In both cases he claimed that someone else coined it (*RP*, 244; Livi, "Interview with Ezra Pound," 44). As with his assertion some forty-five years before that "I am often asked whether there can be a long imagiste or vorticist poem" (*GB*, 94), the speculative person is probably Pound himself, as Bush notes of the *Gaudier-Brzeska* claim (*The Genesis*, 23).

4. Michael Reck, "A Conversation between Ezra Pound and Allen Ginsberg," *Evergreen Review* 55 (June 1968): 29.

5. Norman, *Ezra Pound*, 454.

6. Reck, "Conversation," 29.

7. As Stock, editor of the *Impact* collection, points out in his *Life of Ezra Pound*, 454, Pound had the opportunity to amend anything he wanted in these essays and did partially admit his earlier insufficient understanding of Eliot's *After Strange Gods*. Nothing of the same kind of admission exists in writing for his anti-Semitic and pro-fascist statements in them, though. His dismay over his "stupid and suburban prejudice" could be just a nostalgic rereading of his past in which he attempts to fashion himself as a reformed, and tragically misunderstood man. This kind of fictionalized self-rereading will be one alternative that Pound flirts with during the composition of the *Drafts & Fragments* cantos, though it will be largely replaced by a more honest assessment.

8. For a thorough investigation of the roots of Pound's anti-Semitism and fascism, which suggests that they were inherited attitudes later to dismay him, see Flory, *American*, particularly chap. 6.

9. Ezra Pound, letter to James Laughlin, 24 November 1959, JLA.

10. Livi, "Interview with Ezra Pound," 44, 43, 45.

11. *Paideuma* 10, no. 2 (fall 1981), 331–45. The interview, Pound's last, was conducted in the winter of 1968 as part of a film documentary, and portions of it were reprinted in Ivancich's *Ezra Pound in Italy*. On this occasion Pound was slightly less pessimistic concerning his *Cantos* than he was in the Livi interview. Pasolini's questions, though informed and generous overall, were aggressive (he began with a rendition of Pound's "Pact": "I make a pact with you, Ezra Pound— / I have detested you long enough") and they stirred Pound to defend his poem rather than dismiss it. Still, he stated that the "good lines" in his work "are pebbles. I have not been able to put them into a cosmos" (337) and declared that "One tries to give [the lines] coherence, and . . . I have not succeeded" (337).

Concerning the confusing nature of Pound's anti-Semitism, it is a curious feature of his decisions at the time that within a year of lamenting it to Ginsberg he permitted the inclusion of "Addendum for C" into *Drafts &*

Fragments, a text that still contains the traditional *Cantos* equation of Jews with usury ("S. . . . . ." stands for Sassoon, and "R. . . . ." for Rothschild, the names removed at a lawyer's suggestion).

12. Redman, *Ezra Pound and Italian Fascism,* 77.

13. *Elektra: A Play By Ezra Pound and Rudd Fleming,* ed. Richard Reid (Princeton: Princeton University Press, 1987), xxi.

14. Sieburth, *Instigations,* 142.

15. By 1957 he was forced somewhat more directly to oversee and rectify interpretations of earlier statements by an earlier self, and felt compelled to discourage rumors of his ingratitude toward Hemingway for his support of Pound during the St. Elizabeths years, and toward his publisher James Laughlin:

> in view of a recent spate of attempts to stir enmity between me and several of my friends, in the columns of papers which do not print rectification of their "errors," might I ask the courtesy of your office and the patience of your readers to state that I have not accused Mr. Hemingway of dishonesty, though maintaining my reservation as to the activity of some reds in Spain. I have not accused Mr. Laughlin of selling manuscripts but did mention that he had detected someone else doing so.

"Mr. Pound and His Friends," *Times Literary Supplement,* 6 December 1957, 729.

16. Victor Li, in "The Vanity of Length: The Long Poem as Problem in Pound's *Cantos* and Williams' *Paterson,*" *Genre* 19, no. 1 (spring 1986): 5, argues that this is the governing dynamic of the modern long poem:

> The modern long poem denies genre, if we take genre to mean a set of prescriptive rules that governs a piece of writing and helps to identify it as a distinct literary type for the reader. But in their struggle to surpass lyric limitations and recover an authority based on a truth that is neither merely subjective nor merely prescribed, Pound and Williams evince an anxiety which can be seen to constitute, for the reader, the characteristic which defines the "genre" of the modern long poem.

17. "Rhetorical presence," "words, tags and quotations," and "a complex field of cultural discourse" are from Victor Li, "The Rhetoric of Presence: Reading Pound's Cantos I–III," *English Studies in Canada* 14, no. 3 (September 1988): 296–309. In *Ezra Pound,* 16–17, Durant argues that Pound, even in his earlier poetry, "nevertheless both animates these representations, and fixes them in a kind of proprietary control, becoming the supporting condition of their existence."

18. Kenner, *Pound Era,* 143.

19. Donald Davie, "The Pisan Cantos," in Schulman, *Ezra Pound,* 118.

20. Allen Upward, *The New Word* (New York: M. Kennerley, 1910), 200–201.

21. Abraham Heschel, *Who Is Man?* (Stanford: Stanford University Press, 1972), 39.

Afterword

1. Lindberg shows how Pound dismantles this boundary in his prose writings and replaces it with a "rhetorical economy" arbitrating between the two, which "are never absolutely separable, [and whose] 'perceptions' [are not] reproducible as things seen" (*Reading Pound Reading,* 38).

2. See Joseph N. Riddel, "A Somewhat Polemical Introduction: The Elliptical Poem," *Genre* 11, no. 4 (winter 1978): 467: "The lyric, then, undoes its own frame, or repeats the 'force' of framing with its own metaphorical violence—a play of displacements which the modern 'long poem' only makes explicit. The lyric is irreducibly temporal, a text never present to itself. It represents the flaw of the myths of origin."

3. Olson, in 3.135, uses the same pun on the word *lie* as Pound does in CXVI, to undermine the truthfulness of language and to expose its distortion of him: "as I read a poet say I lie / upon this bank stretched out."

4. George F. Butterick, *A Guide to "The Maximus Poems" of Charles Olson* (Berkeley and Los Angeles: University of California Press, 1978), xlvi.

5. See Butterick's discussion of these poems in *Guide to "the Maximus Poems,"* xxxvi.

6. See Butterick's discussion in *Guide to "The Maximus Poems,"* xlvi.

7. Robert Creeley, "A Note on Poetry," in *A Quick Graph: Collected Notes and Essays,* ed. Donald Allen (San Francisco: Four Seasons, 1970), 25.

8. Gerard Malanga, "The Art of Poetry, XII," *Paris Review* 13, no. 49 (summer 1971): 198.

9. Charles Olson, *Projective Verse* (New York: Orion Press, 1959), 10.

10. Bernstein, *Tale of the Tribe,* 200.

11. William Carlos Williams, "Author's Introduction to *The Wedge,*" in *Selected Essays* (New York: New Directions, 1969), 257.

12. In fact, the language Williams uses to describe his search for form predicts the language with a similar purpose in *Drafts & Fragments.* In a letter to Norman Macleod in 1945 he writes that he wants "coherence in any agglomerate. . . . I want a transfixing light through the whole. But not too blinding a glare, just a candle light" (*SLW,* 239), predicting *Drafts & Fragments'* later "A little light, like a rushlight / to lead back to splendour" in CXVI. And in 1947, while writing book 2 of *Paterson,* an intimation of *Drafts & Frag-*

ments' "gold thread in the pattern": "It's pretty loose stuff, but the thread, I think, is there."

13. As Casillo argues, usury in Pound's understanding and rendering of it continually undoes itself, becoming "an overdetermined concept in which contradictory metaphorical ideas are already embedded. Pound is not the enemy of usury per se, for he is not really sure what usury is" (*Genealogy*, 221).

14. Redman, *Ezra Pound and Italian Fascism*, 20.

15. In his 1928 essay "Dr. Williams' Position" Pound wrote that he was

> not going to say: "form" is a non-literary component shoved on to literature by Aristotle or by some non-litteratus who told Aristotle about it. Major form is not a non-literary component. But it can do us no harm to stop an hour or so and consider the number of very important chunks of world-literature in which form, major form, is remarkable mainly for its absence. (*LE*, 394)

More remarkable than the absence of form noted by Pound in this passage, though, is the exclusive set of examples he goes on to employ in order to make his point: the *Iliad*, Aeschylus's *Prometheus*, Montaigne, Rabelais, Lope de Vega.

16. An example of Pound's dismissive response to Milton is in a 1935 letter to the translator W. H. D. Rouse. Pound sets "the movement with the wind [that] takes the god into nature. . . . [the] raw cut of concrete reality" against the "mere pompous rhetoric in Milton" (*LEP*, 273). It is that very wind Pound removes from his early "115" typescript, displaced by the unstable close that even *Paradise Lost* contains. Though Pound's subject in the letter is the question of adhering to an original text when translating, his statements in it are ironically prophetic of the rereading that will shape *The Cantos'* close: "you shd. run on, in your own way, to the end and then go back and look more carefully at the meaning of each let us say phrase (not word) of the original." For an examination of how the termination of *Paradise Lost* is characterized by self-reflexivity and narcissism, see Diane Kelsey McColley, *Milton's Eve* (Urbana: University of Illinois Press, 1983), chap. 3.

Works Cited

Anderson, David. "Breaking the Silence: The Interview of Vanni Ronsisvalle and Pier Paolo Pasolini with Ezra Pound in 1968." *Paideuma* 10, no. 2 (fall 1981): 331–45.

Bacigalupo, Massimo. *The Forméd Trace: The Later Poetry of Ezra Pound.* New York: Columbia University Press, 1980.

Bernstein, Michael André. *The Tale of the Tribe: Ezra Pound and the Modern Verse Epic.* Princeton: Princeton University Press, 1980.

Brooker, Peter. "The Lesson of Ezra Pound: An Essay in Poetry, Literary Ideology, and Politics." In *Ezra Pound: Tactics for Reading,* edited by Ian F. Bell. Totowa, N.J.: Vision Press, 1982.

Brooke-Rose, Christine. *A ZBC of Ezra Pound.* London: Faber and Faber, 1971.

Bush, Ronald. *The Genesis of Ezra Pound's "Cantos."* Princeton: Princeton University Press, 1976.

———. " 'Quiet, not scornful?': The Composition of *The Pisan Cantos.*" In *A Poem Including History: "The Cantos" of Ezra Pound,* edited by Lawrence Rainey. Ann Arbor: University of Michigan Press, forthcoming.

———. " 'Unstill, Ever Turning': The Composition of Ezra Pound's *Drafts & Fragments.*" In *Ezra Pound and Europe,* edited by Richard Taylor and Claus Melchior. Amsterdam and Atlanta: Rodopi, 1993.

Butterick, George F. *A Guide to "The Maximus Poems" of Charles Olson.* Berkeley and Los Angeles: University of California Press, 1978.

Carpenter, Humphrey. *A Serious Character: The Life of Ezra Pound.* London: Faber and Faber, 1988.

Casillo, Robert. *The Genealogy of Demons: Anti-Semitism, Fascism, and the Myths of Ezra Pound.* Evanston, Ill.: Northwestern University Press, 1988.

Cory, Daniel. "Ezra Pound: A Memoir." *Encounter* 30, no. 5 (May 1968): 30–39.

Creel, Herrlee Glessner. *Confucius: The Man and the Myth.* New York: John Day, 1949.

Creeley, Robert. "A Note on Poetry." In *A Quick Graph: Collected Notes and Essays,* edited by Donald Allen. San Francisco: Four Seasons, 1970.

Dante. *The Divine Comedy of Dante Alighieri.* 3 vols. Translated by John D. Sinclair. New York: Oxford University Press, 1979.

Davie, Donald. "*The Pisan Cantos.*" In *Ezra Pound: A Collection of Criticism,* edited by Grace Schulman. New York: McGraw-Hill, 1974.

Doob, Leonard W. Editor. *Ezra Pound Speaking: Radio Speeches of World War II.* Westport, Connecticut: Greenwood Press, 1978.

Durant, Alan. *Ezra Pound: Identity in Crisis: A Fundamental Reassessment of the Poet and His Work.* Sussex: Harvester Press, 1981.

Eastman, Barbara. *Ezra Pound's "Cantos": The Story of the Text.* Orono, Maine: National Poetry Foundation, 1979.

Ewing, Scott Edwin. "Weighing a Pound of Flesh." *Bloomsbury Review* 6, no. 4 (March 1986): 23.

Flory, Wendy Stallard. *The American Ezra Pound.* New Haven: Yale University Press, 1989.

Froula, Christine. *To Write Paradise: Style and Error in Pound's "Cantos."* New Haven: Yale University Press, 1984.

Frye, Northrop. "Introduction" to *The Tempest.* In *William Shakespeare: The Complete Works,* edited by Alfred Harbage. Baltimore: Penguin, 1969.

Hall, Donald. *Remembering Poets. Reminiscences and Opinions.* New York: Harper & Row, 1978.

Hatlen, Burton. "Ezra Pound and Fascism." In *Ezra Pound and History,* edited by Marianne Korn. Orono, Maine: National Poetry Foundation, 1985.

Herrnstein-Smith, Barbara. *Poetic Closure: A Study of How Poems End.* Chicago: University of Chicago Press, 1974.

Heschel, Abraham. *Who Is Man?* Stanford: Stanford University Press, 1972.

Hesse, Eva. "The End of *The Cantos.*" In *Modern Critical Views: Ezra Pound,* edited by Harold Bloom. New York: Chelsea House Publishers, 1987.

Ismail, Jamilia. "'News of the Universe': ^{2}Muan ^{1}Bpo and *The Cantos.*" *Agenda* 9, nos. 2–3 (summer–fall 1971): 70–87.

Ivancich, Gianfranco, ed. *Ezra Pound in Italy: From "The Pisan Cantos."* New York: Rizzoli, 1970.

Kenner, Hugh. *The Pound Era.* Berkeley and Los Angeles: University of California Press, 1974.

Lewis, Wyndham. *The Art of Being Ruled.* New York: Harper and Brothers, 1926.

———. *Wyndham Lewis on Art.* Edited by Walter Michel and C. J. Fox. New York: Funk and Wagnalls, 1969.

Li, Victor P. H. "The Rhetoric of Presence: Reading Pound's Cantos I–III." *English Studies in Canada* 14, no. 3 (September 1988): 296–309.

———. "The Vanity of Length: The Long Poem as Problem in Pound's *Cantos* and Williams' *Paterson.*" *Genre* 19, no. 1 (spring 1986): 3–20.

Lindberg, Kathryne. *Reading Pound Reading.* Oxford: Oxford University Press, 1988.

Livi, Grazia. "Interview with Ezra Pound," *Epoca,* 24 March 1963. Reprinted in *City Lights Journal* 2 (1964): 37–46. Translated by Jean McClean.

Malanga, Gerard. "The Art of Poetry, XII." *Paris Review* 13, no. 49 (summer 1971): 177–204.

Materer, Timothy. "A Reading of 'From Canto CXV.'" *Paideuma* 2, no. 2 (fall 1973): 205–7.

———. *Vortex: Pound, Eliot, and Lewis.* Ithaca, N.Y.: Cornell University Press, 1979.

McColley, Diane Kelsey. *Milton's Eve.* Urbana: University of Illinois Press, 1983.

McGann, Jerome J. *The Beauty of Inflections: Literary Investigations in Historical Method and Theory.* Oxford: Clarendon Press, 1985.

———. "*The Cantos* of Ezra Pound, the Truth in Contradiction." *Critical Inquiry* 15, no. 1 (autumn 1988): 1–25.

———. "Keats and the Historical Method in Literary Criticism." *Modern Language Notes* 94, 5 (December 1979): 988–1032.

Meacham, Harry. *The Caged Panther: Ezra Pound at St. Elizabeths.* New York: Twayne, 1967.

Montrose, Louis. "Renaissance Literary Studies and the Subject of History." *English Literary Renaissance* 16, no. 1 (1986): 5–12.

Norman, Charles. *Ezra Pound: A Biography.* London: Macdonald, 1969.

Olson, Charles. *The Maximus Poems: Volume Three.* Edited by George F. Butterick. Berkeley and Los Angeles: University of California Press, 1983.

———. Projective Verse. New York: Orion Press, 1959.

Pearlman, Daniel. "Canto I as Microcosm." In *Ezra Pound: A Collection of Criticism,* edited by Grace Schulman. New York: McGraw-Hill, 1974.

Pepper, Curtis G. "The Homesick Poet." *Newsweek* 55, no. 1 (March 1960): 130–31.

Perloff, Marjorie. *The Poetics of Indeterminacy: Rimbaud to Cage.* Princeton: Princeton University Press, 1981.

Pevear, Richard. "Notes on *The Cantos* of Ezra Pound." In *Ezra Pound: A Collection of Criticism,* edited by Grace Schulman. New York: McGraw-Hill, 1974.

Rajan, Balachandra. *The Form of the Unfinished: English Poetics from Spenser to Pound.* Princeton: Princeton University Press, 1985.

Reck, Michael. "A Conversation between Ezra Pound and Allen Ginsberg." *Evergreen Review* 55 (June 1968): 27–29, 84.

Redman, Tim. *Ezra Pound and Italian Fascism*. Cambridge: Cambridge University Press, 1991.

Reid, Richard, editor. *Elektra: A Play by Ezra Pound and Rudd Fleming*. Princeton: Princeton University Press, 1987.

Riddel, Joseph N. "Decentering the Image: The 'Project' of American Poetics." In *The Question of Textuality: Strategies of Reading in Contemporary American Criticism,* edited by William V. Spanos et al. Bloomington: Indiana University Press, 1982.

————. "A Somewhat Polemical Introduction: The Elliptical Poem." *Genre* 1, no. 4 (winter 1978): 459–477.

Rock, J. F. *The Ancient Na-khi Kingdom of Southwest China*. 2 vols. Harvard-Yenching Institute Monograph Series, vols. 8–9. Cambridge, 1947.

————. *The ²Muan-¹Bpo Ceremony or the Sacrifice to Heaven as Practised by the Na-khi*. Monumenta Serica, no. 8. Peking: Catholic University Press, 1948.

————. *The Romance of Ka-Ma-Gyu-Mi-Gkyi: A Na-khi Tribal Love Story Translated from Na-khi Pictograph Manuscripts*. Hanoi: Indo-China, 1939. Reprinted from *Extrait du Bulletin de l'Ecole Francaise d'Extreme-Orient*, 39, fasc. 1, 1939.

Rushing, Conrad L. " 'Mere Words': The Trial of Ezra Pound." *Critical Inquiry* 14, no. 1 (autumn 1987): 111–33.

Russell, Peter. "Ezra Pound: The Last Years." *Malahat Review* 29 (January 1974): 11–44.

Sankey, Benjamin. *A Companion to William Carlos Williams' "Paterson."* Berkeley and Los Angeles: University of California Press, 1971.

Sieburth, Richard. *Instigations: Ezra Pound and Remy de Gourmont*. Cambridge: Harvard University Press, 1978.

Singleton, Charles. *Dante's "Commedia": Elements of Structure*. Baltimore: Johns Hopkins University Press, 1977.

Stock, Noel. *The Life of Ezra Pound*. New York: Pantheon Books, 1970. Revised ed. San Francisco: North Point Press, 1982.

————. *Reading "The Cantos": A Study of Meaning in Ezra Pound*. London: Routledge and Kegan Paul, 1967.

Surrette, Leon. *A Light from Eleusis: A Study of Ezra Pound's "Cantos."* London: Oxford University Press, 1979.

Terrell, Carroll F. *A Companion to "The Cantos" of Ezra Pound*. 2 vols. Berkeley and Los Angeles: University of California Press, 1980–84.

————. "The Na-Khi Documents I." *Paideuma* 3, no. 1 (spring 1974): 91–122.

Toba Sojo (Kakūyu). *The Animal Frolic*. Text by Velma Varner. New York: Putnam, 1954.

Upward, Allen. *The New Word*. New York: M. Kennerley, 1910.

Valesio, Paolo. "The Beautiful Lie: Heroic Individuality and Fascism." In *Re-*

constructing Individualism: Autonomy, Individuality, and the Self in Western Thought, edited by Thomas C. Heller et al. Stanford: Stanford University Press, 1986.

Varé, Daniele. *The Two Imposters.* London: John Murray, 1949.

Wand, David Hsin-Fu. "To the Summit of Tai Shan: Ezra Pound's Use of Chinese Mythology." *Paideuma* 3, no. 1 (spring 1974): 3–12.

Wilhelm, James J. *The Later Cantos of Ezra Pound.* New York: Walker, 1977.

Williams, William Carlos. "Author's Introduction to *The Wedge.*" In *Selected Essays.* New York: New Directions, 1969.

———. *Paterson.* New York: New Directions, 1963.

Yao-hsin, Chang. "Pound's *Cantos* and Confucianism." In *Ezra Pound: The Legacy of Kulchur,* edited by Marcel Smith and William A. Ulmer. Tuscaloosa: University of Alabama Press, 1988.

Index

Adams, John, 11, 20
Agassiz, Louis, 85
Agenda, 171–72
Anonym Quarterly, 65–66, 172
Anti-Semitism, 2, 30, 56, 65, 75, 94, 128, 131, 135–37, 144, 154, 186n, 199n

Bacigalupo, Massimo, 179n, 180n
Baudelaire, Charles, 13
Bernstein, Michael Andre, 179n
Binyon, Lawrence, 95
Bloomsbury Review, 65
Bollingen Award, 9
Bonaparte, Napoleon, 103–4
Brancusi, Constantin, 94, 124
Browning, Robert, 15, 120, 134, 149, 155
Brunnenburg, 85
Bruno, Giordano, 111
Bunting, Basil, 19, 52, 128, 156, 191n
Bush, Ronald, 17, 37, 72, 90, 96, 183n, 186n
Butterick, George F., 158

Cairns, Huntington, 112
Camoens, 88–90, 103, 118
Catullus, C. Valerius, 39, 79, 90, 149
Casillo, Robert, 7, 128, 179n
Cavalcanti, Guido, 23, 81, 95, 126
Chaucer, 129
Clark, Tom, 58–60

Coke, Edward, 27, 35, 80, 154
Confucius, 11, 19–24, 28, 37, 54, 85, 87, 92, 95–96, 102–3, 105, 112, 126–28, 130, 137, 149, 151, 177
Connecticut Charter, 35
Crane, Hart, 156
Creeley, Robert, 159

Daniel, Arnaut, 81, 103
Dante, 11–12, 14–24, 27–28, 37, 54, 80, 82, 84–85, 90, 92–93, 95–97, 101–4, 106, 110–11, 113–14, 118, 121, 126–27, 128, 130, 149, 151, 154, 177, 180n, 182n
Davenport, Guy, 172, 180n, 186n
Del Mar, Alexander, 21
Dickinson, Emily, 155
Divus, Andreas, 121–22, 142, 196n
Doolittle, Hilda, 91, 106

Eastman, Barbara, 189n
Eliot, T. S., 25, 30, 92, 115, 118, 155, 161, 199n
Elpenor, 51
Enville, La Rochefoucauld d', 104
Erigena, John Scotus, 128
Euripides, 140
Ewing, Scott Edwin, 65

Fascism, 12, 20–21, 30, 56, 75, 94, 108, 124–32, 135, 137, 139, 142–44, 151, 154, 192n, 198n

Fenollosa, Ernest, 7, 96–97, 106–11, 116, 119, 122
Fitzgerald, Desmond, 115
Fleming, Rudd, 138
Flory, Wendy, 94
Frobenius, Leo, 18, 20, 124–25, 127, 196n
Frost, Robert, 135
Froula, Christine, 125
Fuck You Press, 34, 58–60, 64, 68, 172

Galileo, 26
Gaudier-Brzeska, Henri, 11, 119
Gautier, Theophile, 93
Ginsberg, Allen, 135
Golding, Arthur, 123, 147
Gourmont, Remy de, 115, 142, 198n
Grosseteste, Bishop, 11, 95

Hall, Donald, 11, 21, 51–61, 76, 135, 140, 171, 180n, 184–86
Hamilton, Sir Ian, 106
Hardy, Thomas, 15, 113
Hemingway, Ernest, 200n
Hernnstein-Smith, Barbara, 179n
Hesse, Eva, 63, 70, 182n, 187n, 192n
Heydon, John, 21, 147
Hitler, Adolph, 119
Homer, 11, 86, 94, 108, 112, 117, 120, 126, 149
Horace, 52–53, 185n

Ivancich, Gianfranco, 66, 199n

Jefferson, Thomas, 11
Jones, David, 156
Jonson, Benjamin, 78, 129, 147

Kaminsky, Daniel, 189n
Keats, John, 111, 167
Kennan, George, 27
Kenner, Hugh, 144
Kitasono, Katue, 63–64
Knox, Philander Chase, 91, 192n
Kohler, Charlotte, 11, 17, 31, 76

Laughlin, James, 30, 52, 56, 58–64, 66–68, 160–61, 171–72, 187n, 200n
Lewis, Wyndham, 47, 91, 117
Lindberg, Kathryne, 113
Linnaeus, Carolus, 85
Li Po, 20, 103, 180n
Livi, Grazia, 105, 136
Lodge, Henry Cabot, 91, 192n
Lowell, Amy, 15, 180n
Lowell, Robert, 156, 164

MacDiarmid, Hugh, 156
Macdonald, Dwight, 9
MacLeish, Archibald, 29
Magna Carta, 27
Malatesta, Sigismundo, 11
McAlmon, Robert, 160
McGann, Jerome, 73, 129
McHugh, Roger, 171
Merker, Kim, 64
Mikhailovitch, Draja, 28
Milton, John, 8, 156, 167, 202n
Monroe, Harriet, 153
Montrose, Louis, 34
Moore, Marianne, 164
Motokyo, 96
Mozart, Wolfgang Amadeus, 85
Mussolini, Benito, 11, 20, 39, 94, 104, 112–13, 119, 124, 126–28, 147

Na-khi. *See* Rock, Joseph
National Review, 171–72
New York Times, 66
Niagara Frontier Review, 172
Noh drama, 15, 96–99, 101, 103, 108, 119
Norman, Charles, 65, 144
Noyse, John Humphrey, 81

Odysseus, 51
O'Grady, Desmond, 171
Olson, Charles, 156; *Maximus,* 6, 9, 156–60; *Projective* Verse, 160

Orage, A. R., 20
Ovid, 11, 123, 147, 188n

Paige, Douglas, 64
Paris Review, 51–53, 58, 184n
Pasolini, Paolo, 119, 137
Paul the Deacon, 11
Pearlman, Daniel, 121
Pearson, Norman Holmes, 31
Perloff, Marjorie, 7, 179n
Pindar, 141
Plimpton, George, 51
Plotinus, 23, 107
Poe, Edgar Allan, 155
Poetry, 171
Pope, Alexander, 147, 167
Porter, Katherine Anne, 65
Pound, Dorothy, 37, 39–40, 130
Pound, Ezra
   A Lume Spento, 144
   "Alma Sol Veneziae," 76
   Cantos
      I: 4, 51, 78, 94–96, 108, 120,
      122–23, 126, 140, 142; II: 15,
      86, 123, 134, 145–47, 188n,
      190n; III: 145–47; IV: 134; V:
      14–15, 86, 89; VII: 12, 86, 96,
      115–17; VIII: 82, 92; XIII: 23,
      54, 127; XVII: 71, 94; XVV: 12;
      XXXIII: 20; XXXVI: 127; XLIX:
      127; LIII: 12, 20; LV: 95; LXII:
      27; LXVII: 12, 27; LXVIII: 12;
      LXXII: 1, 63, 69, 119, 131, 139,
      173, 182n; LXXIII: 1, 69, 71,
      119, 173, 182; LXXIV: 12–13,
      18, 35, 78, 96, 128, 137, 148,
      191n; LXXVI: 12; LXXVIII: 79;
      LXXXI: 91; LXXXII: 168;
      LXXXIII: 138, 148; LXXXVII:
      21, 95; LXXXVIII: 98; XC: 21,
      54, 140; XCIII: 17; XCVI: 21;
      XCVIII: 21, 24, 25, 85, 87;
      XCIX: 11, 21–22, 27, 35, 90; C:
      23, 27, 35, 63, 136, 181n; CI:
      27; CVI: 77; CIX: 16, 76; CX:
      7, 25, 35, 39, 40, 52, 60, 63, 75,
      123, 128, 133, 141, 147, 172,
      194n; "Notes for CXI": 39, 91,
      93, 104, 184n; "From CXII": 25,
      38, 99, 103, 105, 175–77; CXIII:
      37, 73, 76, 80–82, 84–86, 90,
      105–6, 133, 141, 143, 151,
      192n, 194n; CXIV: 12, 47, 79–
      80, 86, 90, 94, 106, 111, 137,
      150; "From CXV": 35, 47, 54,
      75, 84, 95–96, 103, 108, 111,
      116–19, 128, 136, 149, 184n,
      187n, 192n; CXVI: 6, 9, 20, 25,
      61, 64, 71, 75, 78–79, 80, 85,
      88, 90–91, 94, 98, 102–4, 111,
      118–19, 133, 141, 143–44, 148,
      150, 164–65, 190n, 194n, 201n;
      "Notes for CXVII et seq.": 4, 24,
      40, 47, 54, 61, 64, 66, 69, 71,
      75, 86, 103, 105, 107, 111–13,
      129–30, 133–34, 148, 151, 159,
      187–88n; "CXX": 1, 2, 47, 63–
      68, 71, 103, 118, 172–73, 188n;
      "Addendum for C": 61–64, 103,
      165, 199n; "Fragments (1966)":
      1, 68–69, 71
   "Canto 110 (or 111 or 112)," 35–
      36, 38, 40
   "Canzon: Of Incense," 190n
   "DH1," 52–54
   "DH2," 52–61, 186n
   early drafts of "CX," 38
   early drafts of "CXI," 39
   Elektra (trans.), 138–40
   "Exile's Letter," 152
   "first collection," 40–51, 53–55,
      61, 194n
   *Hugh Selwyn Mauberley: Life and
      Contacts,* 89, 145
   *Impact: Essays on Ignorance and
      the Decline of American Civiliza-
      tion,* 136
   "In a Station of the Metro," 8
   "In Durance," 190n
   Indiscretions, 144
   *An Introduction to the Economic
      History of the United States,* 17

Cantos (*continued*)
  "Larks at Allegre," 113, 130
  "Na Audiart," 80
  "Near Perigord," 134–35, 145
  Patria Mia, 144
  Pavannes and Divagations, 144
  Pisan Cantos, 7, 12, 15, 17, 27, 72–73, 94, 116, 137–38, 147–48, 160
  "The Return," 143
  Rock-Drill, 16, 20–21, 23, 24, 27, 39, 76, 144–45
  "The Seafarer," 47, 90
  Spirit of Romance, 14, 16, 17, 88, 110, 113–14, 118, 130, 148–49
  "this part is for adults," 37–39
  "The Tomb at Akr Caar," 80
  Thrones, 11, 14, 16, 17, 20–21, 23, 24, 26, 27, 29, 35, 39, 52, 71, 76, 104, 144–45
  "The Tree," 110
  Ur-Cantos, 15, 17, 79, 89, 90, 103, 120, 188n
  Versi Prosaici, 52–53, 185n
  Women of Trachis, 38, 71, 131
Pound, Homer, 19, 91, 102
Propertius, Sextus, 91

Quemoy (bombing of), 91, 104, 192n

Rachewiltz, Mary de, 29
Redman, Tim, 20, 118, 124
Reid, Richard, 138–39
Remusat, Mme. de, 103
Rexroth, Kenneth, 156
Rihaku, 152
Rock, Joseph, 11, 24–28, 37, 82–87, 93, 95, 105, 175–77, 182n
Rome Radio broadcasts, 25, 94
Rouse, W. H. D., 104
Rudge, Olga, 1, 29, 61, 68–69, 114, 130, 159, 173
Rushing, Conrad L., 182n

Sanders, Ed, 58
Sankey, Benjamin, 179n

Santayana, George, 191n
Sautoy, Peter du, 173, 188n
Schelling, Felix, 17, 22, 180n
Seiburth, Richard, 142
Shakespeare, William, 86
Simon, Jules S., 27
Singleton, Charles, 90–91
Social Credit, 12, 126, 154, 165
Sojo, Toba, 78–79
Sophocles, 149; *Elektra,* 138–41; *Trachiniae,* 138, 140–44
Spann (Booth), Marcella, 29, 37, 38–40, 52, 183n
Spenser, Edmund, 167
St. Anselm, 11
St. Elizabeths, 11, 26, 29, 35, 75, 81, 85, 98, 105
St. Peter's Cathedral, 76
St. Victor, Richard, 21
Stendhal, Marie Henri Beyle, 79
Stevens, Wallace, 163, 194n
Stock, Noel, 9, 179n
Stone Wall Press, 64, 173
Sumac, 61
Surette, Leon, 179n

Talleyrand, Charles, 104
Threshold, 56, 58, 65, 171
Tinkham, George, 128, 192n, 197n
Tiresias, 51, 117
Titian, 12
Torcello Cathedral, 76–77
Truman, Harry, 116

Upward, Allen, 12, 17, 90, 108, 128, 137, 150, 191n
Usury, 165–66, 200n

Vare, Daniele, 118–19, 130, 151
Valesio, Paolo, 198n
Ventadourn, Bernart de, 103, 113, 118
Vice Versa, 63
Villon, François, 23
Vorticism, 109, 116–19, 123–27, 154

Wadsworth, Joseph, 35, 39–40, 128
Whitman, Walt, 128
Wilhelm, James, 23, 179n
Williams, William Carlos, 156; *Paterson,* 6, 9, 73, 122, 126, 159–68; *The Wedge,* 161

Wilson, McNair, 27
Wordsworth, William, 167

Yeats, W. B., 92, 106, 122, 144